RIVERSIDE COMMUNITY COLLEGE
1916

BLACKFOOT MUSICAL THOUGHT : CO

ML 3557 N38 198

P9-BHS-362

DATE DUE

BLACKFOOT MUSICAL THOUGHT

OTHER KENT STATE TITLES IN WORLD MUSICS

The Ethnomusicologist, by Mantle Hood

Music in the Mind: The Concepts of Music and Musician in Afghanistan,
by Hiromi Lorraine Sakata

The Music of the Bauls of Bengal, by Charles Capwell

Blackfoot Musical Thought

COMPARATIVE PERSPECTIVES

Bruno Nettl

THE KENT STATE UNIVERSITY PRESS
Kent, Ohio, and London, England

Riverside Community College
Library
4800 Magnolia Avenue
Riverside, California 92506

JUL '92

© 1989 by The Kent State University Press, Kent, Ohio 44242
All rights reserved
Library of Congress Catalog Card Number 88–28450
ISBN 0–87338–370–2

Library of Congress Cataloging-in-Publication Data
Nettl, Bruno, 1930–
    Blackfoot musical thought : comparative perspectives / Bruno
Nettl.
        p.   cm.
    Bibliography: p.
    Includes index.
    ISBN 0-87338-370-2 (alk. paper) ⊚
    1. Siksika Indians—Music—History and criticism. 2. Indians of
North America—Great Plains—Music—History and criticism.
I. Title.
ML3557.N38 1989   88-28450
781.7′297—dc19   CIP
                                                                    MN

British Library Cataloging-in-Publication data are available.

For Becky
("Red Bird Woman")
and for Steve

Contents

Preface   ix

Acknowledgments   xi

Introduction: Ideas about Music   1

1 Background
   1. On Musical Ethnography   7
   2. The Blackfoot People   12
   3. Sources   17
   4. Fieldwork   23
   5. Songs in Blackfoot Life, 1890–1985   32
   6. Four Musical Events   38
   7. Musical Style in a Nutshell   42

2 Fundamentals
   1. The Concept of Music   46
   2. Songs, the Primary Units   52
   3. The Musical Universe   58
   4. The Essence of Musical Sound   65
   5. Music and Language   68
   6. Kinds of Music   76
   7. Kinds of People and Things   82

3 History: Origins, Sources, and Change
   1. Origins of Music   89
   2. And of Rituals   94
   3. Sources: Composing and Learning   96
   4. Blackfoot Music History: The Early Times   103
   5. And the Twentieth Century   106
   6. The Concept of Music History   109
   7. The Concept of Change   113

4 Music in Human and Supernatural Societies
   1. Uses and Functions   116

	2.	Social Groups and Songs Groups	124
	3.	The Power of Music	128
	4.	Medicine Songs and Words	133
	5.	Music and the Heroic	136
	6.	Ownership and Control	140
	7.	The Humorous Side	143
5	Musicianship		
	1.	Terminology	147
	2.	Musical Form and Function	152
	3.	Ensembles and Drumming	155
	4.	Ideas of Performance	159
	5.	Theory and Practice	160
	6.	Questions of Evaluation	163
	7.	Cultural Values and Musical Values	166

Conclusion: A Blackfoot Theory Text?   170

Discography: Chronological List of Recorded
            Collections of Blackfoot Music (1897–1986)   174

Appendix A: Blackfoot Song Types by Use, as Found
            in the Various Recorded Collections   179

Appendix B: Three Blackfoot Songs:
            Methods of Text Setting   181

Appendix C: Responses of Non-Western Musics to Western
            Influences: Development of Concepts in
            Three Studies   184

Bibliography   186

Index   194

Preface

This study attempts to carry out two main tasks. One is to describe an aspect of the musical culture of the Blackfoot Indians, the ideas and concepts that define and surround music. The other, equally important, is to carry out an exercise in method and technique of musical ethnography, particularly in finding and communicating ways of studying and presenting comprehensively the musical culture of a society. My hope is to provide an interpretation that emphasizes the relationships between music and other domains of culture, between ideas about music and the themes that broadly characterize the life of the Blackfoot.

I would like to direct myself to several groups of readers. Specialists in Native American music will understand readily why Blackfoot culture and the questions with which I deal are worthy of interest and concern. Others, who are approaching the subject from a knowledge of Western music, may find a broadly comparative framework helpful as an approach. For them in particular I have tried to relate the Blackfoot musical culture to others for which there is comparable ethnomusicological literature, or to societies in which I have some direct experience. I feel that I can best say something significant about Blackfoot music by viewing Blackfoot culture against a backdrop of the realm of world music, including the academic Western musical culture with which most readers will be acquainted. The comparative remarks will hopefully make clear why a particular question in the area of musical ethnography is interesting and why one should be concerned about an issue. In several chapters or sections the procedure is, therefore, to use data from Western and other societies—the world perspective—as a way of leading the reader to appreciation of the Blackfoot. The account at hand is based about equally on my own fieldwork and on the large amount of research about Blackfoot culture and history that has been carried out and published by others. I can certainly make no claims of being comprehensive, and while I have tried to speak to or at least touch upon many aspects of musical thought, my emphasis is less on the presentation of a complete ethnography than on interpretation. My ultimate purpose is to show that the musical culture of the Blackfoot, even those aspects about which the people themselves seem disinclined or unable to talk, is an organic whole and a complex of interrelationships; and in this respect I hope to contribute to the growing literature that shows musical culture to be a coherent system of sounds and ideas. I have a sense that the statements made here and the relative weight given to observation, statements, snippets of data, and allusions in ethnography and myth would be agreeable to thoughtful members of Blackfoot society; but there is no question that much of what I say is an interpretation of what they said, what I have read, and what I observed. In this sense, I feel that what I write is methodologically and conceptually consonant with much of the standard ethnography published since the 1960s.

Although I tried to follow several approaches to this study, there are important procedures of research that I could not carry out and methods that I was not qualified to use. Chief among these are various avenues of linguistic inquiry. While I do touch upon matters of language and borrow here and there from the arsenal of cognitive anthropology, I cannot claim expertise in these fields and must leave much of what they could contribute to other researchers.

I would like to provide an accurate picture and a reasonable interpretation. But just as important is my desire to stimulate an appreciation of the complexity of the system of ideas and of the amazing degree of continuity (in a period of wrenching social change) that characterize musical culture. I therefore hope that the reader will develop respect for the significance of music in the cultural system and the degree to which it has been maintained—and respect, also, for the people and their particular way of combining a magnificent cultural heritage with the realities of life in late twentieth-century North America.

Acknowledgments

Some of the kinds of things ordinarily included in a preface have been incorporated in the body of the text: sources, venues of fieldwork, discussion of purpose and scope. At this point, however, I should like to acknowledge at least some of the large amount of help that I have received in the course of a long period of interest in Blackfoot musical culture.

First, and most, I wish to acknowledge the help of many Blackfoot people in Browning, Montana, and nearby communities, in their willingness to teach me, to permit me to record their songs and some of their statements, and to discuss many matters not particularly familiar to them. I have tried to interpret their ideas synthetically, but I have also, in a good many places, quoted or paraphrased what they said (while avoiding direct attribution). Although brief quotations inevitably suffer from lack of context, I feel that these statements provide authenticity while also relieving the academic narration. They help, further, to underscore and clarify the difficulties of moving from field interview to interpretive ethnography. Using my notes, I have selected these quotations and presented them intact except for smoothing out sentences and grammar to make them more compatible with academic prose.

In my text I am preserving the anonymity of speakers, as I am sure most of them would want it, but I wish here to remember several of my principal consultants who are at a very advanced age or no longer living: Tom Many-Guns, Mary Ground, Calvin Boy, Darryl Blackman, John Tatsey, Percy Bullchild, and Pete Stabs-by-mistake. There are many others. I hope they will regard my interpretation of their culture as at least sympathetic and reasonable. I also wish to thank two directors of the Museum of the Plains Indian in Browning, Dr. Claude Schaeffer and Loretta Pepion, and the long-time Chairman of the Blackfeet Tribal Council, Earl Oldperson, for introducing me to consultants and for other kinds of help. Over the years, I have received support of many kinds from the University of Illinois toward my work with Blackfoot music, particularly in the form of grants that made it possible to appoint research assistants and to free my own time, and I should like to thank the University Research Board, the Center for Advanced Study, the Department of Anthropology, and the School of Music for many kinds of help. Funds from these units made possible research by Stephen Blum and Robert Witmer in the 1960s, research that is tangentially yet significantly relevant to this study. For making possible field trips in 1967 and 1984, I wish to express gratitude to the Wenner-Gren Foundation for Anthropological Research, which provided grants-in-aid and funding for equipment.

I am especially grateful to Victoria Lindsay Levine, who worked as my research assistant in 1982–83, abstracting and organizing a large amount of data about musical culture culled from many works of ethnography. Finally, I wish to thank Charlotte Frisbie, Robert Witmer, Charles Capwell, Victoria Lindsay Levine, Carol Babiracki, and Robert Carlson for reading earlier versions of these pages and providing many helpful criticisms and comments.

Ideas About Music

There is a strand of literature in the history of ethnomusicology that is devoted to interpreting the relationship of music to the rest of the culture of individual societies. Largely of recent origin, it was inspired significantly by Alan P. Merriam's classic musical ethnography, *Ethnomusicology of the Flathead Indians* (1967), to date probably still the most comprehensive and successful holistic description of the musical culture of a tribal society. It is interesting though only slightly relevant that the Flathead were for several centuries virtual neighbors of the Blackfoot, separated from them (as their reservations still are) only by the Rocky Mountains, sharing aspects of culture and yet, because of their primary associations with the Salish-speaking peoples on the West Coast and the Intermountain Plateau, different in important ways. Merriam draws many comparisons between Flathead and Blackfoot cultures and musics and has thus been particularly important as a guide to this work.

But more influential than this incidental relationship of cultures is Merriam's method of making a presentation of Flathead musical culture. The work is divided into two categories, modestly labeled "ethnography" and "songs and analysis," but this organization makes clear Merriam's view that the musical domain consists of the "music itself," as well as the way music relates to the rest of culture. In Merriam's presentation, the categories are relatively self-contained and separable, at least for purposes of anthropological description and interpretation.

In thus dividing Flathead musical culture in 1967 into two parts, Merriam actually retreated from one of his most influential statements in *The Anthropology of Music* (1964:32–33), the description of his three-part model, which interprets the musical universe of a culture as composed of concept, behavior, and sound, each affecting and affected by the others.

Following Merriam's leadership, I have in this study accepted his division of music for the purpose of exploring the "concept" part of the model. As Merriam would have expected, I have found it difficult to establish and maintain the boundaries between the sectors and have constantly had to draw on sound and behavior to provide insights into conceptualization. The focus of my study is what the people think about music—the conceptions, ideas, and assumptions that underlie the songs themselves and that govern the kinds of behavior that lead to the production and consumption of musical sound.

As the previous sentence suggests, I have modified Merriam's model of 1964. He presents the three parts as being somehow equal and analogous in their interrelationships, but to me, instead, difficult as it is to illustrate in real life, the concept part of the model is first and governs. There is a chronological implication in this theoretical model. We know that in all societies, people are constantly and simultaneously performing music, doing things to bring music about, and thinking about music. Yet for the understanding of culture, it seems to me helpful to think of musical life as a sequence: The society first develops concepts, ideas that derive from central themes and fundamentals of the culture. It then creates, on the basis of these ideas, the observable facts of musical culture, composed of songs and pieces, instruments, style characteristics, and occasions and contexts for performance. The identification of these ideas in Blackfoot culture is my primary task.

It is relevant here to ask whether, instead of Merriam's three-part model, there is not a model available in Blackfoot thought that would be appropriate for our purposes. In a sense, identification of such a model would have to follow the reading of this essay, as it tries to establish the Blackfoot ways of thinking about their music. At a number of points, readers will be presented with taxonomies of song, performance, and musicians, and they might be tempted to ask why these were not used in the first place as the basis of organization of my effort. But in order for ethnomusicologists to communicate with each other, they must agree on a way of presenting information that is compatible with the modes of thinking used in many cultures. A fundamentally comparative perspective is required in a framework for the description of a variety of musical cultures. Merriam's model is sufficiently general to provide this framework.

Finding ways in which concepts of music and musical life are related to the guiding principles and general themes of culture would be difficult even in a society whose members write explanatory books on the subject. Much literature of historical musicology—and surely most of that of the sociology of music, or history and analysis in a Marxist framework, or aesthetics and criticism—deals in one way or another with this problem for Europe and modern America. That literature, based on a plethora of explanatory and analytical work provided by the culture being studied, has surely not been conclusive. For a small tribal society such as the Blackfoot, the task is still more difficult. There are, after all, only some 25,000 of them, there has been much forced discontinuity in their culture, they had no written documents in earlier times, and they still have only rudiments of an articulated music theory and little inclination to verbalize about music.

Why then the Blackfoot? I am tempted to give the reply about scaling a mountain: because they are there, and in the long run, every culture ought to be thus examined. More honestly, for myself, their selection relates to early assignments in my undergraduate studies, to my love of mountains, and most important, to the discovery, three decades ago, that for these people, much music had been recorded and a vast amount published by way of ethnography and history, while no one had carried out ethnomusicological analysis and synthesis. But in a more general sense, the question of why I am concerned with music and society in such a study leads us briefly to aspects of the history of ethnomusicology: the special role of tribal peoples, the importance of a holistic approach to musical culture, and the ideal of the comprehensive description of culture.

In part because of the time of its emergence, sociocultural anthropology began by concentrating on tribal societies around the world at a time when many of these were on the verge of disintegration. Many anthropologists (and to an extent even anthropology as a discipline) were motivated to some degree by concepts that are now considered not wholly laudable, such as cultural evolutionism and its social consequences, the curiosity of the exotic, and the idea that tribal cultures were on levels of development different from the anthropologists' own cultures and thus deserved the colonialist treatment they were receiving (Harris 1968:516–17; Stocking 1968:110–32). Another strong (and probably more laudable) stimulus to anthropologists was the desire to show humanity in its diversity, to demonstrate that the Western way of life was not the only worthwhile one. For this, too, the tribal societies, being the most distant, were the most relevant. But more important, there was the belief that in small societies investigators might be able to do in a kind of microcosm what might be much more difficult in the macrocosm of an immense population such as that of the West, or China, or India. Anthropologists appear also to have assumed, probably with less justice, that in a small culture, the technical knowledge that would ordinarily be required of a scholar wishing to study the art, music, technology, theology, or architecture of the world's major societies could be obviated, and that one researcher could therefore with confidence deal with all domains of culture and their interrelationships.

In the beginnings of ethnomusicology, too, tribal cultures played an exceptionally important role, and they were featured in general works of the field even into the 1960s (Stumpf 1911, Sachs 1930 and 1962, Merriam 1964). As in anthropology, here too evolution and the exotic surely played a part in determining this balance. So also did the basic assumption that tribal or "primitive" culture—including of course musical life—was homogeneous and therefore that one could receive, even from one informant, all of the knowledge necessary to describe the entire musical culture.

Related was the belief that in studying a tribal society, an individual researcher could comprehend the entire musical system. Such a view characterized anthropology in earlier times, and although anthropologists today no longer regard this as an attainable goal, it is at the basis of the strong interrelationship of domains, in pulling together disparate parts of a culture to provide generalizable insights. Scholars such as Alan Merriam, John Blacking, and David McAllester surely have not underestimated the complexity of a tribal musical culture; and yet they and some of their colleagues seemed to believe (justifiably, at least to an extent) that with a substantial amount of fieldwork and study they could at least go far toward this goal of comprehensiveness. In China, India, or Europe, with their huge and diverse populations, where classical music systems live alongside the vernacular musics, where there are complex stratifications of musical life, such comprehensive work is much more difficult. Making studies that come reasonably close to comprehending totality by viewing some of the world's tribal cultures is therefore a service that ethnomusicologists can provide for musical and cultural scholarship at large.

My own experience conforms somewhat to that of the tribally oriented scholar. To be sure, Blackfoot culture (like tribal cultures generally; see Hood 1985) turns out not to be so simple either—far from it. Yet, looking at the whole culture has to a certain extent been possible but not easy. It is an approach that presents problems not only in the gathering of data but also in the structuring of results, for its purpose is to clarify the internal connectedness of parts, such as the relationship between the significance of music in the cosmology and the role of the musician in culture, ideas about composition or learning music and the way in which words are used in song, symbolism of instruments and length and structure of songs (to give artificial examples).

To most Americans or Europeans, Blackfoot music is likely to sound interesting for a few minutes, though a handful may be forever fascinated. The suggestion that it might be a system of sound and structure worthy of comparison with the classical European tradition or perhaps even with the repertory of rock and roll probably seems ludicrous to many. In certain respects this kind of comparison appears ridiculous even to Blackfoot people today, as they know both of these traditions and in many ways keep them thoroughly separate. If I may anticipate (and also generalize very broadly), I would argue that the Blackfoot people consider Western or "white" music as something interesting and enjoyable to hear and also technically admirable and difficult, while the significance of Indian music lies principally in the ideas with which it is associated, in its meaning at many levels. To be sure, many Blackfoot people may not appreciate that Western music is important to whites for similar reasons, and they may suspect (with good reason perhaps?) that the whites whom they know do not have a music as significant to themselves as have the Indians. But the point is that if I am to present Blackfoot musical culture and make it credible to an audience of non-Blackfoot readers, I can do it best in terms of the ideas behind it, of the way in which it operates in its culture. If Western society has developed a technically and technologically complex system of music with which Indian music cannot compete, the fundamental ideas about music in Blackfoot culture are nevertheless of an order of sophistication comparable to those of the West. We want to know about these ideas because, for one thing, they may explain why the music sounds as it does. But also, we sometimes find that they contradict what we learn from sound and behavior and that they instead reflect other and possibly deeper meanings, functions, and ideals.

Let me briefly illustrate by mentioning three events that led me to observations culminating in an interest in the study at hand. In the 1950s and early 1960s I was doing what was then very conventional fieldwork in ethnomusicology, simply recording songs and asking the singers to comment on the individual items they were providing me. At one point during this work, a Blackfoot singer made comments that spoke to his perception of Western music as laying its major emphasis on words. "Our songs don't have no words," he said, "American songs all got words." The statement was not totally correct, but it led me to realize that the presence and absence of words played an important role in the very conception of music in culture. I knew of course that Plains Indian songs often had only a few meaningful words, and that many were sung to vocables exclusively. Yet now the fact that the absence of words was conceived by Blackfoot singers as a positive force struck me as a matter of great import, and its investigation probably more worthwhile than the collection of more data in the form of songs.

The background for the second observation is the belief, once widely held in ethnomusicology, that music in tribal societies changed slowly and new songs or pieces came into existence only rarely. Before my first visit to Montana, I had read that the main source of music in the traditional culture was visions in which guardian spirits appeared, but I understood that human composition was now recognized. On my third day in Montana, I asked an old man whether things were not very different now, with new songs being composed by people all the time. "Not so different. The Blackfoot nation has always been recipient of many songs," I was told by this consultant, who had a somewhat ceremonial way of expressing himself. In the nineteenth century it appears that visions in which guardian spirits appeared—the principal sources of songs—were regarded as frequent and numerous events. Not only in the present but also in earlier times it was the Blackfoot conception that a musical repertory could change, that there were always more songs to be learned. Might this have something to do, I asked myself, with the concept of a universe that provided never-ending resources? Was music therefore either a symbol of the principles guiding the universe or simply a typical component of everyday life?

For the third observation, I move to a visit to the Blackfeet Indian Reservation in the later 1960s. Some people told me that they learned songs in one hearing. I knew that this was not always really so, as I could see singers recording songs on cassettes, but some nevertheless insisted on the theory. I began to ask myself whether this might have something to do with the way in which songs were said to come to individuals in visions and with the structure of songs, a structure that, though not really simple, might almost have been calculated to enable people to learn songs quickly, in a single hearing.

Asking whether a song has words, whether a song is new, and how a song is put together are questions of a sort that have been conventionally asked for many decades in various styles of ethnomusicological inquiry, including the simple collecting of songs; but they are also the kinds of questions that may lead to a discovery of underlying ideas about music. These, in turn, while serving to explain musical sound and behavior, may also help to illuminate the pervasive themes of a culture.

CHAPTER ONE

Background

1. ON MUSICAL ETHNOGRAPHY

Culture could well be defined as what people take for granted, or as those things on which the members of a society agree (but see Kroeber and Kluckhohn 1952, for an early indication of the multiplicity of definitions). Even given the validity of such a rather oversimplified approach, it still turns out to be difficult to determine what precisely it is that a whole society takes for granted, what kinds of information can be regarded as authentically part of a culture, and what degree of agreement must be found before an ethnographer can claim, as it were, to have captured a culture. In much of their research, ethnomusicologists have established the character of musical cultures through intensive study with one or a few informant-teachers or consultants, and even where contact was more extensive, they have usually avoided the kind of approach that would blanket a population with questionnaires. According to some anthropological literature (e.g., Schneider 1980:11–12), the honest statements of an individual consultant may always be credited, as all members of a society, virtually without exception, share at least the most essential guiding principles of their culture. For most fieldworkers, statements by one consultant are not enough, however; extensive residence and intensive exposure as a participant in a culture are therefore usually accepted as techniques coming closest to ensuring reliability. Determining who speaks for a culture and how much consensus is required to define culture is only one of several problems of theory and method faced by an ethnographer of music.

Whether through the account of a scholar who studied with just one consultant or teacher, or of another who established extensive contact, a reader of ethnography usually assumes that he or she is being informed about a culture as it existed at the time of field investigation. Actually, much published American Indian ethnography reconstructs a picture of the past. The classic studies of Lowie (1935), Wissler (1910, 1912a, 1912b), and Kroeber (1902), for example, gave detailed presentation of social structure, religion, warfare, subsistence, clothing, and housing that applied to societies whose lifeways at the time of study no longer conformed to the descriptions, and the investigations were carried out largely on the basis of accounts given by a small number of consultants. But it is assumed in such ethnographic works that some elements from the culture of earlier times provide continuity into the present.

In the most technical sense, ethnography describes culture synchronically. Following the mentioned work by classic ethnographers of the Plains such as that of Clark Wissler, a description of Blackfoot musical culture might well deal entirely with the songs, events, and ideas of the period before 1900. But there would be insufficient data for making this description comprehensive. On the other hand, an account of Blackfoot culture based on more recent observation alone would have to exclude much from the past that would explain the present, and vice versa, and would omit much of what it means to be Blackfoot. Despite obvious methodological flaws, therefore, I was attracted to trying to sketch a composite picture, proceeding from the assumption that there is still a close relationship between the Blackfoot culture of a hundred years ago and that of today. Few of the songs of this earlier time are still known, and the most characteristic kinds of musical events of today are recent innovations. Nevertheless, I believe that the core of Blackfoot culture, as it existed in the nineteenth century, is still at least partially intact and that there is some kind of fundamental continuity of culture that draws together the greatly differing periods in the history of these people. Is this belief justified?

The degree to which any society retains its culture over a period of time has not really been explicitly addressed in ethnomusicology (but see A. Schneider 1984, Knepler 1982, and Dahlhaus 1977:91–118 for relevant discussion from the history of European music). The issue enters into the basic methodology of all kinds of musicological endeavor, and a look at the way historians of Western music look at their subject may be instructive. They appear to share a belief that rapid change is part of the character of Western culture, fundamentally contrasting it in this respect with most other societies which are thought to possess greater stability and consistency unless disturbed by the intrusive Western culture. But this set of beliefs centering on changeability is contradicted by the Western humanist's typical faith in the unbroken continuity of Western culture. Many music historians regard Medieval and Renaissance music as directly ancestral to the Western music of the present, and some therefore believe that they can listen to such early music with their contemporary ears, reacting much as did the listeners of those times. Among Western musicologists, cultural distance among periods of history is not considered an obstacle, compared to the cultural distance between European, African, and Chinese musics in the twentieth century of which contemporary scholars must take account. To historians of Western music, consistency of culture almost implicitly involves a function of biologic inheritance.

It is thus widely believed that one can reconstruct the musical life of the European Middle Ages from the fragmentary information available and that it can be properly interpreted by Europeans because the Middle Ages is thought to be part of their culture.

Whether such a procedure is justified or not, its benefits and weaknesses are similar to those with which the end of the "early" days of Blackfoot culture, the period ca. 1890, can be described. From that time on, Blackfoot culture has been internally consistent in one respect: it has constantly been under the pressures of white people and their culture, and its development is driven principally by the need for adaptation and survival. Thus, drawing a picture of that period by relating facts from 1890 and 1950 to each other may not be very different from producing a synthetic picture of medieval music that is drawn by relating facts from 950 and 1100, in a changing and yet internally consistent situation.

We will see some evidence that in culture the concept sector of Merriam's three-part model of music has had substantial consistency since the late nineteenth century, while behavior has changed greatly and, to a smaller degree, musical style as well. The three parts of the model are of course at best difficult to separate, and because of their mutual influence, as Merriam presents them (1964:32–33), they work to some extent in tandem. If the culture concept of anthropology can be interpreted in part as something tending to give stability to human life, with its core of a set of values that direct the more specific and practical domains of culture, then music in its totality can be interpreted as a microcosm of the total culture determined by the values and principles in *its* "concept" sector. For example, assuming that a major abiding value in Western music since the Renaissance is the importance of the ensemble, this value has certainly been expressed at different times in various ways. If, in the principal conception and framework of the musical culture, the composer is central and compositional innovation the driving force, that will be encountered in different guises in the various historical periods and sectors of society. In this study, it has been convenient to look at Blackfoot musical culture along somewhat similar lines.

It is fundamental to my account and analysis that there is such a thing as *a* Blackfoot musical culture, early and recent, and that it is principally to be sought in the ideas about and concepts involving music. These are related to broader principles that characterize the culture as a whole and that retain a certain degree of stability even over periods in which the more external aspects of the culture undergo fundamental change. The fragments of information of varying degrees of validity available from many sources and times can cautiously be drawn together to form some kind of unified whole. But if the cultural differences within the last one hundred years must be reconciled in order for a holistic picture of culture to emerge, there is also uncommonly great variation within Blackfoot society at any one time within this period. Indeed, one might be tempted to suggest that if culture is what the people in a society overtly agree upon, then in the present period of Blackfoot history, possibly there is not much of a Blackfoot culture.

But it is the discovery of central values and themes of culture and the central concepts of music that enable one to reject such a suggestion. The general ideas about music seem to have been maintained more consistently than have the facts of musical life and sound, just as the *idea* of being a Blackfoot people has had more consistency than the various ways, over the last hundred years, of being Blackfoot.

Separating the ideas about music from other parts of the musicocultural system has a long tradition in Europe and much of Asia, where the writing of theoretical treatises and philosophical speculation about music have for centuries been established practice. For some decades of the much shorter history of ethnomusicology, there was little interest in this kind of separation. Early research, to the 1950s, most typically involved presentation of music in notation and explanation of the music itself and, at most, of the technical theory developed for some Asian art musics. The kinds of interest motivating my study are represented mainly in more recent publications.

But there are occasional earlier ventures. A particularly influential though short example of ethnomusicological attention to musical thought in tribal societies is found in the work of George Herzog, in an article entitled "Music in the Thinking of the American Indians" (1938). A product of the later part of Herzog's scholarly career, it appeared in an obscure periodical and seems to have been presented as a kind of apologetic adjunct to what Herzog regarded as his more central research, analysis of musical style and sound. A more extensive and comprehensive approach to music as a set of ideas did not really make a significant appearance before the presentation of Merriam's mentioned tripartite model of music.

But a considerable number of publications followed Merriam's general orientation and thus helped to provide the framework for this study of Blackfoot culture. While these works all show their dependence on Merriam, they nevertheless exhibit differences in method and approach, depending both on the authors' disciplinary orientations and on the characters of the cultures studied. Let me mention a few. Steven Feld's analysis of the Kaluli of Papua New Guinea (1982) is in the first instance an ethnography of the soundscape of their culture. In dealing with singing as one of a number of types of sound recognized by the Kaluli, along with speech, weeping, and bird song, it relates music principally to myth and to the symbolism of birds. Berliner's study of Mbira music of the Shona people of Zimbabwe (1978), on the other hand, deals with a rather complex system of music theory related mainly to ritual but is much more concerned with the technical aspects of music and the way in which it is described and analyzed by Shona musicians.

Sakata's study of the concept of music in the Persian-speaking culture of Afghanistan (1983) is about the nature and evaluation of music as a concept and as a set of ideas as they relate to the practice of music by various types of musicians coming from a number of social contexts. Neuman's work on the Mirasis of northern India (1980) concerns ideas about music as derived in various respects from social structure. Charles Keil's study of the Tiv (1979) deals with music as embracing a number of functions in a society of Nigeria. Monts (1983) provides similar sorts of data, in less detail, for the Vai culture of Liberia, deriving some of his conclusions from analysis of musical structure.

All of these studies are based substantially upon the terminology used for music and the system of ideas it lays bare but also on behavior of musicians and audience as they suggest conceptualization. Terminology, however, is even more explicitly the subject of Ames and King (1971), who provide a glossary of Hausa musical terms that includes hundreds of words, all conceivably related to musical activity and thought. Here the terms provide a panorama of the musical culture, principally concentrating on sound and behavior. Powers (1980) analizes the terminology of the Oglala Sioux to deal more specifically with the concept sector of Merriam's model. Haefer (1981) for the Papago, Lah (1980) for the Arapaho, Zemp (1978, 1979) for New Guinea and Rice (1980) for rural Bulgaria all approach the question of technical musical thought through examination of text, behavior, and musical structure. Each using different aspects of culture to provide a principal focus of organization, they illustrate together some of the many ways in which a study of ideas about music may be carried out. Any one culture could surely be viewed in several ways; but also, for each culture there may be a limited number of approaches that would work.

Less concentrated and more interpretive than most of the above-mentioned publications, this study about the Blackfoot tries to use four different handles to grasp the universe of ideas about music: (1) conceptions of the general character of music; (2) ideas about music as it exists in time—its origins, history, sources, and changeability; (3) music in society—the society of both humans and supernatural figures; and (4) conceptions of music as a system of sound, as an art. Let me say a word about the organization of what follows. Whether or not it is a plan that might work as a framework for describing many cultures, it is in any event not derived specifically from Blackfoot musical thought. Yet it has compatibilities in Blackfoot culture. History, for example, is to the Blackfoot mainly a matter of origins and of change from times of origin, and so it is reasonable for me to combine origins and change in one chapter. Likewise, the Blackfoot use music to communicate with both humans and supernaturals, justifying my combination of ideas about music as social event and as religious communication. The Blackfoot have a concern for the technicalities of music, but it is an interest relatively minor compared to their concern with music in society and ritual, a situation paralleled in the relatively small proportion of this study devoted to musicianship. The Blackfoot, like many Native American peoples, conceive of much in nature and culture as occurring in groups of four and would therefore probably find my four categories appropriate. And as the songs in some Blackfoot ceremonies appear in groups of seven, I have tried as well, for symbolic and aesthetic reasons, to follow their example in subdividing my chapters.

2. THE BLACKFOOT PEOPLE

The following paragraphs provide a brief introduction to the Blackfoot people for readers of this study. Much has been written about the culture and history of the Blackfoot. Those wishing to read more, seeking reliable but nontechnical literature, are best directed to five publications: *The Blackfeet: Raiders on the Northwestern Plains* by John Ewers (1958) is the most accessible yet authoritative ethnography and history. McFee (1972) gives a thorough description of life on the Blackfeet Reservation in Montana in the late 1960s, while a comprehensive photographic record of this history from the late nineteenth century to World War II is provided by Farr (1984). Samek (1987) makes a comparative study of the relationship of the Canadian and U.S. governments with the Blackfoot people in the period in which the essence of the contemporary culture was established, 1880–1920. And among the writings by Blackfoot authors, the detailed account of mythology by Percy Bullchild, with extensive commentary (1985), stands out.

The Blackfoot language belongs to the Algonquian language family whose speakers lived largely in the eastern section of the continent; the closest linguistic relatives are the fellow-Algonquian Arapaho and Cheyenne. Language relationships suggest that the Blackfoot, about five hundred years ago, were located in the area of the western Great Lakes, living a partially nomadic life but engaging in some agriculture and even making pottery. Later, as a result of various pressures as well as the introduction of horses and guns, they moved westward, taking up a prevailingly nomadic lifestyle and giving up agriculture and associated crafts.

In the nineteenth century, the Blackfoot were among the northernmost peoples sharing the typical Indian culture of the Great Plains. There were three major groups, the Blood and the Northern Blackfoot, both now located largely in Alberta, and the Piegan (*pikuni* in Blackfoot), living today largely on the Blackfeet Reservation in Montana. This Montana reservation is the locus of most of the work on which these pages are based. The Blackfoot had much in common with other Northern Plains tribes such as the Crow, Cheyenne, Arapaho, and Gros Ventres, but they also shared customs and other culture traits with the Flathead, a Salish-speaking people on the western side of the Continental Divide in Montana, and with the Algonquian-speaking Cree, directly northeast of Blackfoot territory.

It is estimated that there were about 20,000 Blackfoot people in the early nineteenth century, and at the present, there are perhaps 25,000. But in the intervening time there were often far fewer, as the population was periodically decimated by disease, starvation, and warfare. The area they inhabited shrank, through wars and a series of unfavorable treaties, from large sections of Alberta and Montana in the early nineteenth century to the Delaware-sized reservation established around 1890 in Montana and three smaller reserves in Alberta. Many members of the tribe live in communities near these reservations, and of course many also live far away, notably in Great Falls, Seattle, and Minneapolis.

After 1800, the Blackfoot developed effective styles of warfare and dominated the area, defending their territory against whites and other Indian peoples. They followed the nomadic life typical of Plains peoples: hunting buffalo on horseback and using them for food, clothing, housing, and ceremonial objects; living in small bands during winter and joining together in the summer; and maintaining an informal political structure with "chiefs" who were usually respected older men with temporary authority.

In Blackfoot tradition, the cosmos consisted of the real world, inhabited by humans and animals, and a supernatural world, inhabited by spirits whose forms were like those of humans and animals, but which might also be abstractions. The portion of the supernatural world above ground was dominated by the sun, who was sometimes personified by the figure of Old Man or Napi, a figure consisting of creator, partly human culture hero, and folkloristic trickster all in one. Below ground, the dominant figure was beaver. The numbers four and seven play a major role in Blackfoot cosmology, standing for the four cardinal directions and the six principal points (plus center), and represented widely in the organization of rituals and in the music theory. The cosmos also included non-Blackfoot humans, but in general it was tribe-centered. Supernatural figures had relevance only to the Blackfoot themselves, yet they were in a sense outside the tribe. As we will have occasion to explain, one of the functions of songs was and is to mediate between Blackfoot humans and the rest of the cosmos.

Blackfoot religion was based largely on personal experience in revelation and ritual. A man tried to have visions, and if he was successful, these would occur in a series in which a guardian spirit—usually an animal but sometimes a person, spirit, abstract concept (thunder), or object—appeared, taught songs and prayers, and gave instructions for carrying out the ceremonies that would provide supernatural help in curing, bringing good weather, or helping to bring buffalo. Powerful medicine men had "medicine bundles" of many objects each of which was often accompanied by one or several songs. A ceremony would usually begin with the telling of the origin myth of the bundle; then the owner opened it and took out each object, carrying out the required action including singing the appropriate songs.

Medicine bundle ceremonies took place at various times of the year, but the other major rite, the Sun Dance, which the Blackfoot shared with many other Plains and other Indian peoples, was carried out in midsummer. A large, nine-day ceremony in which everyone participated, it consisted of many events, some simultaneous, as the subdivisions of the tribe united for individual vision quests and a large variety of social activities, dances, and athletic contests. The Blackfoot had a series of eight age-grade societies into which men were successively initiated roughly every four years, each society having its ritual and playing particular roles in warfare and social life. The women had only one analogous society. Warfare was carried out in different forms. Tribal wars were waged for territory, property, or defense. A smaller kind of conflict was the war party led by an individual, the purpose being to "count coup," that is, to show courage rather than inflicting major damage. Economic life involved the personal accumulation of wealth in the form of horses, buffalo robes, skins, and ceremonies, but also the obligation to share it with poorer relatives and others. Athletic contests, social dances, and gambling dominated recreational activity.

Generally speaking, men and women played greatly different cultural roles. The men took care of hunting, ceremonial life, and contact with the public and outside worlds, human and supernatural; women performed most of the day-to-day labor, including moving the tribe's belongings in the constant nomadic life of packing and unpacking, remaining out of the limelight. Male bravado and female modesty were mitigated by a group of "manly-hearted women" (Lewis 1941) who in their attitudes and activities approximated more the role of men, and possibly of male transvestites, berdaches, whose existence in Blackfoot culture is not well documented.

This is a rough sketch of Blackfoot life valid perhaps for the early nineteenth century. The Blackfoot people in Montana today live very differently, but regard themselves no less as Blackfoot. A majority of the population of the reservation and surroundings is "mixed-blood," that is, Blackfoot people with partially white ancestry. The Reservation is a microcosm of an urban area, with Browning and its surroundings holding half of the population, while outlying towns, including Heart Butte and Starr School, are smaller and tied to Browning as the center of employment and commerce. Blackfoot people work as ranchers and on ranches, in the tourist trade generated by nearby Glacier National Park, on the Great Northern Railroad which cuts through the reservation, for governmental agencies located in Browning, and in small industries, notably the pencil-manufacturing Blackfeet Indian Writing Company. A substantial white population live on the reservation, and a good proportion of the businesses are owned by whites. On the surface at least, relationships between whites and Blackfoot people are generally, though not totally, friendly. The reservation has its share of unemployed—largely among the full-blooded population—and the social problems common to impoverished minorities, but since my first contact, there has been some improvement in the economic and social welfare. To most tourists stopping in Browning, it is not clear that this is a Native American town, as in most respects Blackfoot life is much like that of other rural Montanans.

In a sense, the Blackfoot people live in two worlds, and their social and political organizations reflect this bifurcation. The office of mayor of Browning is usually held by a white person, and Montana laws govern driving, education, and marriage. The school system is integrated, with some attention given to the Indian background of the majority of students, including the teaching of some Indian songs by the music teachers. The tribe is governed, under a written constitution, by the Tribal Council, also called the Business Council, which has the job of caring for tribal land, fishing and wildlife resources, and tribally owned enterprises, while older traditions are carried out under the informal authority of an "honorary council" of elderly men. Older tradition and modern life are held together also by the Museum of the Plains Indian, an institution under the Department of the Interior, whose visitors are equally white tourists and Indians, and by the Blackfeet Community College, whose largest department is Native American Studies.

The visitor to the Montana Blackfoot (and the reader of these pages) may incidentally be confused by various forms of the tribal name that are found in publication. In libraries one will find the Blackfoot-language term *Siksika,* derived from *Siksikáikwan* ("a Blackfoot person"); anthropologists typically use the singular, *Blackfoot,* for one or several persons, noun or adjective, and we will here ordinarily follow this practice. The U.S. Government opted for *Blackfeet,* and the official name of the location is Blackfeet Indian Reservation. A member of the community is likely to say "I am Blackfoot," but just as likely, "I am a member of the Blackfeet tribe." If one person is a Blackfeet, then one may occasionally hear it said with unmistakable logic (if also with a grin) that "we are all Blackfeets."

The degree of current use of the Blackfoot language is briefly discussed in chapter 2, section 5. Suffice it here to say that most Blackfoot people speak it somewhat, but not many very well; and virtually all speak English. Its use is reserved more for ceremonial than for everyday speech. The character of the language is agglutinative, and even simple, basic concepts are expounded by combining several morphemes. For example, the word for a medicine pipe song is *natoaskúiinyemainxksini,* derived from *natóas* ("sacred"), *kúiin ("pipe"),* and *nínixksini* ("song"); *ikotsí-piksák(i)x* ("red bird woman") is derived from *ekotsí* ("red plume"), *piksí* ("bird"), and *akéwa* ("woman"). Words are long, few have less than two syllables (e.g. *nitókska* = "one"; *nátoka* = "two"; *niuókska* = "three"). In the phonology, there is a tendency to have long consonant clusters, making the language difficult for speakers of English to pronounce. There are unvoiced vowels, phonemic stress, and length. An utterance in Blackfoot requires more time than its typical English translation, and as the Blackfoot people are prone to be expansive in conversation, the impression one receives in Browning or Heart Butte is quite the opposite of the stereotype of the "taciturn Indian."

In the few instances in which the Blackfoot language is used on these pages, I have opted for a transcription based on Uhlenbeck and van Gulick's system (1930 and 1934) that uses the continental values for vowels and the English values for consonants (exceptions: x = velar fricative [as in German *ach];* ' = glottal stop). Length (in vowels and consonants) is represented by doubling. Stress is indicated by acute accents, and unvoiced vowels are enclosed in parentheses.

The aspects of Blackfoot culture that go back to earlier times are used by the people of Browning more as emblem of ethnicity than as cultural lifestyle. Their "Blackfootness" functions rather like the "Polishness" or "Italianness" of ethnic groups in New York or Detroit. There are T-shirts emblazoned "Blackfeet Indian Reservation," the Browning High School football team is the "Indians," and signs at the entrance of the reservation welcome the driver to "Blackfeet Indian Territory." All this is mildly frivolous. But in a more serious vein, when the Blackfoot people, whose lives are not easily distinguished from those of the white Americans among whom they live, wish to show to themselves and to the world that they are Blackfoot, they do so with their language, with their dances and costumes, and perhaps most, with their songs.

3. Sources

Having suggested to the reader that there is a dearth and spottiness of information for putting together a comprehensive picture of Blackfoot musical thought, I am now obliged to contradict myself. The Blackfoot have actually been the subject of an unusually large amount of historical and ethnographic research and publication. The quantity of writing that deals with the Blackfoot is considerable in the context of literature about American Indian peoples, to say nothing of tribal societies in many other parts of the world. As indicated in the discography at the end, their songs have been recorded by anthropologists, ethnomusicologists, casual visitors, and by Blackfoot people themselves, over a period of ninety years. It is, indeed, the relative wealth of this material that lends emphasis to the many gaps and the uncertainty and tentativeness of much that is said, making those all the more frustrating. Let me briefly touch on some of the literature available for ethnomusicological study.

In view of the many ethnographic publications and the plethora of recordings, one of the curious gaps is the absence of works that deal explicitly with music and musical life. The only work before the 1960s is a short article by the composer Arthur Nevin (1916). Since about 1960, publications include a few articles by myself (Nettl 1967, 1968b) devoted largely to description of musical life in Browning and some summarization of data from earlier publications, along with discussion of certain problems of musical style. In 1982, Robert Witmer published the most important study of Blackfoot musical culture, based on research done in 1968 on the current state of musical life on the Blood Reservation in Alberta, and of great value for the present study. But there is much about music in other sources. Several ethnographers, travelers, and others who had occasion to find themselves in northwestern Montana or southern Alberta in the late nineteenth century contributed to what eventually became a rich literature on Blackfoot culture, rivaling in quantity the large amount of writing devoted to other well-known tribes such as the Dakota, Navajo, and Iroquois.

In this early period, ca. 1890–1910, four figures stand out. Walter McClintock, whose most famous book, *The Old North Trail* (1910), was read by generations of Boy Scouts and Indian hobbyists, spent portions of several years beginning in 1896 with the Blackfoot. *The Old North Trail* gives colorful accounts of many events involving music and, better than other books, shows its important role in many aspects of life, even in that most difficult time in Blackfoot history. It is of particular interest that some Blackfoot individuals considered it important for McClintock to learn about their culture, get the facts right, and help to make their values and customs known. A master photographer and raconteur, McClintock also made some recordings in 1898 and 1900 and included nine transcriptions of songs in his book. But it is his vivid accounts of singing at dances and ceremonies and the context of singing that were most helpful in this study.

A second figure of importance in this early period was George Bird Grinnell, renowned naturalist, folklorist, and ethnographer, who spent much of his life and especially the last two decades of the nineteenth century studying Indian tribes, particularly Pawnee, Cheyenne, and Blackfoot, along with their natural environment. His role in the history of the Blackfoot country is especially distinguished, as it was he who did much to alert Congress to the desirability of establishing Glacier National Park (Grinnell 1892 [1962]:311; Farr 1984:12). In particular, Grinnell spent parts of several years between 1890 and 1898 with the Blackfoot, producing a major collection of folklore that includes the longest version of the origin myths (Grinnell 1892 [1962]) and making in 1897 what is probably the earliest collection of field recordings of songs. Like McClintock, Grinnell recognized the importance of music in Blackfoot life.

Grinnell received substantial help from a man who identified himself much more closely with the Blackfoot people, James Willard Schultz, a trader in the area from 1878 to 1904, who married into the tribe and took the Blackfoot name of Apikuni. Schultz eventually became a highly prolific author, writing many articles in the naturalist magazine *Forest and Stream* as well as thirty-seven books, the most famous being *My Life as an Indian* (1907). Much of his material is autobiographical, some may be fictionalized, and thus the authenticity of his information for ethnographic and historical purposes appears to be less solidly established than that of Grinnell's and McClintock's works. The quantity of material about music in Schultz's writings is modest in comparison to that of the other authors, but his descriptions of events and accounts of myths and tales are helpful here and there.

Most important by far in this period or, for that matter, in the entire anthropological literature dealing with the Blackfoot, are the publications of Clark Wissler. Taken together, they provide well over a thousand pages that give a thorough accounting of several domains of Blackfoot culture as it may be presumed to have existed before the heavy Westernization of the period 1880–1900. Wissler's publications include a collection of mythology (published with a part-Blackfoot consultant, D. C. Duvall, 1909) and studies of religion (1912a), social organization (1912b), material culture (1910), societies (1913), the Sun Dance (1918), and other aspects of life. Much of Wissler's work is based on the large collections of the American Museum of Natural History, but of course most of his findings result from fieldwork carried out in the first decade of the twentieth century. Like others of his time, Wissler includes substantial information about songs, musical life, and instruments, and much of the information about this period in Blackfoot history presented in my essay comes from his pages. In particular, the collection of myths (Wissler and Duvall, 1909) and the extremely detailed description of the medicine bundles and their rituals provide unprecedentedly broad coverage and include many indications of the use and content of songs. A section devoted specifically to the ethnography of songs (mainly in religious context) (1912a:263–72), based on a rather detailed recitation by one authoritative consultant, is an important feature of Wissler's *oeuvre*. The works are liberally sprinkled with Blackfoot song texts translated into English. In 1904, Wissler also made what was up to then the largest collection of recordings, 121 cylinders, which include the songs of several of the ritual materials he described.

These four figures rather dominate the study of Blackfoot culture in the early period of ethnography, and as they are well known to some of the more thoughtful and interested Blackfoot individuals, they may be said to maintain, even now, a towering presence in Browning and its environs. This early period of research, to 1910, then, provides a large body of ethnography, history, and observation from which one can draw much information about the sound of songs and music, a great deal about its cultural context, and here and there facts that can become ingredients of a picture of musical conceptualization.

In addition to the recordings made by Grinnell, McClintock, and Wissler, two more collections date from this early period, one by Joseph

K. Dixon as part of the Second Wanamaker Expedition, in 1908–1909, and twenty cylinders made by Edward S. Curtis, renowned ethnographer and photographer whose best-known work is a multi-volume survey of Indian cultures. Curtis (1911) includes thirteen song transcriptions by Henry F. Gilbert and gives accounts of contexts of music. Transcriptions were also made, though not published, by Arthur Nevin, who spent the summers of 1903 and 1904 near Browning; his occasionally quaint remarks (Nevin 1916) provide insights into patterns of musical life in early reservation culture. According to Gillis (1984:327–39), the amount of recorded material for this period exceeds what was available from any other North American Indian culture except for the Pawnee and the Hopi. Gillis lists 251 cylinders (plus two collections whose size is not known) for the "incunabula" period of ethnomusicological field recording, before 1910.

A less productive period of research followed. The decrease in interest may have come from the belief that the early scholars, in particular Wissler, had done it all, or the rapid Westernization of the Blackfoot resulted in a withdrawal of scholarly interest. Nevertheless, a number of researchers did work in Blackfoot country between 1910 and 1945, and some of their publications are helpful in this musicological project.

Of particular importance were the publications by the Dutch linguist, C. C. Uhlenbeck, about the Blackfoot language. Between 1911 and 1930, he published the most important descriptions of the language and its grammar, a set of texts including folkloristic material, and a large dictionary, all helping to provide insight into the musical culture (see Uhlenbeck 1911, Uhlenbeck and van Gulick 1930). Also noteworthy is a short monograph by Julian Steward (1934), but of special interest is the doctoral dissertation of Oscar Lewis (1942), carried out under the supervision of Ruth Benedict. Lewis makes only occasional references to songs and singing, but the reason for the significance of his work is its stature as one of the earliest studies making explicit the role of Western culture as an ingredient in culture change, in this case, Blackfoot life of the nineteenth and twentieth centuries. Also significant is Lewis's study (1941) of "manly-hearted women" among the Blackfoot, carried out in Canada in conjunction with his wife, Ruth Lewis. It is about women who in social life behaved more like men than did women as a whole and who also played a different role in musical life.

This "middle" period includes the beginning of a large number of publications by John Ewers, ethnologist and historian of the Blackfoot who resided for many years on the Blackfeet Reservation in Montana, and who in 1941 became the first curator of the Museum of the Plains Indian. Besides the mentioned synthesis of culture and history (1958), it is important to mention his detailed study of the horse in Blackfoot culture

(1955) and of the horse medicine ritual, which incidentally gives much information on songs and singing. Furthermore, the work of Lucien Hanks and Jane Richardson Hanks resulted in one of the few collections of recordings of this period, and their major monograph (1950) makes many references to musical life and associated ceremonies and to culture change.

Around 1950, there began a period of more specialized research carried out by a number of anthropologists coming from a variety of directions and with many purposes, and some of it was in the realm of ethnomusicological collecting and documentation. Substantial collections were made by Howard K. Kaufman and Donald Hartle, but neither resulted in significant publications. A number of projects carried out under the auspices of the Museum of the Plains Indian included specialized studies of an essentially ethnohistorical and historical nature, producing pamphlet-size publications (see e.g., Schaeffer 1962), with relevance to musical life.

Also noteworthy are serious if not scholar-oriented publications produced for tourists and for members of the Blackfoot community explaining rituals and traditions. Some of them are by an adopted member of the tribe, Adolf Hungry Wolf, a man of German origin, and by his Blackfoot wife, Beverly (see e.g., Hungry Wolf 1982). The detailed account of mythology and personal interpretation in an extensive volume already mentioned, by one of the older men of modern times (Bullchild 1985), is of special interest. My own fieldwork (see below) and that of Robert Witmer (see Witmer 1982) belong to this period. So also does the large amount of recording made for use in the contemporary musical culture by Blackfoot people or for a Blackfoot audience. The dozen LP records of Blackfoot music extant (in 1986) and the many prerecorded cassettes entirely or partially by Blackfoot singers provide well over two hundred songs, largely in the category of social dance and intertribal powwow material. While these commercial recordings can be discographically documented, there are probably also hundreds of hours of recordings made by Blackfoot individuals and by other residents or visitors to the Blackfoot communities. But I have no way of documenting or using these.

Two other publications illustrate the types of research and thinking characteristic of the last fifteen years. In contrast to the early and middle-period ethnographies, which (excepting Lewis 1942) strive to construct a picture of Blackfoot culture before and without Western intrusion, these recent works concentrate specifically on the interaction of the two cultures. McFee (1972) deals with traditional and Western cultural values, extracting these from behavior patterns and events, and showing how they help to shape two subdivisions of the contemporary Blackfoot society, the Indian- and the Western-oriented. Farr (1984) produced an anthology of photographs from the enormous photographic record of recent Blackfoot history, a record resulting in part from the proximity of Glacier National Park and the role of its development in Blackfoot history. This collection of photographs shows in exemplary fashion the gradual and the sudden changes in Blackfoot culture against the backdrop of an abiding Blackfoot ethnic identity.

In addition to the materials specifically devoted to the Blackfoot, I found it useful and sometimes essential to extrapolate from ethnographic publications dealing with neighboring or related cultures or to use them as guides. The homogeneity of the Plains culture area and of its history since the late nineteenth century is debatable, but whatever the eventual conclusions of anthropologists on that issue may be, the Blackfoot appear in several ways to be on the northern and western edge of the area. Even so, for a general picture of Blackfoot culture, the gaps in the Blackfoot literature can provisionally be filled by what is known of Plains tribes at large. At the same time, the relationship of the Blackfoot culture to American Indian peoples outside the Plains cannot be ignored.

Among the classics of the standard literature on related cultures, the general ethnography of greatest relevance is probably the study on the Arapaho by A. L. Kroeber (1902), a work that is thorough, voluminous, and comparable in time of research and scope to Wissler's work on the Blackfoot. Kroeber concentrates on ceremonial data and includes at least some mention of musical life (see Nettl 1955). As the Arapaho are linguistically related to the Blackfoot and, according at least to some scholars, the point of origin for certain elements of the classical Plains culture (Kroeber 1947:87–88), they are a society particularly suitable for comparison (see also Lah 1980). Another body of literature whose scope rivals that of Blackfoot and Arapaho ethnography is the series of studies by Robert H. Lowie on the Crow (see e.g., Lowie 1935, 1924), neighbors and associates of the Blackfoot. Lowie's lack of interest in social contexts of music, however, rather diminishes the value of his work for my study. The large body of ethnography on the musical life of the Dakota, beginning with Frances Densmore's distinguished study of the Teton Sioux (1918) and continuing with a series of publications by William Powers dealing with religion, music, and twentieth-century developments (Powers 1968, 1975, 1980, 1982), is also important.

All of these studies indicate that while there is, very broadly speaking, a Plains musical culture, tribal differences are great and significant, and except for a few general concepts such as the vision quest, the existence of men's societies, and the Sun Dance, what is true of some peoples may not be of others. The same applies to ethnographies dealing with two non-Plains culture groups associated with the Blackfoot, the western Woodlands peoples and the easternmost Salish. The likelihood that the Blackfoot once resided near other western Algonquian-speaking peoples in the Great Lakes region is generally acknowledged (Ewers 1958:6–7). But the degree to which one can gain insight into earlier, pre-Plains stages of Blackfoot musical culture from the recent accounts of Menomini, Winnebago, and Chippewa musical cultures by such authors as Densmore (1910, 1913), Radin (1920 [1963]), and Vennum (1982) is uncertain. Surely one may at least gain an occasional bit of insight.

Somewhat more helpful is Merriam's classic and already cited study of the Salish-speaking Flathead, which throughout makes a strong case for similarity and relationship to the Blackfoot (eg., 1967:315). Once the Blackfoot arrived on the western Plains and in their present locale, they proceeded to establish a great deal of friendly and also less friendly contact with non-Plains tribes. They evidently learned about horses from the Shoshoni and received many products of Western culture first through the Cree (Ewers 1958:21–23). A period of close and frequent interchange with the Flathead, living across the Continental Divide and immediately opposite the Blackfoot habitat, had begun by the nineteenth century and continued into recent decades. Thus, much of what Merriam says about the Flathead in the twentieth century virtually parallels what may be said about the Blackfoot. In the intertribal powwow culture of the 1960s and later, the contact intensified.

For the student of Blackfoot musical ideas, it is fortunate that so many scholars have studied and written about the culture at various times and recorded its music, and equally helpful that the Blackfoot have lived among other Indian peoples whose culture and music have also been well documented.

4. FIELDWORK

The published material on the Blackfoot and the amount of recorded music, then, is very considerable and covers a period of a hundred years. It has been essential to this study, but what I wish to offer here also depends substantially on my own fieldwork carried out over a period of almost thirty-five years, in several short installments, and so I feel that I owe the reader a summary accounting of these several excursions.

In 1950, I spent much of the summer working with Tom Many-Guns, an elderly resident of the Montana reservation who was temporarily working at Indiana University as a consultant for language study. My main purpose then was to record songs and to write down dictated texts, but I also asked him many questions, more or less at random, involving musical life. In these interviews, the songs he sang were usually the points of departure.

Much later, in 1965, I went for the first time to the Montana reservation for a few weeks, becoming generally oriented in the traditional musical culture, making recordings and becoming acquainted with a number of the individuals with whom I would later work more intensively—and, incidentally, renewing acquaintance with Tom Many-Guns. This work continued in 1966, when I spent the entire summer in Montana, trying to assemble material for a general ethnography of modern Blackfoot musical life and making recordings. I returned in the summer of 1967 to work mainly with one singer in order to explore his total repertory and to reconstruct his musical biography.

In the summer of 1982 I paid a brief visit again and returned to spend several weeks in 1984 and 1986 in order to redirect my questions and conversations from a focus on events and behavior to an emphasis on concepts and ideas that characterizes this monograph. I also wished to learn about changes that had taken place in the previous two decades. In this work, I tried to refer to earlier field workers and the questions that they raised, to engage in the most general kinds of conversations about music, to ask questions that might or might not be relevant to the re-spondent, and to work with some degree of intensity with a small but varied number of Blackfoot people. On these latest visits, I also recorded a modest quantity of music and a few conversations.

Throughout these visits I worked almost exclusively with people from the Blackfeet Reservation in Montana, and my fieldwork essentially rep-resents the views held there. Most of the fieldwork was actually done in Browning, but some 30 percent of the time was spent in other communities, particularly Heart Butte and Starr School, villages in which, as it happens, some of the most prominent singers resided. The ethnographic literature also tends to deal mainly with this largest group of Blackfoot people, but Witmer's findings (1982) on the Blood Reserve in Alberta support my belief that there is fundamental consistency among the branches of the Blackfoot nation.

Having briefly described the earlier written and recorded sources, I should now briefly describe the kinds of data that my own fieldwork provided me, or, for the reader less acquainted with ethnomusicological methods, of some of the kinds of things on which an anthropologist of music may base his or her work.

I cannot claim to have followed any specific method, and the approach would have to be described as eclectic, especially considering that it covered sporadic visits of more than two decades. It was a miscellany of activities that involved observation, conversation, and recording, fairly characteristic of what many ethnomusicologists do. Most important was living on the reservation for a number of months and the kinds of observation thus made possible. There is no doubt that living among a people constantly provides one with many insights, even when one's attention is not directed toward specific subject matter. The approach of an anthropologist is to try to connect observations from a diversity of cultural domains and to see whether they illuminate general principles or themes. It is often hard to derive much concrete data from this aspect of fieldwork, and yet it provides a backdrop for the more specific.

Like most ethnomusicologists, I spent a good deal of energy recording songs. I collected some of them in the course of attempting to record events as they took place, but I also had sessions in which I recorded songs sung especially for me. These sessions were generally under the control of the singer; he would decide what to sing, in what order, and I might try to derive some insights from these actions. But I ordinarily did not say, "OK, let's do the Medicine Pipe songs," or things of that sort. Rather, I would say something like, "Well, you said you would sing some songs and let me record them. Would you like to start, or are there some things you want me to know first?" I did try to record the entire repertory of a singer on two occasions, once with (I hope) reasonable success. In a few cases, I elicited songs by playing recordings made previously by myself and asking the singer whether he could also sing that song, or knew it, and whether he would sing it for another tape recorder. In the case of songs with words, I asked singers to dictate the texts to me in Blackfoot after the singing, song by song, and to translate them.

Beyond being generally present and observing what went on, and recording songs, I engaged in many conversations about Blackfoot culture, music, musical life, and related matters, with a large number of persons. Although I recorded a few of them on tape, I did not keep a precise record of all, usually taking notes either on the spot or—more frequently and conveniently—later the same day, noting particular points of interest. It is difficult even to estimate the number of people with whom I spoke, but all together, I have notes about statements made by a total of forty-one persons who were Blackfoot, and there are probably some two dozen more with whom I had conversations, but for which I did not make specific notes. Of these forty-one persons, twenty-seven were men; thirty men and women were middle-aged or elderly; three were around twenty years old. In addition, I spoke with and made notes of conversations with six white members of the community, including three elderly women who had lived in Browning most of their lives, one music teacher at the local junior high school, and two teenagers. These conversations lasted from ten to sixty minutes and consisted largely of my asking questions which were then answered with relative brevity, with the occasional exception of more extensive narration. Except for three instances, in which a middle-aged man translated the statements of an elderly person from Blackfoot, they took place in English.

In addition to these general conversations, I also conducted, from 1966 to 1984, a total of forty detailed interviews with seventeen elderly consultants. These interviews consisted of attempts on my part to focus on specific subjects: composing or making up songs, visions, the Sun Dance, more general ideas about music, and medicine bundles. But I tried to avoid too much in the way of specific questions. Some of the conversations were, in effect, song recording sessions in which extended explanation was included with singing, and in such cases, the verbal commentary was recorded. In most instances, however, I took written notes or wrote impressions afterward, finding that most consultants were less inhibited if surrounded by as little record-keeping apparatus as possible.

Of special interest from these sessions were the two mentioned attempts to record the total repertory of a singer and two attempts to elicit autobiographies focusing on musical life. These detailed interviews were not based on standard lists of queries, and I tried as much as possible to restrict myself to general questions and to persuade the consultants to narrate and to speak about the subjects in their own terms. In many instances, however, I had to try to make clear what I wished to learn, and there were many occasions on which my questions led nowhere and my purpose was evidently incomprehensible. Generally, my consultants were friendly and patient, but I do remember at least twice being scolded for asking "dumb questions."

Much of what is said in this study about contemporary musical thought derives from these conversations and interviews; it is therefore appropriate to comment on the way in which Blackfoot collaborators and consultants were selected and on the amount of agreement among them. Selection was made in part on the basis of availability and expressed interest in music and ritual. When I presented myself to various individuals on the reservation as someone interested in musical matters, I would be directed to two particular groups of people—mainly men—one of whom was designated either as "singers," while the other was said to "know a lot about our ceremonies" or "about old times." To state the situation in its most general terms, in the 1960s a group of older men had made a bit of a specialty of keeping traditions alive, and a group of younger ones were actively adapting these to the needs of contemporary life, but there were substantial differences of attitude and opinion between these two groups. Both are represented among my consultants.

There is, in any field situation, a tendency for consultants to select themselves. Certain individuals are drawn to an outsider or need attention that is lacking in their community or have time on their hands. They may or may not be the most representative of their culture. A few such individuals are present in my group of consultants, but two in particular turned out to be helpful and reliable. On the whole, I found it necessary to seek out consultants and, as an intruder into people's lives, spoke with anyone who seemed to be available. There was no attempt on my part to make a scientific sampling beyond my general desire to be evenhanded and to get substantially, though not exclusively, involved with people who had a special interest in songs and singing.

I cannot claim to have learned much of the Blackfoot language, and some insights that could be provided from the vantage point of a linguist are lacking. I received a number of lessons in the language from an untrained but patient middle-aged friend, and I recorded (on tape and in writing) texts and vocabulary. There is a dearth of published vocabulary and instructional material for learning the language. As I write these pages, textbooks are being prepared by the Blackfeet Community College; in my work, however, I was largely limited to the studies and texts by the linguists C. C. Uhlenbeck and R. H. van Gulick. Presentation of Blackfoot terminology comes from interviews with consultants but was checked against Uhlenbeck. I did not use methods developed by cognitive anthropology and linguistics but adhered to my mixed and informal approach, trying when possible to persuade consultants to determine content, context, and structure of what they told me and, when they were willing to be expansive, letting them speak for themselves.

Having said something about conversations and interviews as a major source of data, I should also mention two more kinds of material that played a role in the fieldwork. One is the observation and recording of certain events in the form of sound taping, still photographs, and verbal description. The events include four celebrations of North American Indian Days at Browning, 1966, 1983, 1984, and 1985, five extended gambling games, six other powwows or social dances, one reconstruction of a medicine bundle ceremony, and two rehearsals of singing groups, as well as several events at which Blackfoot singers entertained at hotels and gathering places of tourists. The other kind of material is statements by Blackfoot people about their own and other singers' recordings. I spent some time playing recordings previously made by myself and others for my consultants and asking them to comment, occasionally checking the documentation provided by the collector against their views. My questions were ordinarily in this vein: "Do you know this song? Do you know who is singing it? This song was sung by so-and-so; what do you think? Can you tell me something about this song?" It was of interest to learn that there was frequently strong disagreement about song functions, attributions, and other background data, but that there was general acceptance of these songs as Blackfoot music.

These two ways of gathering data represent extremes of the continuum of fieldwork. Describing what takes place and would take place in any event, recording it, and avoiding intrusion contrasts with a technique in which a field worker asks individuals to think about and comment on songs sung by others, perhaps decades earlier. Each of these approaches, as well as those intermediate, provided certain kinds of information, and together they illustrate the diversity of possible approaches in fieldwork, for they include elicitation, observation, creation of artificial conditions, participation of a sort by the observer, the use of texts, ethnographies, and recordings produced earlier by others as a point of departure, and more.

Let me now turn to some of the special problems of acquiring information needed for a description of a culture's ideas about music. On various occasions, in connection with teaching courses in the anthropology of music, I have tried informally to elicit from various persons who are members of my own society and who share my culture, some generalizations about the concepts and values that govern its musical domain. Few people knew what I was talking about. General synthesis and abstraction did not come easily to them. In their replies, people selected different things as points of departure, and they often disagreed about substance and value. Attempting, on the basis of such responses, to draw a picture of even a culture which I know well, which is fairly homogeneous, and which makes a habit of talking about its music turned out to be frustrating.

One should not be surprised to find similar diversities of attitude, knowledge, and evaluation among the Blackfoot. If indeed in my earlier fieldwork I found these people to be unexpectedly heterogeneous, it was because I had at some point come to believe the old wives' tales about homogeneity of tribal cultures, had read ethnography in which culture is described in positive and unequivocal terms, and had expected that as it was so difficult to get much information from any one consultant, what he or she said simply must be true. From the first feeling of joy that I could elicit anything at all, I quickly moved to a belief that all statements must be correct, and that those which seemed to be incorrect simply came from individuals who were ill-informed, or who, for their own reasons, wanted to mislead me. Later on, I became convinced that there was some distance between this way of evaluating the statements of Blackfoot consultants and the more realistic picture of culture, in which there might be absolute agreement on some matters, difference on some others, and continuing argumentation and conflict on yet a third group of issues.

The members of a society share a culture, which must mean that certain fundamental knowledge, beliefs, values, and ways of doing things are held in common. This sharing implies several degrees of convergence. Let me start by giving an example from close to home. All members of my society in a small university town in Illinois eat with silverware, and all believe that you can buy things with money and that the ability to read is important. A good many, but not all, believe that one should go to church and that working hard is a good thing. Most also regard music in general as a good thing, but they differ on what kind of music is best. Most think that an electoral system of government is best, but a few disagree totally. The great majority believe that one must not steal or lie, but obviously again, a few totally disbelieve this.

Looking at shared knowledge rather than beliefs, everybody except small children knows that one drives on the right, and most people know who Lincoln was. But fewer know about Bach and Mozart, and only very few, about Alban Berg and John Cage. Does this mean that driving is more a part of the culture than knowing about Bach, and that Berg is not a part at all? Fifty years ago, many Americans knew about Wilson's Fourteen Points; now there are few who have heard of them, and one might be inclined to ask whether this knowledge has ceased to be part of our culture.

Beliefs and knowledge. How about evaluation? An election of the greatest composer might give you a three-way tie. Whether jazz is a good thing or not is a point to be argued; whether rock music or country and western are good is even more an issue. No need to belabor. The important point for us is that, contrary to earlier beliefs about tribal societies, differences of this nature are also part of Blackfoot culture, maybe even to a greater extent than in my Illinois town. While the Blackfoot people are a society, one may question whether they still share a culture. I believe that they do, but it is not particularly easy to make the case. Suggesting the opposite, McFee (1972:70–102) pointed out that there are really two sectors of Blackfoot society, white-oriented and Indian-oriented, each with its values, behavior patterns, and lifestyle; that is, two distinct cultures. But even to the Indian-oriented sector, the traditional culture of the Blackfoot in earlier times (the part that might correspond to Wilson's Fourteen Points and to Bach in Illinois) is to most at best known imperfectly. A very few individuals are knowledgeable, but even they reconstruct the older culture from a variety of sources of unequal validity.

In no society do all people know the entire culture; even in small societies, there are varying degrees of knowledge and a number of perceptions and perspectives. There are debates within a culture. But it is reasonable to suppose that there was a greater degree of sharing in the

Blackfoot culture of the mid-nineteenth century than there was in the 1960s. In any event, I had to remain aware of certain possibly insoluble problems, including these: the question of what it required for an artifact or an idea to be a part of a culture; the problem of continuity and change, of reproduction and transformation; the difficulty of determining consistency of ideas and values over a period of rapid change; the interface between fact and belief, between Blackfoot theory and practice; the difficulty of being sure that a small number of consultants is reliable. Differences between theory and practice are a widespread cultural phenomenon, and even a raison d'être for a study such as this. The problem of basing my findings on the statements of a few individuals is shared by many of the classics of ethnography, and the difficulty of determining who is an authority is shared by historiography of Western music. My problems were themselves part of a tradition of research.

Having worked largely in Montana, I cannot be sure to what extent my findings apply to all Blackfoot. But regional diversity may be less a factor than personal diversity of belief and opinion. Let me illustrate how the kinds of information that I am able to present rest upon a number of different perceptions, reminding the reader of my illustration from Illinois.

(1) There are some things on which virtually all Blackfoot appear to agree. For instance, in trying to ascertain the nature of the fundamental unit of musical thought, I found everyone to whom I brought this question (in various forms) agreeing that it was "the song." Some took longer to come to this point than others, and only few seemed to understand why this would be an issue, but in the end, everyone understood what I was talking about and no one presented alternatives. It was a bit like my "driving on the right" example, above.

(2) A statement to the effect that "this is my song," was made by Consultant C. Asked about this, others denied that he really had a claim on this song. But they agreed that persons could own songs. There was agreement on the principle, but not the specific application.

(3) Consultant D told me about a ceremony involving the construction of tipis. No one else to whom I spoke claimed knowledge of this ceremony, but all said that if D was giving me the information, it must be correct. Here a group of statements was not shared by the society, yet one person was accorded the authority to speak for the rest. The informant might be compared to an authority, or an authoritative publication such as the *Encyclopedia Britannica* in standard American culture. Some facts are known only to "it," or claimed by it, and ordinarily we don't question.

(4) The degree to which theories are believed or taken seriously is an issue. Everyone over thirty to whom I spoke about it recognized (and

some could even describe) the composition of songs in visions. Some Blackfoot people unquestioningly accept it as fact that, in earlier times, visions actually took place, and I think they believed that the relationship between human and supernatural was at that time really different from that of the present. A second group maintained—or at least implied—that the vision was an essentially symbolic way of explaining the mysterious side of human creativity. Yet there were others who simply asserted to me that this was just utter nonsense, that it was people who composed songs, and that the notion of visions was just something they made up. A fourth group regards the whole vision quest with reverence, not as empirical truth but as a kind of tribal tradition, without considering the rationality of the concept, but maintaining that the important thing about it is that its memory today serves to enhance the Blackfoot ethnicity.

(5) A related example comes from interpretations of the typical Blackfoot song form. It was described to me in three different ways, with emphasis on three aspects of the form, all "objectively" accurate. People agreed on the "notes," that is, they may sing the song in unison, or upon hearing it, agree that it was sung properly; but they may then diverge in their explanation of what has been sung.

Culture, then, as we said, is that upon which the members of a group of people agree, but it also includes those things upon which they have, in effect, agreed to disagree. It consists of fact, approved interpretation, common knowledge, the acceptance of authority in knowledge or action, and also issues or areas of disagreement. The subjects of debate may be just as important in characterizing a culture as those subjects which are accorded the status of truth by all in the society. Indeed, the longer one remains acquainted with a society, the more prominent as characterizing agents the issues and arguments may become. And yet, while some of the things that I am able to say about Blackfoot musical culture are known only to one or a few individuals, and others the subjects of a diversity of opinion, I could confidently maintain that in general, and unlike Western urban academic culture, the contemporary culture of the Blackfoot is not one in which the future of music is argued and in which many viewpoints contend for attention and allegiance. Those whose orientation is toward white culture and those who wish to live more closely by traditional values tend to go their own ways. There is no arena for musical conflict, and there is a certain seeking for leadership and for individuals who would help the tribe to rebuild a coherent musical culture—and this might include non-Blackfoot persons and even ethnomusicologists. The prevailing mood is the desire to recapture the past and to make it serve the needs of the present.

5. SONGS IN BLACKFOOT LIFE, 1890–1985

The principal task in this study is to present ideas about music and musical life, but one is motivated immediately to ask what kind of music, and to what kind of musical life, these ideas are related. This question leads quickly to another, the degree to which musical life and style have been consistent over a long period. It is of course an issue for the student of Blackfoot life as a whole. Is there really such a thing as Blackfoot culture worthy of the same designation in, say, 1850 and in 1980, or are there just Blackfoot societies in these two periods, each with a culture? General ethnographies and histories tell us that culture underwent vast changes in that time; the question is whether music and musical life followed the same pattern.

The large amount of recorded and ethnographic material from the period around 1900 and from the present or recent past should provide a reasonably reliable guide to consistencies and changes. The remainder of this chapter is devoted to this question. We turn first to an account of song uses through a period of 95 years and move briefly to musical instruments; section 6 then describes four events using music, early and recent; and section 7 summarizes the musical style.

Looking at musical life alone, it seems that we can talk about one Blackfoot culture, reasonably consistent, throughout this period. Surely there has been substantial change, but comparisons of early and recent recordings, and of recent ethnography with the earlier, show that much has remained. We are dealing with one, though a changed, culture. The history of recordings provides some evidence. The total amount of music recorded among the Blackfoot is, compared to the quantity of recordings done in other tribal societies, exceptionally large. Over 1,400 recorded song performances have been identified, including those recorded in the field by early researchers, field recordings of more recent periods, and commercial records and tapes produced largely for American Indian patrons. A list of collections and records is given in the Discography, and information about the collections is provided in Appendix A, which divides the contents of the most prominent collections by song use or designation.

The Discography shows a total of seventeen collections of field recordings, one round dozen of commercial disks, and another of prerecorded cassettes. Chronologically, they fall rather readily into five groups: (1) about 350 songs recorded between 1897 and 1914 by Wissler, McClintock, Grinnell, Dixon, and George Curtis; (2) approximately 80 songs recorded between 1926 and 1939 by James Willard Schultz, Jessie Donaldson, and Jane Richardson Hanks; (3) approximately 95 songs recorded by Don Hartle, Howard Kauffman, and myself, 1950–52; (4) my own recordings, approximately 200 songs, from 1965–67; and (5) commercial materials produced in the 1970s and 1980s and recordings of my own of 1984, a total of about 450 songs.

In virtually all cases, catalogues of these collections (and probably the performers as well) designated the songs by use; by association with ceremonies, dances, and games; and usually by performer. A comparison of these five periods, with ethnographic literature as supplement, tells us about the kinds of songs in use or known and thus something about the musical life of these periods, and perhaps also about continuity and change. These periods have things in common. For example, with the exception of social dance songs, which account for the majority of the recent commercial recordings, much of the same kind of musical material has been recorded and has been available to be recorded throughout the eight decades that constitute this history of recording activity. But the five periods also contrast significantly. Using the collections of the period 1890–1915 as a point of departure, we find a very large number of song designations. Many songs derive from the vision quest and the medicine bundle cults, central to religion and ceremony. Although ethnographies (e.g., Wissler 1912a; Bullchild 1985:267–390; Ewers 1958:163–67) imply the existence of numerous medicine bundle types (and also of "idiosyncratic" bundles, each owned only by one individual), the great majority of recorded medicine songs come from the beaver cult, though, to be sure, many songs are designated as being from various specific parts of the beaver ceremony but associated with different animals. The Medicine Pipe cult also accounts for a large number of songs, and Wissler appears to have recorded an entire set of these, over sixty, each with specific designation (Wissler 1912a:140–46).

Fewer songs come from the large public tribal ceremonial of the Sun Dance (or as the Blackfoot call it in English, Medicine Lodge). Considering its prominence, that may be surprising, but the small quantity of the songs may also be due to suppression of the Sun Dance during this period (Ewers 1958:310–11; Samek 1987:127–33). Songs of several of the men's societies are common in the early recordings, some of them recognizable from lists of age-grade societies, others not as easily identified. A number of uses of music that are explicitly or by implication mentioned in the literature are not represented in the recordings. The number of social dance songs is small, and the social dances most common in the 1960s and 1980s are, at least by their most recent designations, not present in these early collections. Of some interest is the fact that words are relatively common, that the song designations are usually specific, and that there is also evidence of some songs being used in more than one ceremony, as a few of them are designated as being "either this or this." There is, however, a characteristic consistency in an aspect of song designations throughout the collections of this early period that may be significant. In all of the collections one finds the same song uses predominating—Beaver Bundle, Brave Dog Society, and so on.

There is no question but that in the period from 1890 to 1915, Blackfoot society shared a musical culture at least in memory. No doubt, many songs in these collections were no longer frequently sung in ceremonies or other proper contexts at the time they were recorded. But the various singers represented in these early collections (somewhere around twenty-five individuals) knew if not the same songs then songs from the same contexts. In that sense, we are talking about *a* culture.

It is a culture in which music may have had certain broad functions (to be discussed much more later) such as the relationship of human beings and supernatural or mediation between Blackfoot and outside world, but overtly, music was used to accompany activities. While a comprehensive list of these activities in the Blackfoot taxonomy, even as carried out or known in this period of 1890–1915, would require many pages and much explication (and we will have some occasion to deal with it), a brief introductory grouping of the song uses can be provided by placing them along a continuum at one end of which are those of a mainly sacred character, and at the other, secular or social songs. The points of the continuum, with illustrations, are these:

(1) Most specifically religious—songs of the medicine bundle cults, the most powerful of which is the extensive Beaver Bundle, and the best known, the Medicine Pipe bundle. These two ceremonies are well recorded; the others exist largely in description. In this (very large) category are included songs whose function is principally worship (e.g., with texts stating the sacredness of something), songs whose purpose is to cure illness, and songs which bring good fortune (e.g., rain) or ward off disaster or alleviate crisis. There are no recordings of songs of the Horse Medicine, despite its prominence (according to Ewers 1955).

(2) Religious with significant social components—songs of the Sun Dance, an event most importantly religious, but of course a major symbol of ethnic identity already in the late nineteenth century (Samek 1987:117–20), to which significant social events are attached.

(3) Religious narrative—songs sung as part of the telling of myths. Very few have been recorded, but texts are given in several early collections of folklore.

(4) Ceremonial and partially religious—songs associated with warfare and death. These are usually not religious in the narrow sense of the concept. A few of them, usually identified as "Scalp Dance," sung after a victory to describe events of the conflict, have been recorded. Few if

any songs sung at time of departure of a war party or during crises in time of conflict are present in the collections. Songs of mourning for the dead and songs or ceremonial weeping associated with funerals are included in this category.

(5) Secular ceremonial, with religious aspects—songs of the societies, mainly the age-grade societies. These are moderately well represented in the early collections.

(6) Secular, performed at secular ceremonies—social dance songs. These very likely existed in large number around 1900, but are not well represented in the early collections. The Grass Dance, most prominent, was probably the chief social dance practiced at that time.

(7) Secular and formally recreational—music associated with games. Gambling songs are likely to have been sung frequently, but were not recorded in large numbers.

(8) Informally recreational—children's songs, mentioned in some of the literature as "lullabies" and game songs, but hardly ever recorded.

(9) Informal without audience—occasional songs, such as "walking songs" or "riding songs." These are mentioned occasionally in the literature, and a very few have been recorded.

The collections from 1897 to 1915 give us a broad if not comprehensive picture of uses of music, institutions, and events of this period. From this listing we can see that there were many types of events associated with or even dominated by singing and that there were many uses of music. It is further likely that the early collectors of music recordings, though evidently presented by their consultants with substantially the same set of song uses, failed to record songs from a number of repertories that ethnographies lead us to believe existed. All together, there is considerable evidence that in the twenty years or so before 1900, the Blackfoot had a large repertory of songs, that one heard a great deal of singing, that music was associated with many types of events, that many men knew songs and were willing to sing. The configuration in the recordings shows that while much of Blackfoot culture was breaking down, certain groups of songs continued to be sung or known, or perhaps valued more highly, and thus found their way into the recorded collections; others, to be sure, did not. From ethnographic descriptions we surmise that there was something roughly like a musical calendar, with certain songs and ceremonies appearing at particular times of the year.

Following this early period, that is, after about 1900, the rich musical life of the nineteenth century was in various ways translated into a much poorer and restricted version of itself and then into an expansion of this more restricted musical culture. In important ways, the kinds of things that characterize the early collections and are noted in the classical ethnographies had their continuations and successors. The collections of the period 1926–52 are smaller and included fewer uses or contexts of music. There are fewer songs of the medicine bundle cults, still not many (but proportionately more) Sun Dance songs, and also a larger proportion of social dance songs. The collectors' designations of the individual songs are less precise. The collections from around 1950 still contain some ceremonial material, particularly Medicine Pipe and Sun Dance songs, but they include far more from social dances, in particular the so-called War Dance (an alternate name for the Grass Dance, a social dance introduced in the late nineteenth century), and the Chicken Dance. And there are a few songs labeled as love songs, some of them with words in English. There is more evidence of an intertribal or at least pan-Plains repertory.

My own recordings from the 1960s show a continuation of the same trends. Ceremonial materials are less specifically labeled; there is little from the Beaver Medicine Bundle cult, still a few songs from the Medicine Pipe ceremony, and a large quantity of social dance material. For the first time, there are many gambling songs, a category of songs said by consultants to be very old, readily available in my experience but evidently less commonly heard (probably less valued by singers or collectors) than in earlier times. In the 1960s, few of the songs of any type had verbal texts.

In the 1980s, the large quantity of field and commercial recording shows the musical culture to have substantially changed but in no way to have become extinct. Intertribal powwow events, gambling games, reconstructed ceremonies, the introduction of special song types such as the theme songs of individual singing groups—practices evidently derived from white American culture—show a vigorous yet greatly changed ambience. The commercial recordings principally include songs of the Grass, Chicken, Rabbit, Feather, Owl, Fast-and-Fancy dances, all from the intertribal social dance powwow complex. There are also gambling songs, but very few religious or ceremonial songs. Although some of these are still known and sung occasionally, they are presumed not appropriate to commercial records—and few people have much interest in them. Much of the traditional culture, to the extent it is known, lives in memory, and enjoys little visibility. In any event, the history of the recordings shows a greatly changed musical culture.

Nevertheless, a comparison of the five periods of collecting or of statements in early ethnographies, such as the lengthy discourse on musical life by one of Wissler's consultants (Wissler 1912a:263–66), with my more recent experience, shows that in important ways we are indeed still dealing with the same musical culture. We can make a case for the identity even where the actions of 1900 are now only memories and the facts of 1900, only distant ideals. That they are known at all lends them significance. Thus, my consultants, like Wissler's, insisted on the importance of being able to learn a song in one hearing. The idea of songs learned in dreams played and continues to play a major role. The identification of songs by use remains consistent. The consultants in the earlier literature and in my experiences agree on the importance and also the complexity and difficulty of the Beaver ritual, the greater popularity of the Medicine Pipe ceremony, the comings and goings of social dances, the separation of gambling songs from the rest of music, and the conception that imparting words is not the principal task of songs. Almost a hundred years ago, and still now, such ideas were part of Blackfoot musical thinking. Even the great importance ascribed to songs by Wissler (1912a:263) in the human relationship to the supernatural is still reflected at the powwows of today in various attitudes toward songs and singing.

The calendar of musical events in the recent period would be similar to that of the nineteenth century. Large, tribal events took place in the summer. There was a kind of musical climax at the time of the Sun Dance in the nineteenth century, and of North American Indian days in the twentieth. Informal events took place more or less at any time, but more during the warmer seasons. In winter there is characteristically little activity other than rehearsing.

Musical instruments were not numerous in the early period and, in the time since 1950, have been largely or entirely restricted to drums. Wissler (1910:84–86) lists a small number of instruments as being used around 1900, and the other ethnographers indicate the presence of drums and of different kinds of rattles. Flutes were evidently not used or used so sporadically that one must question their existence as properly part of the culture, an interesting point to which we shall have to return. The various kinds of drums and rattles have different sorts of significance in terms of their contexts of use and symbolism, but not in musical terms. In earlier literature there is reference to large drums beaten by several men in unison, to the use of a piece of rawhide suspended from four stakes for the Sun Dance, and to small hand drums. All were decorated elaborately but used for the same kinds of accompaniment to song. The observation that singing is almost always accompanied by percussion is corroborated by Wissler's (1912a:264) special consultant on musical matters. There appear to have been many kinds of rattles, some of them parts of medicine bundles, distinguished by shape, decoration, and sound-producing mechanism. Container rattles and rattles made of strings of objects such as doe claws were used. Bells, introduced in the nineteenth century, played and continue to play a role in music, mainly because they were attached to the legs of dancers. On the whole, however, instruments appear not to have been a major factor in the system of ideas about music, and were totally subordinate to singing.

6. FOUR MUSICAL EVENTS

To continue providing some background for the discussion of musical thought, this section describes, in the briefest possible way, four types of events at which music was and is used, from earlier times to the present.

The Medicine Bundle rituals are described in Wissler 1912a, Ewers 1958, Bullchild 1985, and other early sources. The descriptions of medicine bundle ceremonies as performed before 1900 are rather detailed, but they do not, of course, tell in all respects precisely what happened. Most come from verbal accounts by consultants rather than from observation. Several features were held in common by all or many medicine bundle ceremonies, and these apply as well to cults involving painted tipis, whose contents also resulted from instructions in visions. The ceremonies began with the telling of the origin myth of the bundle, which in itself sometimes included songs that were, in the myth, performed by supernatural characters or even objects, or by humans. The ceremony itself is to be understood, according to Wissler (1912a:251), as a "formal interpretation of the original transfer from a supernatural to a natural person." It consists of opening the bundle, taking each of its objects, and carrying out with or before it a prescribed act. The objects included dressed animal skins, peculiarly shaped pieces of wood and stone, rawhide objects, musical instruments, and tobacco pipes. The actions carried out with the objects normally included singing; the one thing that objects in the bundles had in common was association with one or more songs. But also included might be dancing, smoking, eating, praying in heightened or ordinary speech, face painting, and more complex actions such as the ceremonial cooking of food. Dancing, according to Wissler (1912a:250), was common but incidental. Some of the important medicine bundle ceremonies were preceded by the erection of a sweat house and purification of the principal participants through a steam bath.

Ordinarily, one main participant carried out the actions, with some help from his wife or other relatives, as in principle, the medicine bundle ceremonies were relatively private affairs. But it seems that in many cases, an audience of some size gathered, and by 1900 passive audiences may have transformed these small ceremonies into virtually tribal rituals. In a sense this seems to have been the case in the Horse Medicine, a cult established in the nineteenth century, different from the other medicine cults in its use of many participants, its secrecy, and the prominence of the number three (Ewers 1955:257). But even in earlier times, the medicine bundle cults were on the whole not secret.

A medicine bundle ceremony often took several days to accomplish, but sometimes abbreviated versions were carried out. Despite general similarity, the ceremonies varied in detail. In the case of the Beaver Medicine, whose bundle ideally consisted of the dressed skins of all wildlife of the area, each object had at least one song, and the early recordings specify the identities of the individual musical numbers. In the ceremony of the Medicine Pipe bundle, which included seven or eight principal objects including rattles (according to various descriptions; see Ewers 1958:172–73; McClintock 1910 [1968]:252–70; Wissler 1912a:138–39), there were eight groups of seven songs. Originally, all of these were said to have been sung by the principal, but by McClintock's time several singers took part, performing both solo and in unison. Some of the songs had words, others had only vocables. And the songs found in one group are often melodically very similar to each other and might easily be regarded as stanzas of the same song. The various incomplete descriptions of the ceremonies and the songs recorded in the period around 1900 make it clear that these rituals were lengthy, that they were events in which music was always highly significant, and that the ceremonialist was knowledgeable in a complex of rituals. Individual versions existed, but the various ceremonies that had the same name were largely variants of the same material and structure. The medicine bundle ceremonies were multimedia events of modest scope but considerable drama.

The Sun Dance, or as it is often called in literature and by the Blackfoot, the Medicine Lodge (or Honor Lodge, in Bullchild 1985), is a ceremonial type widespread in the Plains and adjacent culture areas, and widely described for the Blackfoot and other societies (Wissler 1918; Spier 1921). Although medicine bundles exist in many North American Indian societies, the Blackfoot medicine bundle cults had no exact analogues in other cultures. The Sun Dance of the Blackfoot, however, is essentially a version of the Sun Dance ceremony of other Plains and neighboring peoples, but it differs from some of these because built into it, as well, is a medicine bundle ceremony, that of the *Natóas* ("supernatural" or "sacred power") bundle. The Blackfoot Sun Dance can therefore be interpreted as the largest and most prominent portion of the general Blackfoot religious system. But it could also be seen as a result of syncretism of the characteristic medicine bundle cults and the large, tribal ecstatic dance ceremony of the Plains. Because of its complexity, its course of action is not as clearly documented as that of some of the medicine bundle events, and we can here touch only on a small number of characteristics (but see Wissler 1918; Ewers 1958:174–84; and others for more detailed accounts).

It was a nine-day ceremony, the first four days of which involved moving the entire tribe to four different campgrounds, a ritualized search for the proper place. On each of these days, ceremonial singing would accompany arrival at a campsite. The remaining days included the *Natóas* bundle ceremony, the erection of the Medicine Lodge, dancing around the central pole by men seeking visions, each day for many hours; as well as ancillary events such as the ceremonies of age-grade societies, athletic events, social dances, and gambling games. All of these had their songs. There was group and solo singing, and the simultaneous singing of songs for different purposes within earshot of each other is described. Some parts of the ceremony, such as the *Natóas* bundle opening, evidently had a rigorously prescribed series of songs. In the parts of the ceremony involving the erection of and dancing in the Medicine Lodge, certain songs had to be sung at particular times. The literature and the older recorded collections indicate that one song had special significance. Entitled "Raising the Pole" by McClintock (1910 [1968]:308–9), it was sung by a large group, possibly even all who were present. And there are other indications of occasional singing by masses of people. As far as I can tell, however, much of the singing was of songs selected by the singers on the spur of the moment, from a repertory of eligible materials. At the Sun Dance, one would probably hear Blackfoot songs associated with many uses, in a number of musical styles, and with a variety of performance practices.

North American Indian Days is the most prominent powwow, i.e., social event with singing and dancing, of the contemporary Blackfoot. It takes place annually for four days after July 4 and is attended by people from all parts of the reservation, by Blackfoot people from Canada, by members of the tribe from various parts of North America who have chosen this time to visit their tribal home or birthplace, along with some Indian people from other reservations and white tourists from Glacier Park, as well as a few white Indian hobbyists who follow the powwow circuit from reservation to reservation in the summer and participate as dancers. The event is in some respects a successor to the Sun Dance, as it too is a broadly tribal event centered on singing and dancing but accompanied by ancillary events such as gambling games and social life. It is secular, but has significant ritual aspects, such as ceremonial entries of the dancers, some speeches, special ceremonial dances to accompany the picking up of an eagle feather that has been dropped by mistake from a dancer's costume, and a variety of contests to determine the best dancers in various styles of dance, the best costumes, best singing groups, and so on.

Held in an arenalike enclosure with seats on risers for spectators at the edges, the North American Indian Days singing and dancing begin shortly after noon and continue until about midnight. A master of ceremonies, ordinarily the chairman of the Tribal Council, announces and directs action. Music for the dancers is provided by singing groups, called Drums. The dancers do not sing, and singers do not ordinarily leave their drums to join in the dancing.

In 1984, twenty-five singing Drums were distributed around the dance ground, about a third of them from other tribes. Each of these groups consisted of five to ten singers, its nucleus often several members of one extended family. The singers were middle-aged persons or young adults, and included a few teenagers; there were very few elderly people. About a third of the groups had one or two female singers, and one group consisted entirely of women. The groups took turns, singing one song at a time— in contrast to the practice of the 1960s, when one group would sing for one or two hours before being relieved by another. Each singing group had a leader who was distinctly identified. The singers and drummers neither wore costumes nor danced, but each dancer had some kind of costume. Members of the singing groups, many wearing farmers' visor caps and T-shirts lettered with the names of the singing groups recorded each others' songs on cassettes. All of the music was amplified. Most of the singing at the 1984 event consisted of "intertribal" songs, the kinds that had been called Grass Dance or War Dance in the past, each rendered four, sometimes five or six times.

The dancers, over a hundred of them, were elaborately costumed. About two-thirds of them were men, who danced individually and flamboyantly during most of the numbers, while the women proceeded in groups of twos or threes, dancing in a more subdued style. Hardly any of the songs had words. After two or three "intertribal" songs, there might come one of a different kind of dance: Owl Dance, danced in ballroom style by couples; Circle Dance, performed by concentric circles of men and women; a special ceremonial song for the entry of the dancers or to commemorate a deceased member of the tribe; songs to accompany dancing contests.

In the course of the event, the names of the singing groups, but not of songs, were announced by the master of ceremonies. If at any time there was a pause in the live music, recordings of Plains social dance songs were played on the loudspeaker. With the exception of the "Star-Spangled Banner" sung at the beginning, no non-Indian music was heard.

North American Indian Days can be considered a composite "cultural performance" in the sense that in it, the Blackfoot people express very explicitly to themselves and to the world the principal values of their culture. But included in this cultural performance are events taking place outside the dance enclosure, and the relationship among these, and among their associated musics, may give us important indications of the Blackfoot peoples' view of themselves. Closest to the dance enclosure are traditional gambling games with gambling songs. Elsewhere outdoors, a block away, a dance with country-and-western music (performed by a Blackfoot band) is held. A half mile farther is a small rodeo, billed explicitly as an "Indian Rodeo" (though not different from mainstream events of the genre), and accompanying it is recorded U.S. patriotic music, e.g., the national anthem, "God Bless America," and marches.

The various associations of the Blackfoot are combined in a parade on the third of the four days; here floats of government agencies, local businesses, and churches alternate with those of tribal organizations, and music is provided on them in a variety of styles—pan-Indian singing, rock music, country and western, jazz, and hymns. This is to my knowledge the only context of significance at which the various Indian and non-Indian repertories are combined.

The Hand Game or stick game, a traditional form of gambling, commonly took place in the 1960s on Saturday and Sunday afternoons in various spots on the reservation. In earlier times, such games had major social significance and received widespread tribal attention (Ewers 1958:155-56), and they now continue to be popular secular pastimes.

The typical kind of game opposes two teams of five to eight people, sitting in lines facing each other. One side has the task of hiding a pair of bones or similar objects in the hands of one or more of its members, while a representative of the other team tries to locate it, indicating choices with elaborate gestures. The team that is hiding the objects sings and accompanies itself by beating on a plank. The songs are short, have no words, and conform to the general style of American Indian gambling songs described by Herzog (1935:29–30). A song may be sung dozens of times, as it is repeated until the seeking team makes a choice. The entire hiding team joins in the singing, but in each of the games I observed, one person was clearly the leading singer. A number of different songs would be sung, but in any one game, some songs would reappear periodically. During the game, players and bystanders conversed, there was a good deal of coming and going, and sometimes a blackjack game took place a few yards away, without any singing. The hand game was played mainly by men, but about 20 percent of the participants were women. Most male and all female players and singers were middle-aged or elderly.

7. Musical Style in a Nutshell

This study does not propose to analyze songs or groups of songs and is not devoted to discussion of the musical style except where such analysis may illuminate ideas about music. Nevertheless, a very brief summary of musical style characteristics is appropriate.

As a whole, Blackfoot music (or rather, the "Indian" music repertory of the Blackfoot people) has a highly unified style, more so than is the case for other Plains tribes that have Peyote and Ghost Dance songs, as the Blackfoot did not participate in these religious movements and their musical repertories. The singing style of the Blackfoot approximates that of Plains Indians generally as it has been widely described. It is more intense and uses a higher tessitura than does southern and central Plains singing. In the typical songs, after beginning in falsetto, the singers move to a head voice. Pulsations on longer tones, the audible effects of tension, nasality, substantial rasp, and some ornamentation are characteristic. When singing for a tape recorder indoors, but also in gambling games, and evidently in recordings of some of the medicine bundle ceremonies as well, the singing tends to be considerably lower in both pitch and volume. Women's singing is distinguished from the men's vocal style in the lower quantity and intensity of pulsations and in its greater amount of ornamentation (see Hatton 1974 and 1986 for comments on singing style).

Looking at the musical style with the use of older analytical conventions and providing a few generalizations, we find that scales are typically pentatonic, sometimes tetratonic and hexatonic, and in rare cases, heptatonic. The tones are distributed evenly, and the principal scalar intervals are major and minor thirds, major seconds, and rarely, semitones. There is no single predominant modal pattern. Composition includes the reuse of motifs through outright repetition. Transposition of major subdivisions of songs, of shorter units, and of motifs is an important technique in composition. A motif may be moved down a fourth or fifth, and a section, an octave lower to provide a structural framework for a melody. Some other composition techniques of the Blackfoot are discussed in some literature (e.g., Nettl 1968b:11–24), but in the use of motifs, scales, and rhythm, this music is similar to that of other Plains tribes.

The older part of the repertory has a variety of formal types, although many of them can ultimately be reduced to a binary form in which the second section is a variation and/or reduction of the first. The Sun Dance and social dance songs almost invariably conform to that sort of arrangement, described elsewhere as the "incomplete repetition" song type (Nettl 1954a:30). In all of these respects, Blackfoot music shares the style of Arapaho, Cheyenne, Dakota, and Flathead music, as summarized by Merriam (1967:324–30) and at least generally of other Plains and adjacent cultures (see Nettl 1954a:24–33).

To the non-Blackfoot listener, the most characteristic thing about rhythm is the importance of drumming, which is regularly slightly off the beat (but see Pantaleoni 1987 for an alternate interpretation of Plains rhythm). Strong emphasis of accented tones, a large variety of note values, and rhythmic organization of the melody through a gait equivalent in length to the pulsations of the singing style are further characteristics. The concept of meter in the Western sense may not be applicable to an understanding of melody; organization of the rhythm depends substantially on the interrelationship of sections. The phraseology is irregular, as a song may consist of several phrases of different lengths all of which may begin with the same group of note values. The medicine bundle and gambling songs are usually simpler rhythmically in the sense that isometric and isorhythmic structure may prevail or in their use of a smaller number of note values.

Hatton (1974:132) has proposed four musical areas of performance practice in the modern powwow repertory of the northern Plains, and assigns the Blackfoot to an area together with the Crow, Shoshone, Northern Arapaho, Chippewa-Cree (Rocky Boy Reservation), Assiniboin and Gros Ventre (Fort Belknap Reservation), and Flathead, all in Montana. Their performance practice contrasts with that of the peoples of North and South Dakota and of the Canadian Plains (Cree). The differences principally involve practices of drumming and points of changing tempo in the social dances. Blackfoot drumming often begins with regular beats on the rim, goes on to regular beating on the skin, and ends, in the last rendition of a song, with omission of beats, alternating accentuations, crescendos, and other devices of intensification.

If we can believe elderly informants as well as older recordings, the style of the music has changed by an increased emphasis on the Plains singing style in its extreme sense and a reduction of the variety of formal and scalar types. A detailed statistical description of stylistic elements would no doubt indicate that Blackfoot music is not significantly different from that of other neighboring societies. But to make such a determination would be difficult in view of the rapidly changing repertory, the introduction of new songs, and the problem of deciding, in the case of intertribal songs, to which tribe a song should properly be assigned. Keeping in mind the special roles of Ghost Dance and Peyote songs in some other Plains repertories, there is no doubt that Blackfoot music fits readily into the stylistic picture of Plains music and that differences among Plains tribes would be of degree more than of essence.

The material presented in this chapter summarizes, in effect, the bone from the tail of the dinosaur (songs and behavior) from which we want to reconstruct the rest of the animal (musical concepts and ideas). As dinosaur tails go, it is actually very massive; the amount of ethnographic literature, especially from the period around 1910, is unusually large in comparison to what has been written about most individual tribal societies, and there is a substantial body of recorded music. I myself can draw on three decades of sporadic fieldwork. But the metaphor of the fossil is not inappropriate: the answers to many questions are given in the literature only by implication, because they are not easily articulated by consultants and because it is often difficult to determine who speaks authoritatively for the culture. We are looking at a society in a period of rapid, forced culture change, with strands of continuity in a sea of interruption. Yet the answers to questions of this sort are not always readily available in Western culture either, despite the attention its music has received from scholars. Musicologists are only beginning to learn how to deal descriptively and analytically with the systems of ideas about music that are at the center of the world's musical cultures.

CHAPTER TWO

Fundamentals

1. THE CONCEPT OF MUSIC

The task in this chapter is to sketch the Blackfoot conception of the general character of music. We wish to inquire into the nature of music in earlier and recent Blackfoot thought, asking some very fundamental questions. For example: What are attributes of music; of what does it consist; what are its principal categories?

These questions can be asked about any musical system and certainly they might be among those one would ask first in a comparative study of musical conceptualization. But on the other hand, it is also quite possible that such questions, at least if stated directly, might mean nothing to members of a particular society, or that they could be irrelevant or unimportant. A researcher can try to mitigate these uncertainties by using a number of approaches, including looking at early ethnographies, myths, recent interviews, vocabulary, an outsider's description of events and behavior. In the end, however, it is impossible to avoid the fundamental dilemmas of ethnomusicology that these questions highlight, the issues of translating music into language and of translating one culture into the medium of another; we can do little beyond acknowledging the problems and speaking cautiously, remaining ever mindful of their presence.

Let me try to provide an intercultural perspective for a look at the question in Blackfoot culture. Music is a cultural universal, so one reads in much of the literature of ethnomusicology (see Wachsmann 1971:381–84; Seeger 1971:385–98; Harwood 1976:521–33; *World of Music* 1977:2–141). If we use a sufficiently broad definition of music, there is certainly no society without it. The conception need not be all that broad. Definitions of music in dictionaries of English (or French, German, Spanish, and so on; Nettl 1983:15–16), conform strikingly and ethnocentrically to the principles of Western art music and, even more, to Western academic ideas of what music does, should be, and is. And yet, examining the societies of the world through records and musical ethnographies, we are forced to admit that everywhere there may be heard something whose sound is in certain respects like that of the music to which we as Westerners are accustomed and, further, even where the concept of "music" is not made explicit, that in each society there is a kind of human sound production that is expressly distinguished from speech.

Even so, Westerners may take an exclusive view. In its article defining music, the third edition of the distinguished *Riemann Musik Lexicon* (Gurlitt 1967:601–5) asserts that the concept properly exists only in Western civilization. It is doubtful, actually, that the author of the article regards all non-Western music simply as barbaric screaming and banging. More likely, he had in mind the suggestion that the *concept* as it exists in Western art music culture is peculiar to Western civilization, composed as it is of certain conceptually essential ingredients such as composition, notation, a special sort of expressiveness, and in particular the idea of music as a unified phenomenon including sacred and secular, vocal and instrumental, old and new, beautiful and thoughtful—a unique configuration of ideas and criteria. If other societies have music, so the article implies, the nature of the concept and the configuration of its characteristics are likely to be quite different.

Different in what way? Take for example the scope of the concept of music. In Western culture, music is something good and beautiful. It is in the first instance instrumental ("You're a musician? What do you *play?*") and still in essence unified; that is, all forms of music have the same degree of—how shall we best put it—"musicness" about them.

Not so in the urban culture of Iran (see al Faruqi 1979:56–61; Sakata 1983:35–38; Zonis 1973:7–8), where the degree of "musicness" varies by genre and repertory: at one end of a continuum, Koran chanting is simply not regarded as music but is highly valued; classical improvised song, more musical but a bit less exalted; classical instrumental metric composition, definitely in the realm of music but somewhat suspect; popular dance music, music in the most specific sense but definitely viewed with ambivalence.

So, while Western and Iranian cultures both surely have the concept of music, and while each has a word or words to represent the concept, the nature of music, the idea of what it is or of what it consists, is different. In Iran, the negative ambience derives from religious approbation of the normal social context of music, and thus the definition of music is narrow, all kinds of things are eliminated from it. Koran chanting is not considered to be music although structurally it is hardly very different from classical singing. Music is carried on by people of low status and members of non-Muslim minorities (or, by extension, certain Muslim minorities); it is more acceptable as intellectual activity such as the writing of treatises, than as performance (see, for example, the vast collection of treatises listed by Shiloah 1979). It is interesting to find that a large proportion of these deal in good measure with the justification and defense of music. And on the whole, Iranians are amused to think that an aspect of life or culture can be enhanced in conversation or literature by being compared to music, something frequently done in the West.

In Persian there is a term, *musiqi*, which is best translated as "music," but which does not include all of the things that the English word encompasses. There are, of course, many societies in the world that have no term for music as a whole. Keil (1979:27–29) suggests that West African languages do not have a term for music and yet asserts that the general conception of music exists. Even in the language of a Western society such as the Czechs, the word for music, *hudba*, denotes instrumental music primarily and is only by implication extended to singing. Terminology can thus shed light on the nature of the concept of music in a society, but examination of behavior and sound also yield important insights.

This bit of comparative introduction leads us now to seek in Blackfoot culture the fundamental nature of the concept of music, its boundaries and principal characteristics. First, to the language: There are many Blackfoot words that denote parts of the musical system—words for song types, ways of singing and drumming, instruments. But is there a word for music? Well, only in a way. There is a term for singing ("I sing" = *nitsínixki*) and one for song (*nínixksini*). In the traditional culture, all or almost all music was vocal, and so it is to be expected that there is no additional term for "music." In the twentieth century, the word for song has been extended to mean music at large, and to include European-derived or "white" music. Thus in modern Blackfoot culture, the word for "song" includes all those things that the older tradition had to offer that might also be included in the European concept of music, and also everything denoted by the English word "music."

And maybe more. There is another term of relevance, the word for "dance" (*páskani*) which, while denoting the act of dancing, also connotes the concept of ceremony, an activity consisting of several domains, dancing and singing among them. The concept of dancing is extended to ceremonies in which only a small portion of the time is devoted to actual dancing and much, instead, to singing. So the two terms in Blackfoot that come closest to the English "music" show us that music has a particularly close conceptual relationship to ceremony and dance and that it is a unified whole. Although I made no specific efforts to test this hypothesis, I did not find different degrees of "songness" in the repertory, in the way one can find degrees of "musicness" in Iranian musical culture. Some Blackfoot songs may be more powerful or prominent than others, and there are many differences among them, but all are equally songs. And on the other hand, the vocabulary suggests that the central activity of ceremonies is dancing inevitably accompanied by singing.

A good deal of value about the general conception of music can be gleaned from casual conversations, from noting what people choose to mention and what they avoid. Let me comment on the way in which the Blackfoot people today use English in speaking about their traditional music and about musical culture at large, considering that virtually all are at least bilingual. They use the word "music" without hesitation, applying it equally to Indian and to European-derived music. In saying, for example, that there are "white" and "Indian" musics, they include under each of them all of the sounds that ethnomusicologists traditionally consider to be music. They use the word "song" to speak of individual units, but when they are taken together, the word "music" is used. Possibly their willingness to use the Western way of talking about music is related to the fact that music was all along conceived of as a unit in a way compatible with the Western conception.

In English, and in the present, the Blackfoot refer to the performing of Indian music as "singing" or "drumming." In my experience, the former term was more common in the 1960s, while the two were used equally in the 1980s. Considering the fact that music making most frequently consists of the two activities carried out simultaneously by the same person, the prominence of the term "drumming" is of interest. I was not able to inquire specifically in 1984, but in an earlier conversation I was assured that the two mean essentially the same thing, that is, both were used to denote singing with drum accompaniment. "Drumming, singing, it's all the same to us; you can call me a drummer or a singer, it's OK," I was told by a member of a singing group. And also: "All our songs, they've got to have a drum." In earlier times, rattles were widely used, and at least some songs had no percussive accompaniment. I can only guess at the reason for the increased prominence of the term "drumming" but suggest several sources: terminology used in the intertribal powwow culture (Powers 1968; Howard 1951, 1955; Hatton 1974), white Americans' conception of Indian music as consisting principally of drumming, the decline of song texts in the Blackfoot language, or the decrease in the use of rattles and other idiophone percussion accompaniment.

The idea of music as a unified concept in Blackfoot thought is supported by statements and behavior suggesting a wide separation between music and speech. This relationship must be discussed, further on, in more detail, but here it is worth pointing out that to the Blackfoot, both in earlier times and recently, singing seems to have been something very different from speaking. There is an absence of intermediate forms. There are no spoken words at beginnings and endings of songs, as is sometimes the case—for example, in some Anglo-American folk ballad singing before 1940. The physical attitude of singers is distinct from that of other activities. The attitude that singing is or should be separate from speech also becomes evident when Blackfoot people talk about Western music which, they said critically, is curiously close to speech and, in their view, far too much associated with words.

The relationship of Blackfoot to white music is instructive in other ways. We have already noted the different roles of language in the two repertories. But further, the importance of technical complexity and notation in the Blackfoot conception of Western music, with the associated belief that a great deal must go into the learning of it, establishes it as a phenomenon indeed very different from Indian music—and yet definitely also music (Witmer 1982:113–14). The absence of a repertory that makes substantial use of stylistic elements of both Western and Indian music suggests this as well. In 1984, Blackfoot people still regarded the performance of their traditional Indian music as somehow a more ceremonial kind of event than the performance of white music.

If a case has been made for the existence of a Blackfoot concept of music with certain fundamental attitudes, the next question should inquire into the main characteristics of music in the Blackfoot view of the world. Broadly speaking, this is the question addressed by this entire monograph, but here we need to take the first bite out of the apple, looking at a few issues of primary concern.

In investigating a musical culture, one of the first questions ought to be, of what does music consist? In a variety of cultures, answers could conceivably range from "tones and scales" to composers to modes, from pieces to styles, and more. For the classical musical culture of India, the first line of response would surely involve "ragas." Among the Amuesha of Bolivia, it may have been lengthy song cycles or genres (Smith 1984). Participants in the classical music culture of Iran say that their music consists of the twelve "dastgâhs;" but Iranians in the mainstream of 1960s society might have said, "of songs." Europeans and North Americans whose principal allegiance is to classical music think in the first instance of composers, then of styles or periods, then of pieces.

What now of the Blackfoot? Like members of many of the world's societies, when talking about music, Blackfoot people speak of "songs."

While I do not have the results of a questionnaire, all of my conversations point to the conviction that to the Blackfoot, their music consists of songs. They are the basic units of musical thought and, as suggested above, they are all equally music. They are given to the tribe and to individuals as units, learned as units. As individual units, they may also be represented by objects and sticks in the ceremonial medicine bundles.

The Blackfoot conception is that their music consists of a large number of songs, but, in particular, of discrete songs. In conversation, little attention was given to the ways in which the components of these songs may be manipulated. In contrast to some Indian societies, the Blackfoot make little of ideas such as the existence of a song in several variants or breaking down and recombining the ingredients of a song in different ways to make new songs.

I asked, "When your grandfather sang the songs of the Medicine Pipe, did they kind of sound alike?" "Yes, kind of," I was told, but couldn't progress further. I tried to do better: "If I were to play a medicine song for you on my recorder, could you tell the bundle it came from?" "I used to know some of them bundles real well, but I wouldn't be so sure any more. Each kind of medicine had its own songs." Attempts to direct conversations with consultants toward the notion of song cycles or to units shorter than songs were rarely successful. This is not to say that Blackfoot songs did not have stylistic and genetic subdivisions or that they are not recognized. And of course we will have occasion to examine ways in which all songs are not equal in power, popularity, or significance. But these differences play a relatively minor role in past and present as compared to the conception of the integrity of the song. Dividing or multiplying songs is not a major concern.

The concept of song as discrete and stable unit leads us to the Blackfoot conception of stability and changeability of songs and of music as a whole, an issue discussed in chapter 3, but surely also relevant to a discussion of the general nature of music. To frame it again in a broader context, in many societies, the matter of change is a major issue. In Western academic and popular musical culture of the twentieth century, change is not only tolerated when it occurs but, rather, virtually required, something necessary for the normal health of the musical system. Change is permitted in two principal forms: (1) the style of music changes, new music that is different from the extant not only in individual identity but also in its overall characteristics may be (and indeed must be) created; and also, (2) new music in an extant style may be composed. On the other hand, change via the establishment of variants or the presentation of new interpretations is less part of the Western classical system, but of course it is an essential part of the picture of musical change in folk music and jazz.

The Western art music culture regards its units to be a set of immutable masterworks, and the changeability it ascribes to the individual works of folk music, jazz, and non-Western music, to improvisation and oral tradition, confers on these other repertories a lower status. By contrast, in the art music of the Middle East and North India, music as a whole—style and repertory—is thought to change but little, while improvisatory change, performance to performance, is greatly valued.

The Blackfoot view of musical change is closer to that of Western culture. Songs once composed are thought not to change. Songs that are similar to each other are not recognized simply as variants of the same song, or as members of a tune family, but as independent units. Oral tradition is not thought to be a vehicle for improvisation. The coming of new styles into Blackfoot life is accepted but not thought to be common. In contemporary Blackfoot society, people do speak of gradual changes in the style of their traditional music, but they speak of this music as consisting of a discrete number of broad and relatively stable categories. In their rhetoric, they deal with large groups of songs—medicine songs, Sun Dance songs, gambling songs, white music. They make rough comparisons among these groups. People of my acquaintance did not usually talk about the changing of these songs or their styles, only about their appearance, presence, absence, disappearance.

2. SONGS, THE PRIMARY UNITS

If the principal unit of musical thought is the song, the next question may well concern the kinds of songs that exist in Blackfoot thought, the ways in which they are classified and identified. The general principles of taxonomy in Blackfoot culture might provide clues. How do the Blackfoot conceive of human culture and of nature? Observation of events, conversations, ethnography, and myth suggest three basic principles.

First, I want to argue that the Blackfoot think of their culture as consisting of a large quantity of things or units. An object such as a tent, an animal such as an elk, or a ceremony such as the rite of a medicine bundle are in a sense equivalent. Each is a unit that may be discussed as such but is not divided, something one may own, sell, give away, move, and compare in value to other things. The fact that concepts and ideas such as songs, kinds of supernatural power, and stories can be exchanged and are sometimes symbolized by physical objects strongly suggests that this is so.

Second, the tendency of Blackfoot rhetoric is to deal enumeratively with groups of objects, ideas, persons, and other classes. People spoke of towns on the reservation this way, of relatives, of events in a ceremony, in accounting for points in a sequence of events, in listing song types, and in telling me about local wildlife. A life history would enumerate events in order rather than beginning with central or significant events; an accounting of song types did not come to me in order of major classes followed by subdivisions. There seemed in most conversations to be approximate equality of emphasis in the listing of classes of virtually anything. But there is a tendency to say that in any cultural category, there are several or many classes, many animals, relatives, ceremonies, song types.

The third principle is related to the first two: The components of a group are more or less equal. Culture is not presented hierarchically (Ewers 1958:96–99). The songs, animals, ceremonies enumerated for me in conversations or listed in myths and tales, were usually presented as if they were equal. To be sure, there are ceremonies, songs, and persons more powerful than others, but this is not a distinction upon which my Blackfoot consultants dwelled. All of this corresponds closely to traditional political and social organization as described in standard ethnographies. There was no class structure, and political power was temporary and informal. Economic dominance resulted from personal effort rather than inherited status and would be temporary in any event, and an individual was simultaneously a member of several sometimes overlapping social groups. Obviously, these three principles are interpretations derived from field observations; standard ethnographic accounts help to make them credible. (See, for example, Lewis 1941:214–15; Lewis 1942:180–83; McClintock 1910 [1968]:167–71; and Wissler 1912a:280, 282).

My attempts to discern the taxonomy of music in Blackfoot culture are based on a mixture of techniques including observation and simple questions. Asking things like "what kinds of music can a person hear in this town" provides the first large breakdown of repertories, the division of the musical universe into Indian and white music. As already pointed out, to the Blackfoot these are both music, but music of very different sorts. Even in 1984, the question of where songs come from was treated in distant and somewhat mysterious terms for Indian songs and in a much more matter-of-fact style for country music and rock ("Some of the players and singers, they make up the songs"). The two kinds of music exist on different planes in terms of style and age.

But within the "Indian" repertory (and my Blackfoot consultants always assumed that this is what I meant), the taxonomy most used by the Blackfoot does not follow along the same lines. Replies about the kinds of Indian songs or the identity of particular songs reinforce the truism that Plains Indian societies first associate songs with the activities with which they are normally or were originally intended to be performed. The ethnomusicological literature of earlier times is so full of statements to the effect that in tribal societies, music is something "functional," that is, used to accomplish certain concrete ends, that we may be surprised to find that some Indian people actually conceive this to be the case.

Publications of around 1900 as well as conversations of the 1960s and 1980s do indeed indicate that the Blackfoot classify their songs primarily by overt use (see, for example, McClintock 1910 [1968]:513–15; Witmer 1982:70–76). To them, a song is first of all a Grass Dance, Sun Dance, hand game, or Medicine Pipe ceremony song. Inaccuracy or disagreement on individual songs does not falsify the significance of this taxonomic principle. Asking a consultant more generally what kinds of songs the Blackfoot have or had normally also first produces such categories. When singers sang especially for me so that I could make recordings, and I asked for identifications, this is what I was almost always given first. At North American Indian Days, the master of ceremonies announces songs and identifies them thus, and the same is true of tape cassettes intended mainly for an Indian clientele. But while all of this suggests that the songs were permanently fixed in rigid categories, that may not actually have been the case. The point, however, is that the Blackfoot tend to think of songs in terms of such categories, and to present to themselves and to others this outwardly rigid picture.

The Blackfoot taxonomy does not divide the songs first by one criterion and then subdivide by another; instead, the approach is enumerative. While a song is identified in the first instance by use, there are also secondary associations, though not in the sense of large categories with subdivisions of increasingly low order. Let me again explain by first providing some comparative background from the academic sector of contemporary Western musical culture.

The principal way of classifying music here is by composer ("What's this music?" "Must be Brahms." "No, it sounds more like Moussorgsky to me" [see Nettl 1963]). Beyond that, subdivision is usually by work, explicitly defined, and not usually by performer, instrument, religious or secular character, or tempo. Though not neglected, such matters are tertiary. Think of the person who switches on the radio and, upon hearing a few notes, says, "That's Bach." A bit later, he may say, "It's Partita No. 3 for unaccompanied violin," but he is much less likely to say, after hearing the first few tones, "Ah, it's Oistrakh," or, "Hurrah, some violin music," or, for that matter, "Good, I'm in the mood for some slow music." There is something of a hierarchical taxonomy in the series of associations. First, the broad category (classical, jazz, rock), then composer, followed by work, and then other traits. Much of the time this kind of sequence appears, but let me add that what I said comes from myself as informant for this culture, not from questionnaires or surveys.

In Blackfoot music, if there is a hierarchy at all, it works differently. For example, if a song is identified as a Sun Dance song and one then requests further identifying commentary, one is not likely to be told from which subdivision of the Sun Dance ritual it may have come, or other things about its function. One may instead be told that it is a song taught to the singer by his father or uncle, or that he learned it under particular circumstances. These associations, however, do not function as subdivisions of the classes established by use or accompanying activity, and they are also, though less frequently, the primary categories of taxonomy.

Thus, while most of the time, in my experience, when asked for identity or association of a song, a Blackfoot person says that it belongs to a particular dance or ceremony, occasionally I was also told, immediately and first, that it is a song associated with a particular person. "This is my own song," I sometimes heard (we will have occasion to discuss later just what this may imply), or, "This song was given to me by my mother," or, "This is George S.'s song." The matter was once generalized by a man in his forties: "Most of the songs I sing, my songs, I got them given to me by my dad, my stepfather, that is." Thus, on the basis of frequency of response—but not as a result of subdividing—we may say that the second level of song classification is by association with persons. Even in the 1980s, singers were willing to entertain such questions as "How many songs belong to you?" even though the era of vision quests and active accumulation of medicine bundles is gone.

A third, less common way of identifying songs is by associating them with events, or attaching them to stories in ways that may be related to (but not identical with) the singing of songs that is a part of telling myths. The suggestion that songs are associated with events comes largely from personal experience from the 1960s on. In a number of cases, while recording songs that I especially solicited, singers said such things as, "This is a song we first sang after Jim F. built a house on Badger Creek," or "This is a song we used to sing a lot when we were working on that ranch near Dupuyer" (a town just outside the reservation); or less specifically, "I learned this song when I visited my cousin at Rocky Boy [the Chippewa-Cree reservation in Montana], and we got together at night with a lot of people and sat around singing." The custom of associating certain songs with particular events may ultimately derive from the association of songs with specific ceremonial activities or the memory of their first appearance in specific visions or dreams, seen as events.

Occasionally a singer went into greater detail in giving an account of an event at which a song was first sung or learned. In my collecting experience, the associational process led from song to story. A consultant would sing a song and then tell a story about it. I was requesting people to sing songs, after all, and in the course of thinking of songs, singers might recall the associated stories. But in real life the association may sometimes have been reversed. James Willard Schultz (1962:155–63) narrates an event at which the singing of a song was instrumental in helping a woman and two men escape capture and death at the hands of a hostile Indian band. When the story was told, the song may have been sung or at least remembered. On the other hand, McClintock (1910 [1968]:410), who gives a thorough accounting of the significance of songs in Blackfoot life, tells of one experience in which a man sang a song and then went on to explain its significance in terms of a past (and possibly fictitious) event.

This relationship of song and story, and the practice of performing them together, was impressed on me at various times. While I made no attempt to collect tales or narratives as such, I was on at least four occasions told one particular story associated with a song. It is a story that is already mentioned in connection with a recording made by the Wannamaker Expedition in 1910 (although the melody is quite different from mine; cf. Nettl 1979: side A, band 5). Evidently very widely known among the Blackfoot, the text tells in capsule form the story of White Dog, a Sioux chief whose band preyed on Blackfoot camps until, their patience broken, a group of Blackfoot men caught and scalped him. I was told that this song of White Dog was frequently sung, and often followed by an account of the story, at parties and small informal powwows. The words are translated thus:

> "White Dog, stay away from our tribe; now you're crying, when they scalp you."

The association of songs with events can be related to the concept of associating a song with a physical object. Indeed, although admittedly this point is hard to substantiate, there seems to me to be some kind of similarity and in specific cases even identity of event, object, and song. Let me start by arguing that it is possible to interpret Blackfoot songs as being most frequently symbols of events or as resulting from events. Consider first, for example, the way songs come about in visions (see Herndon 1980:13–18; Herzog 1938:1–5; Densmore 1918:58–59; Merriam 1967:3–19). It is well known that in many North American Indian cultures, people dream songs or learn them from spirits in visions. To the Blackfoot, visions once accounted for most songs, and the songs that came about in this way were new songs; it's the Blackfoot idea of musical creation. But are all songs that are dreamed actually new songs? All owners of the same type of medicine bundle have presumably dreamed some of the same songs, unless they acquired the bundle through purchase, gift, or inheritance. The published ethnographies do not distinguish between dreams in which the songs that are learned are already known, and others containing (by standards of the outside observer, admittedly questionable) truly new songs (see Wissler 1912a:261, 263; Ewers 1958:161–62; Dempsey 1972:16, 24). Seen from one perspective, a song is an act of creation. So, two songs that are identical are in one sense just that, two versions or performances of the same song. But looked at differently, they are really two songs because they resulted from two acts of creation, their identical sound notwithstanding. You can make the same song twice, as you can make two identical drums or headdresses.

To put it another way, however, the two identical songs are different because they are associated with two different *events*. The custom of telling stories reflecting origin or meaning of a song is quite possibly related to the fact that in the tradition of composing through visions, a song is always the result of an event. One of the most important things about a song, as important as words and melody, has always been the circumstance under which it came into existence for a singer. There is an analogy between the recent scalping of White Dog, the evil Sioux chief, as background for a modern song and the idea of validating a vision with a song and legitimizing a song by telling its origin in a vision. Related to this configuration of associations is the importance of song as symbol and audible counterpart of a physical object in a medicine bundle. Blackfoot songs, then, are associated with general uses, persons, and events in everyday life, in visions, and in ceremony, all in descending order of frequency; but again, the songs do not exist in Blackfoot thought as units in a hierarchically arranged taxonomy with main divisions and subdivisions.

There is one more aspect of Blackfoot song identification that invites comment. Hearing Blackfoot people talk about songs in the abstract, as I said above, one may ordinarily be told that a song is of the Grass Dance, and a bit less frequently that it belonged to a particular person, and less frequently again that it was sung "when this or that happened," and even less frequently that it was dreamed by someone on a particular occasion, or goes with a particular event in a ceremony. But when they are singing together, they do not use these associations very much for identification. The reason is that what we have been discussing places a song in a class, but it does not distinguish it from all other songs, at least most of the time. At one time, I was told by an elderly informant, people spoke more frequently of specific uses of songs, saying such things as "Let's sing now the first song for raising the pole" at the Sun Dance. The discussion of songs in some of the earlier literature, particularly McClintock (1910 [1968]:277–82), supports this contention. But even then, songs did not quite have the individuality enjoyed by works by Mozart and Schubert. And certainly in recent times, Blackfoot people rarely say things such as "let's sing that song we learned from Tom G."

Their way of identifying songs, when it is necessary to be specific, instead, is most commonly by the initial melodic motif of a tune. In singing groups it may be sung by the leader of a song, with others nodding in agreement, thus indicating that they recognize and know it. So, the melody itself, and more specifically its beginning (which incorporates much of what is to follow in the tune) is also in a way the title, the designation of the song. It goes without saying that in contrast to many other societies, the Blackfoot do not use verbal titles, consisting perhaps of phrases from the meaningful texts or vocables, to say nothing of such things as opus numbers, keys, modes, rhythmic peculiarities; not because the structure of the music would not allow it, but because the principal ways of conceiving of music provide access to other associations.

3. THE MUSICAL UNIVERSE

Having considered some of the basic attributes of music and the Blackfoot ways of identifying the units of the musical universe, we turn next to the nature of this universe and particularly to its scope and its boundaries. We are concerned especially with the limitation of music to certain species of beings, and with its total as well as its potential quantity. Understanding the concept of music in a culture surely includes a consideration of the degree to which it is associated with humans and with other beings in the universe. Chapters 3 and 4 are in large measure devoted to this issue, but some of its aspects also belong in an examination of the general nature of music.

The first question may appropriately inquire into the distribution of music in the cosmos and thus, whether nonhuman entities have—in the conception of the Blackfoot of the present or in their mythological accounts of the distant past—the uses of music. Do animals, birds, spirits, or stars perform music for themselves, for each other, or for humans?

For the world's cultures, the answers to such questions are greatly varied and provide interesting comparative insights. One may be reminded of the Havasupai belief system, in which spirits sang to each other before humans arrived on the scene and began to use speech (Nettl 1983:165, with information from Leanne Hinton); and of the Bolivian Amuesha, where the story implies that people don't become properly human until they learn to sing (Smith 1984:137–38). These beliefs may have far-reaching implications, as must the widespread European belief that communication among the members of certain species (e.g., birds) is music, but of others (e.g., cats), not. Some African folklore presents the idea that animals make music. In European folklore, animals and objects such as pots, brooms, and tables may sing, and it is often their particularly important utterances that are presented as songs. The notion in modern Western society that birds or whales may sing seems to me to be related to the protective attitude widely taken toward these creatures. Passive creatures sing, we are perhaps saying, while the sounds of aggressive ones are otherwise classified. On the other hand, in Iran the suggestion that animals sing and that computers, even when instructed by humans, produce music was not readily accepted. The study of the association of music with other beings may tell much about a society's use of music as sound and symbol.

For the Blackfoot, music appears to be associated with humans. It is humans who ordinarily sing, and when other entities do so, it is always in conjunction with humans. The myths which tell of the singing of animals, stars, or rocks do not depict them as singing to each other but only to humans. The sounds made by animals and birds to each other are not regarded as music. In the myths, stars and rocks sing, but the implication is that their songs sound like those of Plains Indians. When I asked them, three Blackfoot consultants replied differently to the question of animals singing. One said, "Only in dreams"; a second, simply "No," and didn't wish to discuss it further; and the third thought it was a very amusing suggestion (for comparative data for Central Africa, see Merriam 1964:64–65).

But if real animals don't sing, what about the singing of supernatural animals and other figures? The Blackfoot concept of music is closely tied to the supernatural, there is no question of that, and this kind of relationship is also emphasized in the literature on other Indian cultures. Merriam discusses its importance for the Flathead at great length; McAllester, for the Navajo; Haefer, for the Pima; Kolstee, for the Bella Coola; and so on (Merriam 1967:3–24; Haefer 1981:163–209; McAllester 1954:63–75; Kolstee 1982:6–10). This is the conventional wisdom about music in tribal societies. And even more, there is a case to be made for the special relationship of music and the supernatural in human culture as a whole, as Nadel (1930:538–44) suggests that religion gave the impetus for the actual invention of music. There seems to be no religious system without its music, the relationship is evidently a cultural universal. Yet in the musical culture of the Blackfoot, and perhaps in that of other Plains societies as well, the association with the supernatural requires special explanation. The sources of music are supernatural, and the principal function of music is to moderate between humans and nonhumans, and music is therefore a domain partly in, but in a certain way also somehow outside, the culture.

I asked an elderly consultant about the differences between Indian music and white music, both of which he knew. His answer revolved about the different functions. White music had all kinds of uses in everyday life, he said. "White people don't make anything special of their music. . . . They listen just any time, doing something else." And also, "They listen but don't pay much attention." The same interview pointed out that white people use music as a way of telling stories and that they don't really think singing is in essence different from other ways of spending your time. Yes, I was told, many Indians now take the same attitude, especially as records and tapes of Indian music are now readily available. But in the "days of the old-timers, when they sang a song, they didn't think about nothing else, only maybe about the person who gave you the song or how you dreamed that song." The implication was that when one sang a song, that *was* something special. This response, along with other similar experiences, made me feel that there is something special about music in Blackfoot culture. While in some respects, music is very much part of culture and tied in with its many other domains, there are other ways in which music is separate, thus in a special relationship to the totality of culture.

Observation of behavior gave me a similar impression. I cannot claim to have data about the ethnography of sound at large and about a taxonomy of the soundscape. But it is significant that the Blackfoot don't try to make the sound of singing similar to other sounds. When they sing, they don't do anything that is like speaking. Singers look to the ground and concentrate on the song. When singing for an audience, they don't directly address it, don't look at the listeners, or sing at them. They concentrate on singing and drumming and even avoid looking very much at each other.

From this isolation of music and musical activity one can infer, only indirectly to be sure, a special form of the common conception of music's relationship to the supernatural. I was shown and sometimes even told that Indian music is a very different thing from white music, used for different purposes; that it is very separate from speech; that in early times it served mainly religious and ceremonial functions; that in theory at least, music had to be treated with respect (and even now, at powwows, ceremonial songs are treated by the audience much like national anthems, standing in silence); and that the songs have much to do with the identity of the tribe. This configuration of beliefs about music suggests its significance as emblematic of the human tribe and yet providing a way of communicating with the supernatural, a part of the universe that the Blackfoot conceive as being both part of and outside their culture.

How much music is there? Is the musical universe limited or infinitely expandable? These questions are important for the characterization of a musical culture and are of considerable interest for further delineating the concept of music in Blackfoot culture. One may ask, for any culture, whether music as a whole is conceived as a static entity, whether it may expand or even shrink, and in what ways this conception can actually be replicated by appraisals made by cultural outsiders or by the Blackfoot people's own objective descriptions of their life. And one will also surely ask whether the concept of an expandable musical universe is reflected in ideas about other domains of culture. Although the literature of anthropology includes unending discussion of culture change, the conception of culture as a quantity which may be conceived as static or expanding has not received much attention; it may be that the quantifiable character of music lends it particularly well to such considerations (but see Sahlins 1976:210–13).

Let me again begin with the familiar. In the classical, popular, and jazz repertories of urban Western society, music is considered to be more or less infinitely expandable, and musicians are obliged to do the expanding. All of this is dependent on the importance of innovation, but further, the concept of preservation, through notation and recording, is also a major factor. New music is created and extant music remains in the system through these technologies and the efforts of the academic music establishment. New pieces and new styles are accepted; the total musical system grows constantly, and the society's conception is that this is a good thing and, indeed, must be so. We do not, however, expect as much innovation in performance. In a sense, the music system reflects what otherwise goes on in Western society, which innovates in technology and economic life but also mass-produces identical units. Assuming resources to be inexhaustible, it uses them up and wants its cultural system to grow indefinitely.

The classical music system of Iran, by contrast, is not expected to expand by its society. The twelve modes, or *dastgâhs*, are thought to compose a perfect system expressing all that can be expressed in music. This is the theory; new materials are known to have frequently been developed. The twentieth century literature on Iranian classical music is in agreement about the existence of the twelve *dastgâhs*. Their interrelationship as regards significance and primacy is not agreed upon, and were it not for the theory of the twelve *dastgâhs* maintained by musicians, an external description of the system might be quite different and indicate substantial change in identity and number of components since about 1900.

The notion of twelve *immutable dastgâhs* may be indirectly related to the significance of the twelve Imams in Shi'ite Islam, and twelve is therefore a kind of perfect number. In South India, on the other hand, it is conceded that new ragas may be created, while it is the general opinion that the general style of Carnatic music should not change (see Nettl 1985b:100–103). And yet South Indians regard their music as having important expandable dimensions.

In this regard, American Indian cultures have a lot of variety. A well-known Inuit song text quoted by Merriam (Merriam 1964:175–77) suggests that in its culture, all songs are thought to have been already composed and new ones can only be made available through recombination of extant materials. In other tribes too, such as the Pima, there is the suggestion that the musical universe is limited. But in the Blackfoot conceptualization, the amount of music that may enter the culture appears not to be restricted. One has, to be sure, no way of knowing how this way of thinking may have affected the actual size of the repertory in comparison to those of other societies. Theory does not always reflect practice, and I find little evidence to suggest that there are far more Blackfoot songs (or styles, or genres) than is the case in Pima or Eskimo music.

My Blackfoot consultants had difficulty understanding the idea that there might be limits to the quantity of music that a culture may have. In principle, there was always the possibility of getting more songs. I asked, "How many songs did some of the oldest medicine men dream," and was given an estimate of seventy or eighty. "If they had lived longer, would they have dreamed even more songs?" Emphatically yes, I was told. A medicine man who had visions could, at least in theory, always receive more visions and more songs. In theory, also, there was no point at which a ritual was complete, although the various standard medicine rituals were in fact unified wholes. There was always the chance that beaver, or thunder, or the singing worm might, in a dream, change the ritual and add songs. Still, discussion of such issues might be dangerous. I asked an authority on rituals how it could be that he was explaining a closed ritual when each medicine man might dream his own version, and was told sharply, "you're talking like a dumb white man."

There was less danger in discussing expansion of the musical system by learning songs from other tribes. These could evidently be learned without limit and incorporated into the Blackfoot repertory. Indeed, the openness of Blackfoot society and its willingness to adopt members of other tribes and even non-Indians is reflected in their willingness to accept songs from the outside. One man put it just that way: "We take other people into our tribe, so it figures we would take other peoples' songs into our songs."

To be sure, the custom of adopting songs from other tribes is common among American Indian cultures, some neighboring and others far from the Blackfoot. In some, songs may be borrowed but the borrowing not acknowledged. In making these comparisons, I am certainly not claiming that these cultures also necessarily are open to adopting strangers or have the conception of an open musical system. Other factors and configurations of attitude may well be at work. My suggestion of relationships applies only to the Blackfoot. The degree to which culture traits and individuals from other tribes may have entered Blackfoot culture and society must have varied with time. In the nineteenth century, the culture appeared to be relatively "open," as indicated by Ewers (1958:310–13). Although in the reservation system, it may constitute an economic burden to adopt members, a considerable number of individuals, some of them white, appear to have entered Blackfoot society and to have been accepted.

The musical system capable of expanding and adding songs without limit is reflected in Blackfoot ideas about the incorporation of new genres of music and of styles. Take as evidence the general acceptance of the fact that various dances—Grass Dance, Rabbit Dance, Forty-nine Dance—were brought into the Blackfoot culture by borrowing from other tribes (Ewers 1958:311–12) and the acceptance of white music as something that could simply be added to the Blackfoot musical universe without greatly disturbing what they already had.

Actually, however, the conception of the music system as infinitely capable of absorbing materials from the outside is contradicted in certain instances by history. The notion of the receptive culture notwithstanding, the Blackfoot may in truth have been less receptive than some other Plains societies. Look again at the Ghost Dance and Peyote.

In the 1880s, most of the Plains Indian societies in the United States became involved in the Ghost Dance movement (Mooney 1896:60–61). This is true especially of some of the northern Plains peoples such as the Sioux and the Blackfoot peoples' fellow Algonquians, the Cheyenne and Arapaho. And yet the Blackfoot stayed aloof. Similarly, when in the early twentieth century many of the Plains tribes took up the Peyote religion, the Blackfoot remained immune to its missionary movements (Davis 1961). The matter, to be sure, is not totally clear; peyote may have been used in ceremonies at some point in Blackfoot culture (see LaBarre 1959:114). In any event, the Blackfoot musical system does not have the musical substyles of Ghost Dance and Peyote music that created variety in the repertories of Cheyenne and Arapaho, Pawnee and Kiowa.

While the Blackfoot may contend that their culture is capable of absorbing outside influences and incorporating genres and even systems additional to their oldest traditions, when compared to that of other tribes in their culture area their style actually turns out to be more homogeneous.

It may be possible (cautiously and speculatively) to relate the concept of expandability of the musical system to the Blackfoot perception of their physical environment and to ways in which they thought about tribal and personal wealth. In the early nineteenth century, before the period of wars, famines, and broken treaties with the whites, the Blackfoot must have experienced a surge of economic well-being (Lewis 1942:170–82, 197– 99). The then recent move to the western Plains, the acquisition of horses and guns and the resulting ability to hunt buffalo more efficiently, the enormous variety of flora and fauna encountered in the Rocky Mountains, the possibility of greatly increased wealth through trade with the whites, success in warfare against smaller neighboring tribes, all of this could have produced a feeling of expanded horizons and of resources that were indeed practically without limit. The religious system of unlimited visions and open-ended ceremonies and a related conception of music could have been developed together. But such conclusions are limited by the absence of information on what music and musical thought may have been like before the emergence of the Blackfoot as a typical Plains culture, in the times of partial agriculture and a less nomadic way of life.

Comparison with the musical cultures of some of the eastern Woodlands tribes provides some help. The most suggestive evidence comes from Woodlands cultures such as those of the Iroquois and Menomini (see Fenton 1953:172–210; Densmore 1932:40–53) as well as Prairie or Eastern Plains cultures such as the Chippewa and Pawnee (Densmore 1910:13– 15; Fletcher 1904), where rituals of great complexity may have remained unchanged for long periods, and in which change, so the accounts imply, is virtually unthinkable. For the Menomini, Densmore discusses adoption dances as exhibiting stability. For the Chippewa, she describes the *Mide*, their principal religious complex, as a somewhat variable ceremony, but her account leaves little doubt that it was expected to be done essentially the same way each time, and that there was no sense that individuals could expand it as a result of dreams. In the eastern Plains, the area from which the Blackfoot may have moved to their final location, the Pawnee *Hako* appears to have been an extremely complex, highly prescribed, and thus possibly very stable ritual. These were not ceremonies in which songs could conveniently be added, and the vision complex, though present, provided less flexibility. The literature speaks of old songs, nurtured and preserved.

To be sure, the pitfalls of this comparison are abundantly evident. For example, the contact of whites with the eastern tribes long preceded that of the Plains Indians, and the vital musical culture of the East may have been so paralyzed by the time recordings could be made that mechanisms for its expansion may have ceased to exist. Yet there were, it may be inferred from the much better documentation of Pima and Havasupai cultures (Herndon 1980:15–17; Herzog 1938:2; Hinton 1984:12–20), societies in which the potential quantity of music was more limited. According to Herzog, the Pima appeared to conceive of an extant musical universe whose songs humans realized as sound, but they also conceived of spirits who appeared in dreams and had a virtually unlimited number of songs they could teach. For the Havasupai, Leanne Hinton described a variety of songs all learned by dreaming, but she points out specifically (1984:19) that they are conceived as part of a closed system. It is certainly possible that the eastern Woodlands peoples, whose cultures are quite diverse, may all along have shared the conception of a musical system in which the number of songs was limited.

It is tempting to suggest that the Blackfoot also thought of music as limited until their environment temporarily expanded. And tempting also to speculate that when the Plains musical culture later on became the focal point of a newly created pan-Indianism, this was a result of the newly-found expansiveness of the Plains musical system which made possible and acceptable the bringing of new songs and styles into the repertories in order to serve the twentieth-century needs of Indian people. If the conceptual expandability of the Plains repertories is exceptional among Indian musics, the ascendancy of these repertories may have been a natural accompaniment to a period in which other resources appeared, for a time, to be virtually without limit.

4. THE ESSENCE OF MUSICAL SOUND

Musical thought in Blackfoot culture involves ideas about what music is, what it can do, to whom it belongs, and of course also the way it sounds. Many ethnomusicological studies are devoted largely to describing and analyzing a musical repertory, to say nothing of transcribing songs, the artifacts of musical sound. Such is, however, not the task of our study beyond the brief description of the style for background in chapter 1 and the discussion of the way in which Blackfoot people think of musical style and its elements in chapter 5. But as the task of this particular chapter is to sketch broadly the general character of music in Blackfoot thought, it must ask what the Blackfoot consider to be the principal characteristics of their musical sound, and how these relate to the concepts of song and singing in language and in folk taxonomy.

Using the Blackfoot people's own comparative perspective of Western and Indian music provides interesting insights. Witmer tells us that "in the minds of many informants, the ideal identity of individual songs was closely circumscribed" (Witmer 1982:61), and goes on to explain the

Blackfoot conception of songs as permanent and unchanging entities, again suggesting one of the abiding themes of this study. Musical sound is something received by humans from an external source and then remaining unchanged in their possession, somewhat like a physical object. In real life a song may often be attributed to more than one function and sung differently by different singers, but this reality may simply not be reflected in the theoretical. In contrast to their own songs, the Blackfoot regard white music much as white people conceive of it—something more flexible and more directly and exclusively associated with humans. In accord with this distinction, one of the principal conceptions of Indian music as sound is that it is, and should indeed be, different from Western music. The fact that there are hardly any social events at which both Indian and white music are heard supports this suggestion. To the Blackfoot, Indian music is something special and its sound does not mix with that of white music. And to be sure, if Blackfoot music has moved toward the white model in concept and behavior, this has not been true of the sound.

The quintessentially vocal quality of Indian music is important to the Blackfoot conception of their music sound. It is a peculiarity of Blackfoot culture that there is no melodic instrumental repertory into which songs can be translated, no attempt (in my experience) to play Indian songs on Western instruments, and no mention of songs as anything but vocal. By contrast, some other Plains tribes have flutes on which vocal melodies may be played, and in some Southwestern tribes, people play certain songs on violins, pianos, and harmonicas. The absence of melodic musical instruments among the Blackfoot is something of a curiosity.

In some of the world's cultures, an instrument is not just a music-making tool, but is thought to create the music. In a poem regarded by Iranians as symbolic of the essence of Persian music, the oft-quoted beginning of the *Masnavi*, the Persian poet Mowlavi presents the reed-flute as the producer of sad sounds because it has been torn from its roots— and ties to it the lamenting nature of Persian music. And so we ask about the Blackfoot: If there is no conception of purely instrumental music, how may this be related to the representation, in visions, of singing by inanimate objects? The myth of the Buffalo Rock (Wissler and Duvall 1909: 85–87) tells us, for example, that a rock can sing, or a tree trunk, and we might think that the Blackfoot are thus telling us that music can be made by objects that might conceptually be related to instruments.

I thus determined to ask: If something like instruments exists in myth, why do the Blackfoot have no melody instruments in real life? I was able to bring this question only to one consultant, and to him, the suggestion that the kind of music made on instruments by white people was somehow related to the singing done by stone and wood in the myths seemed meaningless. He did point out that real Indian music was always singing, as far as he was concerned; but my suggestion met a dead end.

According to Witmer (1982:113) and to my consultants, one of the important characteristics of white music was its technical difficulty. It had to be learned with great care and required notation, and thus consisted of separable elements. By contrast, the Blackfoot see Indian music as having a kind of immediacy, and song as something whose components are integrated from inception (whether or not practice bears this out). In contrast to their own discussion of white songs, the Blackfoot do not talk about Indian songs in terms of ingredients, its words, its relation to white music or other songs. When they talk about their music, each song appears unique and separate, not easily related or compared.

Briefly anticipating here the more detailed discussion in chapter 5: There are some sounds that embody, to the Blackfoot, the essence of their music. Percussion accompaniment is essential, and it must be rhythmically independent. In modern Plains Indian culture, we have already noted, singers may also be called drummers; the terms are interchangeable. In a singing group, drumming in perfect unison is essential, more so than singing in unison. Vocal style is essential; the singing style of Plains music, the particular use of the voice, is integrally part of Blackfoot music, more so than form, contour, or scale. Tunes that may possibly have a Western origin are sometimes used as the basis for Indian songs, and the idea that such songs may enter the repertory was accepted at least by some singers in the 1980s. But the suggestion that they might some day sing some of their Indian songs, such as Grass Dance or Sun Dance songs, using a vocal style characteristic of country or rock music was considered absurd.

The particular vocal style and tone color of Plains Indian music has, in the period of increasing domination by white culture, since 1900, actually become increasingly differentiated from that of white music. The idea that ethnic musical identity can be established through exaggerating the unique characteristics of a style, and particularly singing style or timbre, has been suggested in publications dealing with various cultures (see Nettl 1983:352; 1985b:26, 28, 35; Katz 1968). In Blackfoot music, the characteristic style of Plains singing, with high-pitched beginnings, pulsations, vocal narrowness, nasality may have increased, if comparison of early with recent recordings can provide credible evidence. The change may be due to the interculturally determined "exaggeration" (Nettl 1985b:26), or it may possibly be a result of increased influence from tribes geographically more central to the Plains culture area. Older consultants agreed, however, that the "Indian sound" in Blackfoot singing has intensified: "These younger fellows, they sing higher and louder than we used to."

I asked why the Blackfoot continued to sing their songs in a style so different from that of the whites. "They wouldn't sound like Indian songs if we didn't," was one reply. Another: "We've always sung this way." And a third, with the obvious approval of others present: "Yes, those Indian songs sound different." The general sound of the vocal style is a central, perhaps *the* central feature of Indian music to the Blackfoot. It may even be an object of parody, as it occurs in the songs of a singing group calling themselves "The Indian Chipmunks." There are occasional experiments mixing styles, with harmony, on guitar or piano, the incorporation of modern Indian tunes into rock and roll, the adoption of hymn and popular melodies into the Blackfoot repertory. But what is least tampered with is the singing style (see also Hatton 1986:203–5).

A white music teacher at a Browning school (raised and trained in the Midwest) told me that he taught some Blackfoot songs to the largely Indian student body. Unable himself to sing in the Indian vocal style, he did not try to teach the music with its sound. The vocal style, he said, would be learned by the students at home. There might not be anyone to teach them specific songs in their own families, but once they had learned the tunes and the words, there would be no lack of people to show them how they should be sung.

5. Music and Language

Most societies consider language to be a major emblem of ethnicity. To be considered a "people," one must have a language, and over the centuries, the struggles for national and cultural recognition in places as diverse as Ireland, Czechoslovakia, Turkish-speaking western Iran, and Spanish-speaking portions of Texas revolved substantially about the right to use the traditional language in formal communication and education. The Blackfoot language occupies an important role in the cultural conception of Blackfoot society, but it is not, today, widely spoken or even generally known. In the late nineteenth century, its use was discouraged by Indian agents and the use of English quickly came to predominate in the many mixed-blood households. The intertribal character of reservation life and the need to combine forces with other tribes for political and cultural purposes in the mid-twentieth century pushed the Blackfoot language further into the background.

In the 1960s, I found that most people under thirty knew no Blackfoot, or very little, that only a few elderly people, mostly women, were largely ignorant of English, and that among middle-aged people, most conversation took place in (very slightly accented) English. In the 1980s, although still fewer people were fluent speakers (Blackfeet Community College 1985:7–9), interest in maintaining the Blackfoot language had revived, and a vigorous program of formal instruction in the language had been established in the newly founded Blackfeet Community College. At events such as North American Indian Days, some speeches were made in Blackfoot, despite the fact that the majority of people present did not understand; it seemed in certain instances more important to show that there was a distinctive language than to communicate verbal content. In view of these great changes in the role of the language in cultural life, it is interesting to see substantial continuity in the function of language in the text of songs.

At the outset, it is important to stress that the relationship between words and music in Blackfoot song is quite different from that in Western societies. In European cultures, in the Middle East, and in India, a principal purpose of singing is to impart verbal text to a listening audience. Vocables (or, as they are sometimes called, meaningless syllables) may be found, as in refrains or in melismatic passages, but these are regarded as exceptional. Blackfoot singing, by contrast, makes very substantial use of vocables. The same is true, in lots of different and often highly complex ways, of many other North American Indian cultures (see Frisbie 1980 and Hinton 1980:279–90 for discussion of the complexity of vocable structures and their functions). In some tribes, the entire repertory of Peyote music consists of vocable texts with distinctive syllable patterns that bear a close relationship to the rhythm of melody (Nettl 1953); Frisbie (1980) provides a complex grammar of vocable use in Navajo texts.

The use of nontranslatable texts which are learned and form an integral part of songs would appear to give the concept of song a different cast from that of Western music, in which the existence of lexically meaningful text is essential, even when the performer knows it will not be understood by the audience (as may often be the case in opera, concert song, and rock music for reasons of language, dramatic situation, amplification).

The distinguished anthropologist Oscar Lewis (whose dissertation field research with the Blackfoot in 1939 is barely remembered in the light of his later accomplishments) was also an excellent amateur singer of Italian opera, and in this context told about an occasion at which his Blackfoot friends gathered to bid farewell to him, singing their songs to him and inviting him also to sing. He responded with an aria but was surprised to find the Indians laughing at him while applauding. They later told him that they always found themselves amused when hearing white music because it had so many words. If you want to talk, why don't you talk instead of singing, they asked.

To be sure, Blackfoot and other Plains musics do have conventionally meaningful texts. There are fewer such texts than are found in other American Indian musics, but sometimes they have great dramatic impact. In the contemporary culture, few songs have any meaningful words, but this may be a function of the intertribal and pan-Indian nature of present-day Indian life in which songs travel from reservation to reservation. Or it may be a function of the need to learn songs rapidly and the fact that singing groups may themselves be intertribal. But only in part. After all, in some cultures the intelligibility of texts has never constituted an obstacle to their acceptance. The development of medieval tropes involved the composition of texts in order to facilitate the memorization of tunes. Opera and art song are sometimes sung by artists who are themselves ignorant of their meanings.

No doubt Blackfoot music today has far fewer texts than it did in earlier times, and one might expect the Blackfoot people to comment on this and also to mourn the loss. I was surprised by the rather matter-of-fact acceptance of this change, and can only speculate that it is connected to (1) what I think is a Blackfoot belief that melody is a more important component of song than are words; (2) the traditional substitutability of words in certain songs; and (3) the changing role of music in Blackfoot culture in which communicating with the Blackfoot peoples' own supernatural was replaced by dealing with the outside, non-Blackfoot, world. Instead of decreasing the number and length of meaningful texts, the Blackfoot could have adopted English as the regular vehicle for texts, and they actually they did so for some songs. But more likely, the present state of affairs results from (1) the acceptance, all along in traditional Blackfoot culture, of the possibility of having songs without words, and (2) the substantial loss of culture which took away much of the subject matter about which one sang in earlier times. The mentioned gap between Western and Indian music rests in good part on the differing role of words. Less humorously than Oscar Lewis's friends, my Blackfoot consultants in recent times pointed out to me that Indian music had very different purposes and functions from white songs, and that the way in which whites used words was indicative. The main function of Indian songs, I was once told, was to get help from the supernatural. And the spirits understood, one didn't have to spell things out for them, at least not very much. A word or two would suffice.

All of this supports the contention that the Blackfoot conceive of singing to be a very different form of communication from speech. Let me add a few remarks amplifying this statement. First, this differentiation may also have another interesting ramification: The Blackfoot people rarely use the words of songs in speech. For example, they do not label songs by quoting first lines. When asked to give the words of a song, they are able to do so, but often they were uninterested in quoting it precisely as sung, preferring to paraphrase it. The fact that there is little textual material and that Blackfoot people scoff at the ubiquity of words in white music may imply that words are an unimportant component of songs, but the opposite is probably true. What is said in the songs is important, and indeed, the very paucity of the words lends them significance. Furthermore, the older recordings of Blackfoot songs have a larger proportion of verbal text, and a few are occupied entirely by words, and not at all by vocables.

A consultant commented on the distinction: "When we're singing 'hey-hey-hey' or 'heya-ha-ya,' that's just the words of the song. It's supposed to be like that. . . . That's how they made them songs, in the dreams." I asked about the larger quantity of words in earlier recordings. "There's more words in medicine songs; it's the medicine power."

The vocables used as meaningless text in Blackfoot songs are those used in Plains singing at large. They consist of the consonants *h*, *y*, and *w* plus vowels, and in contrast to some other Indian peoples, they avoid *n*, *c* (*ts*), and other consonants. There is some correlation between *i* and *e* with high pitches, and *a*, *o*, and *u* with lower pitches. In the performance practice of modern singing by groups, a song has the same vocables each time it is sung, and all members of the group sing them in approximate unison. The vocables then tend to constitute a true text, that is, they are memorized and learned as an integral part of the song.

I did not find my Blackfoot consultants interested in the relationship of particular texts to melodies. They conceded that a song might have words in part of its history and lose them or gain new ones, that a song could be sung with or without words, and also that the words of a song could be changed. The suggestion that you would take a verbal text and set it to different tunes made less sense to them. A song was primarily— I got this distinct feeling from various conversations—a melody. Words were incidental and could be changed or replaced by vocables. This is hard to explain in the light of the fact that significant events or statements in myths may be sung and that words are important in certain songs of the war complex.

The way in which words are set to melody may also illuminate the relative importance of text and melody. In several ways, text setting may violate the ordinary way of speaking Blackfoot. For example, an individual word might be interrupted by vocables, and even more frequently, a sentence of song text may have a few vocables scattered among the words. One might expect, as has been suggested for Arapaho songs (Nettl 1954b:198), that this could be a function of the desire to permit stressed or long syllables to match stressed or long tones in the melody. In the Blackfoot material, that may sometimes be the case, but in certain instances, the matching of length and stress hardly testifies to this motivation. Inquiring about the issue did not meet with success, except for the simple comment made by two individuals that words could be sung differently from the way they would be spoken. Appendix B illustrates the characteristics of text setting.

In some of my recording work, I would ask a consultant to sing a song and then to give the verbal text to me in spoken form, along with translation. Sometimes, I found differences between the versions. In the spoken version, particularly in final or semifinal sections of the text, some syllables or words might be missing in the sung rendition. Or sometimes, one or two syllables from the end of a word were repeated. For example, using phonetic transcription from the spoken and sung text without necessarily conforming to Uhlenbeck's form of the words:

Spoken text: akeyé winotámoket tákxyapaapówi takxkyaowimíni
              woman don't worry   I'm coming home   I'm coming home to
              about me   eat berries

Sung text: akeeye wiinootaamoket takkxyaapoyo

I particularly noted that spoken texts were longer, and the sung versions, sometimes simply abbreviations. I inquired:

"When you gave me the words of that song, did you give me what you sang just now?"

"Yes." (Don't argue with informants, my teachers told me.)

"But the end of what you told me, I just took it down; I didn't hear it in the song. Shall I play it for you?"

"When we sing, it's sometimes different from talking. What I told you, that's the real words of the song when I speak'em. Singing might be different."

"You mean, when you sing you don't have to sing *all* of the words?"

"That's right."

I am not sure I followed very good interviewing procedure. Here as in many instances, inquiry did not produce explanation, and I am unable to determine whether the versions that were sung were specific to singing, or whether in speech one could use a considerable number of variants, certain of which had been selected for use in the particular song rendition that had just been recorded. But throughout, I continued to get the impression that it made little sense to my consultants to compare speaking and singing. The conversation reproduced above reinforced my belief that song texts fulfill a function very different from speech and that song texts often deal in brevity and allusion.

If now the Blackfoot feel that there is such a difference between speech and song, one might expect the subject matter or poetic style of sung verbal text to be very different from those of speech. And yet— vocables and the very fact of singing aside—I have no evidence that the way in which things are said in song, in terms of vocabulary and grammar, differs from the way they might be expressed in everyday speech. The point is that there is little verbal text, that one does not simply put any available thought into song, and that songs play a particular role in myths and ceremonies; all of this gives the texts heightened significance.

Songs play a role in many activities, and a description of text content might well follow the lines of their uses in ceremonies, dances, myths, and so on. But a look at the way texts divide themselves into categories on the basis of their content, as presented in early ethnographies and as collected in smaller number in the 1960s, may also be instructive. First, the matter of their brevity. In much of the repertory, particularly songs with the characteristic Plains song form, and especially in the modern songs, texts occupy only the first portion of the second, incomplete rendition of the melody. In old ceremonial or medicine bundle songs, they often occupied a larger proportion of the melody, and sometimes all of it, but in these songs, many of the melodies themselves are short. Here is a small sampling of texts, in English translation, older and recent:

> "Bear is looking for something to eat." (Wissler and Duvall 1909:96; sung in a myth)
> "One-chief, Sun pities him." (Hanks, 1938 recording; Sun Dance song)
> "Old Man saying, my pipe is saying, holy." (Hanks, 1939 recording; Medicine Pipe song)
> "It's a bad thing to be an old man." (Nettl, 1951 recording; Crazy Dog Society song)
> "I don't love anyone, I'm telling the truth." (Kaufman, 1952 recording; war complex song)

These illustrate the characteristic brevity. An idea is stated, concisely and to the point. Even when texts are a bit longer, the statement of a single idea dominates, and there is no extended narrative or lyrical discourse. Thus, in the myth about smoking otter, a swan sings, "The man says, the wind is my medicine; the rain is my medicine; the hail is my medicine" (Wissler and Duvall 1909:99). And in the myth in which the smallest of the seven-stars constellation gives a man a pipe, it sings,

> The Seven Stars say, "my pipe is powerful."
> Old man says, "my pipe is powerful." He hears me.
> (Wissler and Duvall 1909:91)

Or, in a myth in which a man receives supernatural shields,

> Buffalo is going to drink: water is my medicine;
> Buffalo is going to eat: grass is my medicine.
> (Wissler and Duvall 1909:101)

Not only is there a single idea, but the text is often a rather forceful statement and, in some myths, a powerful reinforcement of something already asserted. At this point, it may be instructive to group the texts by the kind of statement that is made. Five groups conveniently emerge:

1. A statement certifying or asserting that something is sacred:

> This lodge is sacred; the ground also, where the Chief lives, is sacred. (McClintock 1910:264; from Medicine Pipe ceremony)
> The earth is our home. It is medicine. (Wissler and Duvall, 1909:98; from a myth about the Bear-knife ceremony)

2. Description of what a figure in a myth is doing:

> Bear is looking for something to eat. (Wissler and Duvall 1909:96; from the Bear-knife ceremony)

3. Description of an act or attitude by a figure in a myth, stated by himself:

> I begin to get restless in the spring. (McClintock 1910:264; from the Grizzly Bear dance in the Medicine Pipe ceremony)
> I don't want them to kill me; These here (straw, etc.) I will fight with. (Wissler and Duvall 1909:104; from a myth telling the origin of the eagle-head charm)

4. Description of an act in which the teller of a myth or a ceremonialist is actually engaged while singing:

> I am now moving around.
> I will take away the chief's (pipe's) robe. (Both are from McClintock's description of the Medicine Pipe ceremony 1910:262; the owner of the medicine bundle describes his beginning of the ceremony by moving the pipe around and then the removal of the outer covering of the medicine bundle)

5. Songs in which someone is told or exhorted to do something, in a ceremony or otherwise:

> Sun says to smoke. (Nettl, 1952 coll.; from the Sun Dance ceremony.)
> Yonder woman, you must take me. I am powerful. Yonder woman, you must take me, you must hear me. Where I sit is powerful. (Wissler and Duvall 1909:85; from the myth of the buffalo-rock, a song sung by the rock to the woman)
> Woman, don't worry about me; I'm coming back home to pick berries. (Nettl, 1951 collection; a song sung by warriors as they left for war parties)
> White Dog, stay away from our tribe; now you're crying when they scalp you. (widely collected since 1910)
> If you wait for me after the dance is over, I will take you home in my purchased wagon. (Nettl, 1951 collection; a text originally in English)

This very cursory glance at types of song text content shows some significant characteristics. The narrators of the texts are often figures in visions and myths, but they may also be humans in stories, or the singers themselves. There seems to be little distinction by narrator in style or type of content. The types of texts are distributed, though to be sure not evenly, among some of the uses of songs: myths, medicine bundle ceremonies, Sun Dance, informal occasions. The number of texts collected for songs sung in the telling of myths and in medicine bundle ceremonies greatly exceeds that known for Sun Dance and age-grade ceremonial occasions, to say nothing of the songs sung for social dances, which rarely have verbal texts. And the song text content categories as described above do not correlate with uses. For example, texts in which someone is exhorted to an action appear in the songs of myths, ceremonies, the Sun Dance, and informal recreational occasions.

It is interesting to see that the Blackfoot do not have lengthy or repetitive texts (as do, for example, the Navajo and the Pueblo peoples; see McAllester 1980:205–07; Densmore 1938:81–86). They do not deal with abstractions or philosophical categories. They are ordinarily not strophic in the proper sense of the word, which would require using repetition of tune for new or at least slightly changed words. They do make strong points. Thus, if a figure in a vision wishes to announce his own coming, he may do so in song. Announcing an important presence in a myth may be occasion for singing, likewise the assertion of supernatural presence or power, or important requests or directions. Within their ceremonial or narrative environments, songs lend importance to occasions, and song texts, brief and unprepossessing in a literary sense, add to their significance, providing formality and emphasis. The nature of the texts of songs, like singing style and behavior, serves to separate music from conversational speech.

6. KINDS OF MUSIC

We have talked about identification, which suggests taxonomy, but the two are not identical, and so we next inquire into the categories of music recognized by the Blackfoot, along with categories of other things that play a role in musical life. And as comparative taxonomy of music is an important avenue to the anthropology of music, we again begin with the contemporary world of Western art music.

This segment of Western musical society tends to classify the world of music in a number of ways. First, there are broad types, styles, or repertories: classical (with subdivisions of standard, early, and new); popular; folk; jazz; and less prominently, non-Western music, church music, and military music, semiclassical stage music, and a few minor categories. Then there are composers; performers; genres (such as opera, symphony, chamber music, solo); instrumentation; and more. For our considerations here, it is important to note that these categories intersect and overlap, but that they also serve as subdivisions one of another, and most significant, that a hierarchy is implicit in all of them. Thus, classical music is above others; certain composers are clearly in a different class from the rest; opera and symphony orchestra ordinarily lie above solo piano; and even instrumental above vocal, in the sense that "normal" music is regarded as instrumental, purely vocal music is regarded as something exceptional, and singers are not seen as musicians in the same sense as instrumentalists. But while these statements may reflect stated and articulated theory about the world of music, the hierarchy is not in all respects reflected in the behavior of Western society. Thus, popular musicians are typically paid more than classical musicians, and the "great" composers are not the ones whose works are necessarily heard most.

It is also interesting to consider the way Western society classifies the world of musicians. There are composers, performers, teachers, scholars, and ancillary personnel such as agents, publishers, record executives, and audio engineers. Composers are central, given great respect but sometimes little reward. Teachers, especially if they are not great performers, are looked down upon, but they are usually paid better than performers. In Western academic musical culture, it appears to be important to have many categories and to arrange them in a qualitative hierarchy, which again may not be observed in real life. The concept of hierarchy is exacerbated by a kind of star system, in which individual classes, persons, or pieces are singled out for a vastly greater degree of prestige than the rest—star performers, great master composers, hit songs, masterworks.

In these respects, music has much in common with the other arts, if not with the total cultural system. And in various ways, the Western taxonomy of music does correspond to other taxonomies in Western culture, presenting as it does certain values of society: for example, a class structure, strong leadership, cooperation and conformity, concern with both quantity and quality. With this in mind, we should now consider how the Blackfoot lay out their world of music, by what criteria their taxonomy is developed, and how it compares to the rest of their culture.

We have already established, because it was essential to a picture of the basic character of Blackfoot music, that the fundamental unit of musical thought is the song and that the principal ways of identifying songs are, in order of frequency, by association with activity, person, past event, and the head motif of the melody. The overlapping but nonhierarchical approaches to song identification have been noted. One might expect such criteria also to be important in establishing the classes of music in Blackfoot thought, although to be sure a taxonomy of the total repertory is not the same thing as identification of its individual units. Asking nine Blackfoot people simply to tell me what kinds of songs they had, I uniformly received answers reflecting use. Only in one case was the bifurcation of Indian and white music mentioned first. Otherwise, it was evidently to be assumed that when I asked a question of that sort I gave myself away as the kind of person who would have only Indian music in mind. Yet the category of white music as a part of Blackfoot culture is definitely there (see also Witmer 1973:76–91).

None of my nine consultants gave me a very long list of uses of traditional Blackfoot music. The categories mentioned were not uniform, but the most mentioned were War Dance, gambling, Sun Dance, and medicine (in the general sense) songs. No one, I think, tried to make a point of providing a comprehensive picture of uses or song types. After being given three or four categories, I was always told that there were a lot of other kinds of songs. I did not receive answers that reflected a picture of principal categories (e.g., sacred and secular, or perhaps medicine bundle, dance, and gambling songs), which might then be broken down into subdivisions. A taxonomy created by an outside observer would very likely, on the basis of behavior and a certain amount of logic, determine that there were medicine bundle songs, social dance songs, and other categories, and then break the medicine bundle songs down into those associated with stereotypical bundles such as the Medicine Pipe and others that are more idiosyncratic and have fewer components. These then might be divided by specific bundle, and further subdivisions according to the use of the songs in the ceremony might be made. Or, social dance songs might be subdivided into War Dance, Owl Dance, Circle Dance, then into fast and slow War or Grass Dance songs, and so on. To the outside observer, the repertory lends itself to a hierarchical classification with successive subdivisions.

Now, my Blackfoot consultants recognized all of these types and categories, and when I presented some of them with such an outline or a statement of this sort, did not find it objectionable. But it did not seem to be important to them to consider and discuss their musical repertory as consisting of major classes which are then divided and subdivided. Rather, they would say, enumeratively, such things as this: that they have powwow songs, Medicine Pipe songs, slow and fast War Dance songs, baby songs, Scalp Dance songs (from the old war song complex). (Indeed, this is just what one man told me.) The fact that some of these categories are much larger than others, or closer to the top of my "outsider's" classificatory scheme, was irrelevant to him. The conclusion must be that the Blackfoot taxonomy of songs consists of a large number of groups all of which are conceived, in classificatory terms, as more or less equal.

It is instructive to inquire further into the nature of this taxonomy and its role in the culture. Do the Blackfoot, as it were, have the whole system in front of themselves in their minds, ready to exhibit it to a questioner? Such a question is not easy to approach in any culture. But let me illustrate from experience elsewhere. Some Iranian practitioners of classical music, asked without elaboration to explain their system, begin without hesitation by saying that they have seven principal and five secondary modes (*dastgâhs*), and that a performance has five main parts. In these and other ways they proceeded to circumscribe the entire system. Similarly, musicians in Madras told me without prompting that there was north and south Indian music, vocal and instrumental, seventy-two main ragas, composed and improvised music, three great master composers, and then, subdivisions of these main categories—morning and evening ragas, for example, or regular and *chapu* talas.

Confronted with the same question, an American classical music performer did not say the same kinds of things at all. It was clear that he did not, as did the Iranians and Indians, come to an initial comprehension of the entire system, all of its classes and subdivisions. Instead, he began with one set of facts about harmony and moved to a second subject, recent composers, and on further, without much regard for the way in which each bit of information might fit into the entire system. These brief characterizations are intended to be no more than just that, and they are surely in no way definitive. But they may serve to suggest that the societies of the world not only have different ways of identifying their units of musical thought but also approach the question of taxonomy of their musical systems quite differently.

The Blackfoot are closer to my American example than to my Asian ones. It is important to them to establish that they have classes of music. Questions about kinds of songs and about the repertory are normally answered by reference to classes by use. In my notes of several years, I recorded five general explanations or accounts of Blackfoot music given by consultants in the form of short lectures. These did not begin with an overview followed by subdivisions; rather, they were enumerative recitals. It seemed important to the Blackfoot to say that there are many classes. Indeed, one woman explained the differences between white and Indian music in terms of numbers. "You just have church songs and the other kind of music, but we used to have a whole lot of different kinds of songs, you can't imagine how many kinds."

This discussion of classification and taxonomy leads logically to the way the Blackfoot conceive of the structure of their musical repertory. What does it mean to say that musical repertories (not styles but the repertories in the sense of a group of units) have a structure? Here are some of the kinds of things I have in mind, speaking as the outside analyst. Some repertories consist of small numbers of units such as tune families, each internally structured through various kinds of relationships but all represented through a spectrum of the music's history. This might be a description of Anglo-American folk music. Some can best be divided into units from different points or times of origin, as the Western classical concert repertory of 1980 might be said to consist of a small amount of "early" music, some music of the eighteenth century, more yet of the nineteenth and less again of the twentieth, the central music being one to two hundred years old. Various kinds of interrelationship of units, such as frequency of performance of each, relative value of genres, composers, instruments—all of these might be aspects of this structure.

But then, if this can be empirically established, it is also important to determine how the cultures of the world interpret the structure of their repertories. There is little literature that illuminates this kind of a question, and even to give illustrations from extant research involves extrapolation from ethnographic literature.

For example, the Navajo consider their songs to be in categories involving the degree of power or danger that they contain; prayer ceremonials are high in such a scale, moccasin game songs intermediate, songs from the latter part of the Blessingway ceremony least dangerous or powerful (McAllester 1954:63). According to McAllester, the Navajo do not have a set of categories, but they do, if asked point-blank, indicate that the question of danger and power is central in their music, and that a song type (by use) can be compared to another in these terms.

In Iranian classical music culture the picture is quite different. A number of hierarchies and other sorts of interrelationship among the three hundred or so *gushehs*, short units that compose the system, are recognized. While they can be shown to correspond to a variety of social values (Nettl 1978a), Iranian musicians usually do not admit that they have much to do with anything outside the musical universe and consider the structure of the musical repertory to be independent. In the case of the American folk music repertory of the lower Midwest (in the first half of the twentieth century), tune families and text families overlap, but the society thought of the repertory primarily in terms of stories, each of which has a main tune (with its variants) along with some secondary, unrelated tunes.

The Blackfoot, I suggest, conceived of the structure of their musical repertory principally in terms of the structure of their culture as a whole. To them it is clearly reasonable to contend that the musical system is a direct reflection of the cultural system. Each major component of culture has its music, and the way in which culture is conceived by Blackfoot people—as a group of discrete objects—is the way in which the musical system is also perceived. Ideally, at least, the Blackfoot take their musical repertory to reflect all activities that are significant to them; for everything, there is the right song. "The right Blackfoot way to do something is to sing the right song with it," I was told in 1965. And categories in life should be matched by categories in music, so that each song has its proper activity. To be sure, as Witmer (1982:76–77) also suggests, real life does not usually correspond to this theory; there is confusion and disagreement about the proper use of a song, and many songs fulfill a number of functions.

Another aspect of taxonomy worthy of consideration is the integrity of classes. Given that a society perceives music as consisting of many songs belonging to a variety of classes, one would wish to ask whether these classes are easily distinguished, whether they are in fact distinct or separated by sharp lines or whether they merge and are therefore better described as a continuum. Again, in an example from Western art music, although the society distinguishes significantly between sacred and secular music, the repertories of church and secular concerts are separate but actually overlap in important ways.

For another illustration, the fact that popular, folk, and classical music are widely conceived as separate classes in Western society is underscored, for example, by their mutual exclusiveness in concerts and by the sharp difference in attire of performers. But in style and in statements of music theory, the three repertories overlap substantially. In Western culture, lines among classes are sharp in theory but less so in practice. In contemporary Iran, these lines are even less distinct, both in style and in conception; the repertory is more of a continuum, and people do not speak of music very much in terms of classes at all.

Wissler (1912a:263–72) tells us much about Blackfoot songs from the time of his research using what is largely the already cited, unanalyzed account by one of his consultants. It is significant that most of what this man had to say about musical culture is stated in terms of classification. He, and other Blackfoot people from whom he gathered his information about music, seem to have talked about songs largely in terms of *kinds* of songs (e.g., 1912a:221, 237–38).

Wissler's experience parallels my own; the Blackfoot people talk about songs to a large extent in terms of kind or type. Conversation about songs which I heard—even when many or most of the classes have fallen into disuse—often dealt significantly with the grouping of songs, the question of whether this group of songs belonged to a particular ritual, the similarity of groups, the overlapping of ceremonial repertories. The question of which songs belong where was evidently significant, and continues to be so. This way of thinking about songs seems related to the conception of music as a reflection of the cultural system, and to the notion that each activity has its appropriate songs. It also suggests that in the Blackfoot conception, though not in practice, sharp lines among categories were important. Consultants admitted (Wissler 1912a:237–38) that there is overlap, that for the ceremony of the snake-painted tipi, most of the songs are "Buffalo rock and buffalo songs," coming from another ceremony, or that "the eagle tipi is said to have originated at the same place and time as the lance . . . and that in consequence the rituals of the two have many of the same songs" (1912a:238). But in Wissler's work, one notes a preoccupation with categories: It appears that he was frequently told such things as that the songs of the Bear Knife ceremony are all war songs, as the bear is a fighting animal (1912a:134), or that all songs sung in the sweat house for the war bonnet transfer ceremony are songs of the Bull (age-grade) Society (1912a:114).

To be sure, of such detailed knowledge there is today only a vestige. But even now, there emerges a picture of musical thought totally different from what one might receive in Western academic musical society, in which one particular piece by J. S. Bach is performed in church and concert and on radio, available on records, piped into a grocery store as Muzak, and accompanies a television commercial, while the various audiences spend very little time worrying about such matters.

We conclude, then, that the Blackfoot have a strong interest in taxonomy, that their classification of music follows that of culture, and that they draw sharp lines among categories in their conceptualization of things. The question that logically follows concerns the way this set of ideas is reflected in real life and in the music. In the rather compact musical style of the repertory, it is evidently not possible to distinguish narrow categories, such as the songs of different sections of a ritual, by such elements of style as pitch inventory, scalar configuration, meter, or form. Nevertheless, were the repertory to be divided into groups by criteria of musical style, it would on the whole fall into classes that coincide with some of the large classes of use. Gambling songs, traditional medicine songs, and the whole group of modern social dances are distinct musically. Within these large categories, musical groupings can be found largely on the basis of tune relationships. Although few songs from the older medicine bundle and other ritual repertories are actually extant, there is evidence that groups of songs, such as the second seven songs, or the third seven songs, of the Medicine Pipe ritual (Wissler 1912a:142–43) were sung to similar or genetically related tunes. Modern reconstructions of the ceremonies confirm the structure, as do the small number of Medicine Pipe songs recorded by myself, although sung by a singer who no longer remembered words. The published texts show the groups to have parallel verbal structure. To some extent, then, the lines of the taxonomy that emerge from use of songs is reflected in musical style—but not by dramatic differences and not always sharply or clearly.

7. KINDS OF PEOPLE AND THINGS

Among the taxonomies of music used by any society, an essential component is the classification of humans by their place in the musical culture. This may concern active and passive roles and include creative musicians as well as audience, composers, performers, patrons, and scholars.

In Blackfoot culture as I experienced it, there is a specific grouping of people in accordance with musical activity and related to the growth of singing groups or "drums" in the pan-Indian powwow culture. Thus, when seeking consultants about music in the 1960s, I was told that some particular men were "singers," and, quite as specifically, that others were not. The idea that certain people were "able to sing" was brought up in 1984; when noting that some elderly or deceased men had made recordings (between 1900 and 1930) and appeared on a record I had edited, a few individuals expressed surprise, saying that they were not aware that so-and-so "could even sing." Asking what was meant by this remark, I was told about such things as good voice and "sounding good," rather than about knowing songs. In 1966, after several weeks on the reservation, I concluded that there were some fifty men who were widely designated as singers; and around a dozen who were the mentioned "old-timers who know a lot" of songs and lore perhaps not known to "singers." Thus, the categories, loosely applied, of singers, scholars, and general audience are characteristic of the most recent period. The number of "singers" increased greatly between 1965 and 1984. In the 1980s, although women's "drums" were recognized and some women were listed as members of singing groups, the title of "singer" or "drummer" was still gender-specific.

Whether there were authorities in matters of ritual and music who did not themselves perform in the nineteenth century is unknown, but if there were such scholarly individuals by 1900, this fact may have had something to do with the then already great decline of ritual knowledge from early times. When Wissler (1912a:263–65) at length cites the consultant who seemed to have given virtual lectures about songs in their ritual and cultural context, the account resembles in style and statement some of the statements made to me by elderly authorities in my time. Hanks and Hanks (1950:78) describe, for the Blackfoot reserve in Alberta, the figure of the "master of ceremonies" who was "able to lead one or two kinds of ceremonial, though some knew many more. . . . For a Medicine Pipe three or four could perform adequately; for the Deer Dance there may have been half a dozen." In Montana of the 1980s, the singling out of such men with special designations such as membership in an "honorary council," or even "ceremonial chief," is a recent development.

If there is no elaborate taxonomy of people according to their musical activity, there is nevertheless much about the taxonomy of music that concerns the identity of the people who perform and use it. There is, for instance, the significant difference in cultural roles between men and women; and while the explicit taxonomy of musical persons does not include gender, my own Blackfoot consultants, male and female, made it clear that men's and women's participation in music is different.

I have no evidence that a sharply separated and distinct musical repertory was used by women. When asked, contemporary women denied that there were special women's songs, or they referred only to lullabies or other songs sung for children. The existence of a women's society, the Buffalo Society, is acknowledged in the literature, but the description of its activities and rituals (Wissler 1913:430–35) indicates that the singing was done by men while women danced, blew whistles and played rattles. On the other hand, there are indications that women had their own songs and singing functions. For example, McClintock (1930:19) describes the Crow Water Ceremony, in which women did "most of the singing while men beat drums and helped in the songs." Wissler's musical consultant (1912a:264) goes into some detail about this matter, indicating that it was not proper for women to sing loudly, or alone, but he mentions some exceptions. McClintock (1910 [1968]:242) describes "night singing," in which young men and their wives or sweethearts ride around the encampment, singing in unison, and Ewers (1958:108) mentions women's mourning chants. Hatton (1986) makes a point of showing that the development of women's singing groups in the powwow culture is to be seen as a continuation of, not a departure from, the cultural tradition. These examples notwithstanding, however, the general implication of the literature is that women participate in the same musical culture as men, but do so to a smaller extent than men, but admittedly, past research is limited by the absence of many female scholars and the use primarily of male consultants.

Oscar Lewis's study of "manly-hearted women" among the Blackfoot (Lewis 1941) provides further insight. These women, whose social behavior, personality, and status were more akin to those of men, and who are thus labeled by the tribe, also engaged in musical behavior more like that of men:

> In song most women have little freedom of expression. . . . Only manly-hearted women are ever heard to sing alone or in the presence of their husbands. Religious songs are sung by women only in chorus, and even manly-hearted women were too embarrassed to sing alone and refused our request. However, Widow G., a very manly-hearted woman, did not wait to be asked but took out her bag of one hundred sticks and sang a song for each of them. She is the only woman who sings men's songs during religious ceremonies. (Lewis 1941:222)

Wissler's consultant does indeed state that women sing alone when playing the stick game or when doctoring, the latter activity evidently related to that of Lewis's Widow G. Nevertheless, despite the presence of many women in singing groups, the conception of women as subsidiary actors in musical life persists even today on the part of men and at least some women. While a classification of people in accordance with their musical participation does not include distinctions specifically of gender, the principal gender-related distinctions of society exhibit their musical correlations.

Blackfoot society consisted of a number of kinds of categories in overlapping taxonomies; there were many types of people and a variety of groupings. There were the principal tribal subgroups; there were bands, men's societies, general distinctions by age, association of individuals with various medicine bundles, full- and mixed-bloodedness, and more. Some of these classes had and have important musical association. In modern Blackfoot society, one hears occasionally about differences in musical practice among the main divisions of the Blackfoot nation. Usually they are expressed by reference to the population groups of Montana and Canada. Thus, I often heard it said (by Blackfoot and local white people) that the older traditions were better remembered and practiced in Canada than on the Montana reservation, and that there were, by implication, important differences between the Piegan and Blood people. I never heard about differences in musical practice that may have separated the various bands—but these are, to be sure, extant only in memory. However, the early ethnographic literature also makes no point of mentioning tribal and band differences in music, and little in ritual practice.

Distinguishing people by age must have played a major role in Blackfoot earlier culture, and to some extent it still does. Old men knew more of the total culture of the society, including more music. Old women could afford to sing alone more readily than young ones (Wissler 1912a:264). The members of the honorary council today are elderly men. Not only must one be old to know the tradition today (this is the theory, although younger men with an interest in reading ethnography may actually be better off), the tradition itself requires that the material must be learned gradually and in a specific order. For example, visions appeared seriatim, or one was gradually initiated into a succession of societies. And while different age groups had their own music, in each case it was music added to a repertory already extant and maintained. If older men learned new songs, they did not abandon the old ones.

In contrast to some other societies (e.g., the Venda; see Blacking 1967), Blackfoot children appear to have had little in the way of a separate song repertory. Here and there, children's game songs are mentioned (McClintock 1910 [1968]:391; Wissler 1912b:58; 1912a:264), and one transcription of such a song appears in the early literature (McClintock 1910 [1968]:515), a song with smaller range and shorter form than is found in the standard Blackfoot repertory. A repertory of Mice Songs, part of a game, may be related to the singing of mice in a humorous myth (Wissler 1912a:64; Bullchild 1985). I myself was unable to collect children's songs, with the exception of songs sung by mothers to babies (see e.g., Hungry Wolf 1982:199), and I was told that children began learning Blackfoot music by listening to adults singing ceremonial and dance songs. In today's culture, young boys, aged about eight to ten, sometimes sit in with singing groups, singing along softly. This absence of a major children's repertory may conceivably be related to the association of music and religion, an area in which children do not participate until puberty.

Dividing the Blackfoot tribe musically is a complicated matter. To be sure, various groups of people—members of a society, members of a class of medicine men, age-group, and more—all have or had their principal repertories. And in modern times, "mixed-blood" and "full-blood" Blackfoot were also in part distinguished by their musical and dance allegiances. But the typical individual would be a member of several groups and have a unique configuration of musical, dance, and ritual interests. Therefore, while classes of people as identified by their musical interests exist in theory, each individual is likely to be a member of several overlapping groups. The theory is that people are grouped into classes that are divided by sharp lines, as are the songs, but again, practice is more complex. The theory and practice of identifying persons appear in some ways to be analogous to the theory and practice of identifying and classifying songs.

In Western academic musical culture, one of the areas in which taxonomy is most used and prominent is that of instruments. Musicians who are otherwise quite removed from professional intellectual concerns make use of instrument classification in teaching and in their performance work. The classes established by Hornbostel and Sachs (1914)—*membranophones, aerophones, chordophones, idiophones*—based on sound production, are widely used, as are *strings, woodwinds, brass,* and *percussion*, a taxonomy based on musical function in the late eighteenth-century orchestra. The cultures of China and India also have produced articulated classifications of instruments.

To the Blackfoot, this is an area of minor significance, a fact that should interest us in view of the importance of song taxonomy in their culture. I spoke with six consultants about instruments. Confronted by a general question, "Tell me about instruments," they tended to say something like, "Yes, we had lots of instruments." Asked about types, they said first, "Drums," and then went on to say in one way or another that each ritual and each use had its particular instrument. It was important for each instrument to have its specific decoration in accordance with its use, and my impression was that instruments were classed individually by ritual, and not grouped further. One man told me first that there were drums and rattles, and then proceeded to explain that there was a rattle used in the Medicine Pipe ceremony, and another in the horse medicine, and so on.

Thus, the Blackfoot accounts of instruments did not include classes such as container rattles and deerhoof (strung) rattles, or hand drums as against large dance drums. The idea that instruments should be classed by their appearance, sound production, or material did not, I think, occur to my consultants, any more than did the classing of songs by form or scale, which also does not occur. Like songs, instruments are grouped by use. Blackfoot terminology provides a general word for drum (*istóki-matsis*), and one for rattle (*auaná*). There is also a general word for instrument (*ninixkiátsis*) derived from the word for singing, but it may not have been used widely until recent times as the dictionary by Uhlenbeck and van Gulik (1930:114, 242) assigns it specifically to the violin, an object that may now be regarded as generic "musical instrument" more readily than the drums and rattles, which have their more specific purposes. I have no further information on this peculiar treatment of the violin. According to Witmer (1982:36), among the Blood Indians in the 1960s, the number of drums available was limited, but he tells us further (p. 136) that drums were by far the most common instruments in his time, that rattles were rare, whistles used occasionally, and sticks used to accompany the hand game, but no indication of taxonomy is given. Witmer's experience was like mine, and Wissler's description of instruments (1910:9, 84–86) also suggests a limited quantity. The very dearth of instruments, even as far back as 1900, may be related to the lack of greater interest in classifying them.

The existence of the very concept of musical instrument is worthy of scrutiny. As the word for instrument (*ninixkiátsis*) is primarily associated with a Western instrument, it is conceivable that the various things that ethnomusicologists call instruments are not really regarded by the Blackfoot as a class. The drum, most widely used and most generalizable of the instruments, appears to be a unified concept. Rattles and whistles, on the other hand, are regarded principally as part of the paraphernalia of certain ceremonies and rituals, and more closely tied to their companion objects—dressed skins, sticks, feathers, pipes—than to each other. It may even be that instruments are not really an important category in Blackfoot musical thought. Certainly I found that they occupied a small place in those discussions of music that I heard. Singing without percussion is uncommon and not usually proper, and drums are major components of Blackfoot culture. But surely, if the Western conception of music is that it is in essence primarily instrumental, the Blackfoot hold an opposite view, that music is song, and whatever else goes into music is somehow secondary.

The general character of music in Blackfoot thought is essentially vocal rather than a tool for imparting words; it is human-specific and consists of integral and indivisible units—songs—that are identified by uses, persons, and events. An unlimited resource, it takes its place among the domains of culture in sharing with them an informal yet complex taxonomy closely related to the Blackfoot methods of grouping people and things. Yet in certain ways it stands outside the culture.

CHAPTER THREE

History: Origins, Sources, and Change

1. ORIGINS OF MUSIC

An important segment of musical thought relates music to the passage of time. Ethnomusicologists have, therefore, despite the often-cited synchronic orientation of their research, been interested in questions of origins from the time of their earliest publications, and since the 1950s they have also concentrated on questions of change. This chapter examines Blackfoot beliefs about the origins of music as a concept or a domain of culture and the origins or sources of the individual units of music, the repertories and songs. It then moves to Blackfoot ideas about the nature of their music history and of musical change. We are dealing with matters that are, broadly speaking, historical.

Myths of human and cultural origin have played a major role in anthropology, providing fundamental insights about a society's view of nature and culture. Myths of the origin of music have not had the same impact on musicology. The issue arises briefly in histories of music and handbooks of ethnomusicology, but authors sometimes deal with it in a modestly embarrassed tone, confessing that while there is some intrinsic interest in speculating about the origins of music, there is no possibility of discovering what really happened.

I suppose it must be admitted that ethnomusicologists' continuing interest in the problem tells us less about the origins of music than about the Western culture from which they come. It is a culture in which the origin of things is of great importance. In its approach to the passing of time, contemporary Western thought packages the components of culture in units with a beginning, a life of some sort, and an end. Historical treatises often view their subjects in terms of these three components, and biology or paleontology sees the history of life partly in terms of units of time encompassing the origin, ascendancy, and demise of species. In Western culture it is also important to know from where, geographically, something has come. Biographers have a great interest in genealogy and the precise place and date of birth. Library catalogers insist that the origin of a work is among its most important characteristics. Dictionaries begin with etymology. The musicologist's interest in origins correlates with ways in which Western society classifies humans and components of culture.

If the attitude toward origins held by a society tells us important things about its culture, a society's approaches to the origins of music might also be suggestive for understanding its attitudes toward music as a whole. Beliefs about the origins of music held in Western society might therefore provide us insights into the set of ideas that make up Western musical thought, and the reader will therefore kindly forgive a digression whose purpose is to set the stage for a look at Blackfoot attitudes about origins.

What, then, are the beliefs of Western society about the origins of music? The size and diversity of the "society" are so great that one can hardly generalize, and I know of no public-opinion surveys, but two types of sources may be helpful. They are domains that are widely used to extract the principles by which members of Western society live—science and scholarship, which in this case might be statements by experts (e.g., ethnomusicologists), and religion, embodied in the Bible. These sources yield several theories which may be examined to see what they may have in common, and what these commonalities indicate about Western attitudes toward music and culture. As we will later wish to examine Blackfoot myths, we may be justified in considering the Bible on the one hand, and the books of scholars and scientists on the other, as counterparts of mythology for modern Western urban culture.

The theories about the origin of music that were developed in the nineteenth and early twentieth centuries have been summarized in many publications (Sachs 1962:33–43; Nettl 1983:162–71). Most of them stipulate some kind of need—to communicate over long distances, to find sexual partners, to communicate with the supernatural, or to aid efficient labor—that could be satisfied by the "invention" of music. According to most of these theories, music was developed by humans after they had already become distinctive by having acquired culture, and it was invented because it was needed by people so they could carry out other more fundamental functions of life. These theories do not assert that music was present among prehumans (although one finds statements discussing the alleged "musicality" of various animal sounds), nor that it was given to humans directly by supernatural or divine forces, or came about as a source of pleasure, or existed for its own sake. And yet the societies from which these theories sprang and the academic establishment that articulated them accepted music as something that could exist for its own sake, as art, with an important purpose—that of providing pleasure.

The mentioned theories then tell us something about the ways in which late nineteenth- and early twentieth-century Western intellectuals conceived of music. To them, it was at least to some degree a secondary commodity whose job it was to help humans to do things that had to be done in any event, helpful but not essential. And they conceived of it as something that came about originally for a particular purpose, but it is a purpose that eventually changed, and along with this change we encounter an implication that the essence of music also changed after its beginnings. Additionally, the fact that there are theories of origin that see music as a unified concept is also important in understanding the Western view of music.

The Bible does not really give an account of the origin of music itself, but it specifies that Jubal was the first musician, implying but not stating that he "invented" music. In any event, whatever the intentions of the authors of the Bible, laymen of the twentieth century who know it may tend to assign to Jubal the act of actually inventing music. Here, too, music is presented as an artifact that may be and was in fact invented by someone. Like the ethnomusicological theories, the layman's view of the Bible ascribes the beginning of music to a specific point of origin or act of invention.

A collection of myths and legends compiled by Wolfgang Laade (1975) presents a variety of music origin stories in non-Western and especially in tribal societies. There one may find explicit invention of music, but more common is the bringing of music to the world intact by supernatural forces, or by the serendipitous discovery on the part of a human of music making in which animals or spirits are engaged. The existence of music in the prehuman past also appears in the mythology of many peoples. The Havasupai, according to Hinton (1967–68; 1984:12), believed that prehuman spirits sang to each other rather than speaking. The well-known star-husband tale of American Indians sometimes has musical content, as among the Amuesha, for whom the bringing of music to humans by the woman who married a star was a symbol of the beginnings of human culture and the cessation of precultural social chaos (Smith 1984:139).

To summarize, then: Western ideas about the origins of music involve (1) the idea of invention by a specific human, (2) the bringing of music to humans because a specific need must be filled, and (3) the notion that music evolved gradually from something else (speech, labor, or mating calls). In contrast, the myths of some non-Western societies indicate that music comes in extant form and has something important to do with the relationship of humans to the supernatural. In both cases, the origin myths give important insights into the system of ideas governing both music and culture as a whole.

It is disappointing, then, but probably also significant to find that the large published body of Blackfoot mythology and folklore does not contain a specific statement of the origin of music. Indeed, it also does not contain much mythology dealing explicitly with the origin of the world, and what is extant consists of a cycle of tales in which the order of events is not completely clear. Grinnell (1892 [1962]:137–44) provides a unified account of the "Blackfoot Genesis," which appears to have been assembled from several tales collected separately. Wissler and Duvall (1909:19–30) give a number of tales that narrate the founding of the Blackfoot world through actions of Napi, "Old Man," the culture hero who is the subject of a large proportion of Blackfoot tales and still plays a role in the aesthetic and folklore of the contemporary reservation life. Bullchild (1985:5–226) provides very extensive if more personal accounts of these same myths.

In these origin myths, Napi the culture hero creates objects of nature such as landscapes, determines natural processes such as death, and defines human customs such as dress and warfare. In some tales, he is also the object of ridicule, and in others, a vulgar trickster. But while in some respects he is cast as the creator of the world in general, he is also presented as the creator specifically of the Blackfoot world, that is, as a person who wanders around the area inhabited by the Blackfoot, entering it from the south and finally leaving it as he walks northward. While he is engaging in these creative acts, the Blackfoot people and, even more clearly, other humans are already in the world. A dual concept is expressed, the world at large and the Blackfoot world as independent of it, and we will see that this concept plays a role in musical thought as well.

The closest thing to a published myth of the origin of music appears in Grinnell's collection (1892 [1962]:141). Napi (Old Man) is said to tell the people: "Now, if you are overcome, you may go and sleep, and get power. Something will come to you in your dream, that will help you. Whatever these animals tell you to do, you must obey them. . . . Whatever animal answers your prayer, you must listen to him." A much more extensive version appears in Bullchild (1985:77–79), but in both cases, Old Man is presenting sleep and the associated concepts of dream and vision as a window to the helpful supernatural. Songs, which play such a major role in visions, are explicitly included by Bullchild, and implicitly by Grinnell. If this is indeed a proper interpretation, the myth's intention may be to say that songs were given to the Blackfoot people to help them in times of trouble, to fill a specific need when culture otherwise already existed but, in contrast to modern Western myths, from a supernatural source.

In the origin myths given by Grinnell and Bullchild, little is said, about the origins of religion as a whole. By contrast, Blackfoot mythology has much to say about the origin of individual components of the religious system, such as the individual ceremonies. The origin of music as a whole is also, by implication, less an issue than the origins of individual songs or groups of songs.

If examination of myths gives us little to go on, the statements about origins of music made by individual consultants in my fieldwork were scarcely more extensive. The idea of following up the origin of the individual song or of a ceremony or a dance could readily be taken up in conversation. People make up or dream songs, dances are adapted from other tribes. Yet the notion of singing or drumming as something that might itself, as a unified concept or activity, have a specific origin, was harder to fix. One elderly man chuckled, saying, in a deprecating manner, "Our kinds of songs are so old, they must go back to the days of Napi." But whether this was a statement about musical origins or an attempt to explain the great difference between Indian and white songs was not quite clear.

My occasional attempts, in informal conversation, to discuss this issue with some older Blackfoot people provided interesting secondary insights, more from what they did not say than from what they did. Thus, singing did not come from speech. It did not evolve from other human activities. It came in the form in which it is now known. It did not come from other Indian tribes, even though the similarities of style were recognized. The idea that the Blackfoot received their music from a supernatural source was considered reasonable even recently, and the fact that it may sound like the music of other tribes, and even contain what sounds like the same song, is not an issue. Consultants corroborated the myth: "You got to understand that our Indian music is not like that white music. We got to have our songs to be Indians. White people think all Indian songs are alike. A lot of Indians think so too. But we get our own songs, they belong to the tribe, doesn't matter what they're like." The bits and pieces in myths and conversations tell me this about origins: Music, as songs, was given to the Blackfoot intact, ready for use. It is not something that evolved from another activity already extant in the cultural arsenal, as in Western myths or theories—speech, labor, religious worship. Thus it is not, as may be implied by these Western theories, just another way of talking or communicating, but an activity more distant from others in the culture. We extrapolate that music is a whole, something given intact, in finished form, not something evolved gradually, although its components and repertories, the ceremonies, came to humans one by one.

2.   AND OF RITUALS

If there is little reference to musical origins, and no detail, in the myths, we may look to the origin myths of individual rituals for further insight into the Blackfoot conception of how things come about. Consider for a moment the principal form of worship in older Blackfoot culture, the "opening" of medicine bundles by their owners or the similarly ceremonial painting of tipis, rites in which songs played a major role. Such events normally began with the telling of the myth of the origin of the bundle or tipi type and its ritual. The two best-known types of medicine bundles are those of the beaver and the medicine pipe.

Wissler and Duvall present several versions of the origin myth of the beaver medicine bundle (1909:74–78). In one of these, at a crucial point, beaver sings a series of powerful songs to a human hunter in exchange for the dressed skins of all local mammals and birds (1909:76). The hunter, whose wife had previously had a child by beaver, thus becomes the first owner of a beaver bundle. Through the common child he cements the bond between animals, humans, and the supernatural. And he is given the songs by beaver, in their complete form, each song with its specific purpose. The fact that he is represented as receiving only songs, not objects or instructions from beaver, while giving up the skins (which he presumably must replace in future hunts) indicates the centrality of the songs in the conception of the ritual.

And yet the casual way in which songs are sometimes mentioned in stories and myths and the lack of detail given about them ought to be noted along with their significance. The origin myth of the medicine pipe ceremony, which was evidently for long (and still is) the most prominent of the medicine bundles (if not the most powerful) mentions music hardly at all (Wissler and Duvall 1909:89–90). It is related to the star-husband complex of tales studied by Stith Thompson (1946:345–48) and found in both North and South American Indian cultures. The only reference to music (and it is indirect) appears in a statement to the effect that when the woman prepares to leave her star-husband in order to return to her human home, she is given the ceremony of the medicine pipe as a token of the experience, as something that will help humans and as a way of establishing her own credibility. Songs or singing, while presumably implied, are not explicitly mentioned. Conceivably, they are so taken for granted that they need not be specified.

The virtual absence of songs in some of the prominent myths can possibly be illuminated by interpreting the body of myths as a cycle representing prehuman and prehistoric chronology. As indicated in the texts of the stories published by Wissler and Duvall, Grinnell, Bullchild, and to a somewhat lesser degree, Schultz, songs were evidently sung in the telling of these myths. A survey of the five types of myth of which the Wissler-Duvall collection consists—stories of Old Man, of stars, of ritual origins, and of other kinds of origins (e.g., "Why dogs don't talk"), plus miscellaneous stories—shows songs playing by far the largest role in the "ritual origins" category, and a secondary one in stories of stars. The chronology of the myths appears to begin with the period of Old Man, followed by a period in which humans interact with stars and supernatural figures, after which there is a period in which nonhuman actors decrease, heavenly bodies, inanimate objects such as stones, and animals falling away in that order. The stories of Old Man, which evidently represent the earliest period in the Blackfoot conceptualization of prehistory, a period farthest removed from that of ordinary human culture, say little about music, dance, or ritual. Songs, singing, and dancing are mentioned more frequently in those of the myths that involve the origins of less prominent medicine bundles. It is in the last period that songs begin to take on the largest role.

Assuming that the Blackfoot corpus of mythology is one of the more reliable sources for an understanding of Blackfoot ideas about the origin of music, it is important to note two points: (1) While there is little about the actual origins of music, songs play a major role in the myths, more so than in the analogous mythology of European cultures. (2) While singing is a practice in which supernatural figures engage, they do so only in their relationship to humans. We have already noted the human-specific nature of music in Blackfoot conceptualization. Songs are either sung by humans, or to them. One does not find supernatural figures, animals, or stones singing to each other. And songs remained, even in actual practice, a principal form of communication between human groups, or between the human and the supernatural world.

Origin myths of music in the world's cultures often involve nonhuman actors. To the Havasupai, prehuman spirits sang, the Pima unravel songs extant in the supernatural cosmos, and African myths tell of the use of music by animals, overheard and imitated by humans (Hinton 1967–68; Herzog 1938:3; Laade 1975:61–62, 70). But Blackfoot music came from a superhuman, but in some way all-too-human, culture hero. In classifying forms of life, the Blackfoot appear to accord Old Man a status closer by far to that of humans than of spirits or animals. He does not appear in visions as a guardian spirit, as do animals and abstract spirits such as thunder, rocks, and clouds. Like humans, and unlike deities in other religions, Old Man is a personage of the past who is no longer around. Songs were given to the Blackfoot by one of themselves and in that sense are, even here, human products.

To summarize, music came to humans, and more important, specifically to Blackfoot humans, for a specific purpose, in the general forms which it still has today. It was not invented by humans, but it was also not something that preceded humanity. The fact that the origin of individual music-bearing activities such as medicine bundle rituals is emphasized over the origin of music as a general concept fits the Blackfoot conceptualization of music and culture. The important presence of music in the myths indicates its significance in and to the culture. The suggestion that Blackfoot songs were given by Old Man at a time when possibly other cultures and their musics were already extant (in the South, whence Old Man had come?) illustrates a certain ambivalence the Blackfoot may have had about themselves, on the one hand, as the quintessential humans (a view many societies hold of themselves) and, on the other, as merely one of many societies.

3. SOURCES: COMPOSING AND LEARNING

A good deal has been written about the ways in which North American Indians compose or appear to compose their songs and about the ways in which they conceive of composition as act and process (see, e.g., Herzog 1938; Merriam 1967:3–24). At one end of a continuum is the conception that songs somehow exist in the cosmos or the real world and that they are put together—in some instances, laboriously—by humans. A stellar illustration is a well-known text of an Eskimo song suggesting that all songs that can be composed have already been composed and that therefore the composer now combines and recombines material from extant songs (Merriam 1964:177). Others are descriptions of the composing of Peyote songs (Nettl 1955:327), at least some of which may result from the combination of material from extant songs and the "untangling" of Pima songs once they have been dreamed (Herzog 1938:3). At the other end of the continuum is the body of tales and myths, particularly of Plains cultures, that present songs as being already in a developed state at the point at which they are provided to humans. There are intermediate processes, such as the Flathead description of visions which suggests that the gradual formulation and development of a song from a germ of idea is symbolized by a gradual approximation of the sound from distant to very close on the part of the supernatural singer (Merriam 1967:9).

In earlier times, the Blackfoot considered most of their songs to have resulted from visions; these are the central concept of a source for music. They also believed that some songs had been with them from prehistoric, mythic times, taught by Napi, and that a third group had been learned from other tribes. In my more recent experience, the notion that songs come in visions was still widely recognized, the concept of songs having an origin in prehistory was mentioned with a bit of laughter, the suggestion that songs could come into the tribe from other tribes was readily accepted, and the idea that humans could actually and directly create songs was recognized, but with the occasional proviso that dreaming played a role. But before Westernization exerted great force, visions and the learning of songs in dreams were the principal sources. In this respect, the Blackfoot are somewhat like the Flathead as described by Merriam (1967:4–19), and a good many of the characteristics of vision learning given by Merriam may also be valid for them.

The central importance of songs and song learning in visions is attested at many points in the mythology of the Blackfoot as published by Wissler (1912a:72–82, 88–90, 268–69). The origin myths of the medicine bundle and painted tipi ceremonies almost without exception include an indication that a vision has taken place and songs have come into existence. "Every man of consequence," Wissler also says (1912a:104–5), "is supposed to have one experience in which he acquired a supernatural helper and received a song." On the other hand, the accounts of the visions and the origin myths treat the matter of song composition itself in a cursory fashion. Never encountered is the suggestion that labor is involved in the making up of a song. The concept of composition rather is one in which songs seem to come into existence effortlessly or reside in the supernatural world, ready upon the right signal to be imparted.

The accounts of visions given by Wissler and other early authors stress the importance of songs. I quote two brief examples from Wissler:

One time at a place where Badger Creek runs into Two Medicine River, I saw two owls on a tree. Each owl in turn sang a song. Then one of them spoke to me, telling me that I would always be fortunate and get much property. They told me to take some of their children for medicine. So ever since that I have kept the head of an owl and I have always had much property. (Wissler 1912a:81)

One night I slept in the open out on the prairie. I heard some rattles beating. There was a strong west wind blowing at the time which carried

the sound to me. I got up, followed the sound and came at last to the top
of a hill. As I looked down beyond I saw many tipis. I approached the camp
and coming near one of the tipis found that I could see through it as if it
were transparent. Inside, was a man using rattles. This was the noise that I
had heard. His body and hair were painted all over with red. This man invited
me to enter and after a while said, 'I shall give you my hair, all the beaver
medicine, and all the songs.' After this I had the beaver medicine and songs.
(Wissler 1912a:75)

The concept of composing in a state of trance or a dream raises many
questions about the nature of musical creation (for detailed discussion,
see Rouget 1985). How did a vision produce a song that conforms so
closely in style to that of the total repertory or, more specifically, to that
of a particular genre or song series in a ceremony? And what of the fact
that some visions appear to have produced songs that are really innovations
to the repertory, while others impart songs that already exist in the repertories of other visionaries? How indeed can we account for the fact that
all medicine bundles of one type, e.g., Medicine Pipe, have the same
songs, although each medicine man seems to have learned them in his
own separate visions? We need to determine what constitutes a "new"
song, and in what ways a song must be different from others to be regarded
as "a song." We wish to know something about the concepts of song
integrity and innovation in Blackfoot thought.

The Blackfoot concept of song may help us here. Wissler (1912a:103–
4, 215–19) reinforces the interpretation of songs as something like physical
objects, not to be divided, and to be given and taken. They can be sold;
given; or treated like pieces of clothing, stones, animal skins. Older ethnographic literature is clear on this, but it is significant that the view has
continuity into more recent times. This can be illustrated in several ways.
I have never heard, or heard of, the breaking up of a song in rehearsal.
The notion of dividing a song into components is difficult for some Blackfoot singers to grasp. They sometimes can be persuaded to talk about the
modern making of songs as the combining of material from different
sources but only in the creation of a new song, while no attention is paid
to what happens to the songs that function as source. Similarly, one uses
components to make an object—a tent or a dress—but once it is completed,
it remains a unit.

In a detailed and interesting transcription of an interview with two
informants who discuss mistakes or stylistically inappropriate musical
gestures in songs, Robert Witmer (1982:62–68) tries unsuccessfully to
lead the conversation to matters of composing. The conceptions of incorrect
musical actions, of correcting mistakes, of some kind of work that may

be involved, are all present when it comes to performance, but the speakers do not know how to react to the idea that a composer may have to do things over or that there is more than one way a particular song could have been composed. This Witmer found even when dealing with people who recognized composition by humans.

An important component of the Blackfoot conception of song acquisition is the idea of the song as something which exists complete but outside the culture, and is imparted to a human—or particularly, a Blackfoot human—in finished form. Composing therefore has a conceptually close relationship to learning, and by extension, the concept of learning songs in real life seems to have been affected by the principles of song learning in supernatural contexts. In the visions, learning of songs not only is ubiquitous but plays a major role. The various medicine men cited by Wissler (1912a:72–82) included the learning of songs, and in their narrations, song learning often occupied a climactic, dramatic, or emphatically conclusive role. But beyond occasionally stating that a song was sung four times, the myths and the accounts tell little of the way a vision being goes about teaching a song. Yet the word "teaching" appears in Wissler's English texts over and over.

We have made a point of saying that the Blackfoot conception does not limit the quantity of music that can be created. Yet the music is there, to be turned over to humans under the right circumstances, and not (traditionally) something that can be made up by humans out of thin air. Songs are things; humans receive them in finished form from beaver, buffalo, thunder, owls, or worms; and the process of teaching is much like that of giving. The song, not materials from which a song can be made, is given. The tone in myths and accounts shows the supernatural beings eager to impart the songs, not hesitant to share them. The idea of laborious composition did not exist in Blackfoot thought, except in the sense that one needed to persist in one's vision quest, even to torture oneself, or in the myths, where undertaking a perilous journey in order to acquire visions, power, and songs may be seen as a metaphor for strenuous creativity.

The suggestion that there is a general conception of composition that is related to the concept of learning leads, therefore, to four observations: (1) The structure of songs is related to the treatment of the origin of songs in mythology. (2) The way in which humans taught songs to each other was adopted for elaboration in mythology. (3) The other methods of acquiring music in Blackfoot culture are conceived in ways related to the central act of musical creativity, the composing in visions. (4) A major difference between Indian and white music, to the Blackfoot, is in the way songs come into (human) existence.

The accounts of visions from the ethnographic literature and informants provide insight into the details of the actual process of composing.
It would seem that the Blackfoot composition was a series of sudden
flashes of insight, a matter of quick thought and rapid decision making,
something in which great care cannot be taken, resulting suddenly in a
song that may or may not be very original. Possibly the characteristic
structure of Blackfoot (and other Plains) songs is related to this view of
the creative process.

Elsewhere (and long ago; Nettl 1956:196–97), I suggested that in
order for an orally transmitted repertory to be viable, it would have to
develop unifying factors that would integrate the individual compositions
in order for them to be easily and efficiently learned, especially in quantity,
and by people who might not have extensive or trained musical memories.
This was necessary in particular in those societies in which there was
broad and general participation in performance, with little or no specialized
musicianship. To be sure, human memory is capable of enormous expansion, but it seemed to me that in order for some parameters of music
to exhibit great variety or complexity, others would have to remain relatively simple. There are certainly problems to this theory, such as the
difficulty of establishing interculturally valid criteria for what is simple
or unified in music. But it may have residual utility nevertheless, for if
unifying factors in the individual work are important ingredients in oral
traditions, they are especially significant in those traditions in which the
nature of learning—learning from humans, or from supernatural forces—
is thought to involve speed and sudden insight.

Earlier Blackfoot music used a variety of different kinds of song
forms, but most can be shown to consist of two sections, the second of
which is in some sense a variation or partial repetition of the first. In recent
times, except for the gambling songs which involve the litany-like repetition of one or a pair of phrases, the principal song form was the "incomplete repetition" (Nettl 1954a:25–28), in which a short head motif,
articulated by the leader and then repeated by a second singer, functions
as a kind of generative unit that is repeated or varied at the end of the
song an octave lower, perhaps thus:

> A A B(a) C A(8) B(a) C A(8); or
> A A B C(b) A(c8) B C(b) A(c8).

Other, older forms, such as those of some of the Medicine Bundle songs
recorded around 1900, depart from this particular kind of strophic structure
in their details but not in principle. One can readily see how someone
with thorough knowledge of the style could, upon hearing the first phrase,

have a rather good idea of what might likely occur in the rest of the song. The overall form makes it possible to predict much of the song from the head motif. It should not be difficult to learn a song of this sort in four hearings, especially if the words are entirely meaningless or include only a short meaningful text. The idea of the sudden, swift insight in a vision is paralleled by the idea of a short initial phrase which is the most significant thing about a song. In actual life, the essence of a song is grasped quickly, and this kind of learning parallels the mythological principle that songs come to humans as finished products. In composing, teaching or rehearsing, in life or myth, a song is not broken up or divided. Furthermore, the idea of a song being transmitted quickly, as a unit, is also paralleled by the use of the short introductory phrase, which in a sense, "is" the song, as a means for identifying songs in singing groups.

The brevity with which Blackfoot song learning, a type of event of great importance to humans in their relationship to the supernatural, is treated in their myths may reflect tendencies of mythologies generally, as these rarely go into technical detail. But to consider Blackfoot culture more specifically, the ways in which the myths treat the learning of songs may be derived from human song learning, its character abstracted and distilled. In the myths we may note the following:

(1) Songs are learned quickly, suddenly, and in one piece, and no mention is made of differential ability among humans for the learning of songs. (2) The learning of songs is sometimes a dangerous, awesome event. (3) The myths tell about the learning of specific songs, not songs or music in general, and the implication is that the learning of a particular song is an event of great significance. (4) Song learning and teaching symbolize the transfer of power or important knowledge. (5) The myths contain events in which diverse song materials are combined in ceremonies of eclectic derivation.

These kinds of events also occur (or used to occur) in real life, or at least this is how music in real life is conceived to exist. It has already been noted that songs are thought to be learned quickly, in one hearing. The ability to learn songs is assumed for all men. If a man is not good at learning songs, it is not ascribed to lack of specific musical talent but to lack of general intelligence. "What kind of a man might make a good singer?" "Should be a smart man . . . has to remember a lot," was one answer. The occasions at which songs are learned from other humans, to say nothing of learning from supernatural sources, are circumscribed by ceremonies such as the transfer of medicine bundles. One learns a song but, in theory at least, also the occasion for its performance, the acts that go with it. The right songs must be sung with the occasion, with the appropriate object in a medicine bundle—in theory if not in practice.

Witmer (1982:72–76) describes the transfer of song series from one context to others, leading to a situation in which a song may have more than one officially recognized use. The idea of a song being considered definitively part of two ceremonies juxtaposed to the notion of functional exclusiveness is confusing, but an aspect of the particular Blackfoot (or Plains Indian) conception of song identity may shed light on it. It is necessary to consider that in Blackfoot culture a song has acoustic integrity but is also defined by an act of creation. This is a concept quite foreign to Western musical thought. Let me explain:

In the myths, songs are sung as if they were new. We don't hear about a mythic character singing a song that has already been sung by someone else, and this supports the suggestion that each creative act, each vision, produces new songs, even if in their sound they are identical to the songs already known to the tribe. There is standardization of the ceremonies involving a medicine bundle, there is such a thing as "the" beaver ceremony with its attendant songs, but on the other hand, each visionary has his unique visions and songs. I find it hard to reconcile these viewpoints, but they help to explain the conception of song learning as significant and unique experiences, while the concept of song variants seems not to be developed in Blackfoot culture.

I confronted some of my Blackfoot friends with this dilemma and got two kinds of answers. In one case, I was told that "we don't know how this worked; it was a long time ago," implying that visions in which songs were composed are now sufficiently rare so that the mentioned duplication does not occur. Another elderly man simple said, "Yes, in a way they are the same song, and in a way they are different songs." And left it at that.

The Blackfoot, as already pointed out, recognize that songs can also come into the tribe from other peoples. The conception is not all that distant from that of songs given at the beginning by Napi, for these songs, the myths imply, were extant and not actually made or composed by Napi. In a way, then, songs learned from Napi and from the Cree Indians are alike, both being the result of learning songs from extant musical cultures.

Here, I believe, as in many instances, the Blackfoot are telling us something about songs that they might, if they had concrete documentation or collective consciousness, say about their whole culture, namely, that beyond its unique core it in fact represents a confluence of elements from various other societies—Plains, Eastern, Shoshonean, Salish—and that much of it is recognized by the Blackfoot as having been "borrowed." In their conception, culture is mainly something "learned" rather than "in-born" genetically determined. The idea of songs that have come into the tribe as things learned rather than created or sui generis may represent the recognition of what has happened in the history of Blackfoot culture.

The matter of learning relates to the differing conceptions of Indian and white music. While the concept of learning is essential in the Blackfoot idea of musical creation, it is not, any more than composing is, learning in a laborious or gradual fashion. Blackfoot consultants, as I already pointed out, stress the greater complexity and difficulty of white music, and to them the existence of notation and terminology and the high degree of critical judgment to which musicians of white music are subjected gives to this music a totally different flavor from that of the Indian tradition. To them, Indian music is not to be taken apart, analyzed, or learned by its components, not because it would not be possible, but because the integrity of its songs and its continuity are taken for granted, and because the notion that there are different ways of performing one song is not readily accepted. White music is practiced; one talks about ways in which various musicians perform a song; one learns its material gradually. To the Blackfoot, white music is something innately man-made, something that fits into ordinary life in the sense that it, like most everyday activities, requires labor, practice, and skill. Indian music, also human but tied to the supernatural, consists of units that come to humans suddenly, from another level of existence, and remain whole, and thus in Blackfoot thought this music has, in certain respects, an existence outside the realm of everyday life.

4. BLACKFOOT MUSIC HISTORY: THE EARLY TIMES

Do the Blackfoot have a music history? Of course they do, but little is known about it certainly, in comparison to the kind of knowledge available about the history of European art music. Studying the music history of a tribal society is usually quite different from standard musical historiography. Ethnomusicology as it existed up to the 1950s distinguished sharply between Western art music and tribal musics precisely on the basis of factors that affect the study of history—oral tradition versus the written, stability versus constant change, homogeneity versus wide divergence in repertory and the musical involvement of people. And it was believed that even beyond the differences in the kinds of sources, the two types of cultures had types of history too different for their students to share many viewpoints.

In historical musicology, the main consideration has usually been change in musical style. Many other kinds of study are carried out, but the most central ones have dealt with such things as the periodization in music history or in the life of a genre or a composer and stability and change in the patterns, methods, techniques, and rules of composing music. There has been much less emphasis (but some) on the history of individual pieces of music (e.g., change in the perception and performance of a Beethoven sonata over 175 years), and studies of the social contexts of music have been carried out largely for the purpose of providing insight into stylistic change. The kinds of things that can be learned about the history of a music in a small or tribal society do involve these same considerations of style, but sources are often meager, and the convenience of better data as well as a different conception of history have led researchers to greater emphasis on other areas of interest.

While our main task here should be to discover the Blackfoot people's own view of the course of their music history, it may be helpful to supply some background about this history as it might be understood by the outside observer or an "objective" Blackfoot individual. There is indeed a lack of conventional data. Unfortunately, except for the last eighty years, what little there is must to a large degree result from conjecture, extrapolation, and speculation. But accepting these caveats, it is worthwhile to attempt a synthesis.

The structure of the Blackfoot repertory and the relationship of its genres and styles provide clues to its historical development. For what may be the oldest portion of the repertory, we turn to a significant study by Herzog (1935), who identifies a number of song types, as determined by use and cultural contact, that are found throughout the North American continent and share brief litanylike form, limited scale, and small range. These appear to constitute, says Herzog, an archaic layer which in each repertory preceded the development of other, more complex music. Among the Blackfoot, it is the gambling songs that are the largest group in this category. Although there is no reason for assuming that the present-day gambling songs are themselves ancient, their style may well be the oldest extant in the Blackfoot repertory.

I asked two consultants whether they could tell me which of their kinds of songs were oldest. In both cases, I was told that it was the powerful medicine songs, one chuckling about their going back to the days of Napi. I proceeded to ask whether the hand game songs weren't pretty old as well. One consultant immediately agreed, saying simply, "Yes, very old too." The other thought and then retorted, "I don't know how old they are, but they're a reminder to the tribe of the old days, make people think about old times." Such an exchange may show the reader some of the pitfalls of asking leading questions, and yet, the two consultants did not contradict my suggestion, as Blackfoot people were often inclined to do.

If gambling songs are the oldest stratum and determined to be so because of the continental distribution of their musical style, the most recent layer is also in an intertribal style. It is the repertory of songs that accompany the social dances traditional in style but of recent origin, such as Grass Dance and Owl Dance. The style is characterized by the ubiquity of the incomplete repetition form, the absence of words, large range, and high tessitura in performance. It too is shared with other peoples in the Plains and elsewhere because of the powwow culture, but it is also, roughly speaking, the style of many songs of older contexts and uses more specific to the Blackfoot, including the Sun Dance and the men's age-grade societies. The surviving songs available from the medicine bundle repertories exhibit a style that is in some respects intermediate between the other two, particularly in ambitus and scale. They normally have words and employ a larger variety of forms. Examining the extant repertory suggests, then, an approximate and no doubt overlapping sequence of three styles which may have entered the Blackfoot repertory at different times.

Events in the history of the Blackfoot people surely affected the history of their music, and what is known about the Blackfoot past may be used as the basis of reasonable conjecture. If indeed the Blackfoot moved to the western Plains from an area near the western Great Lakes, it is possible that their musical style at one time contained elements of the music of that area as it is still extant. These include a less tense, lower, less pulsating and nasal vocal style, a more symmetrical and clearly defined phraseology, a greater tendency toward anhemitonic pentatonic scales.

Once in the western Plains, the Blackfoot are thought by some anthropologists (Merriam 1967:22; Ewers 1955:6–7) to have been influenced in various ways by peoples living on the western slope of the Continental Divide, such as the Salish-speaking Flathead and the Uto-Aztecan Shoshone of the Great Basin. Just what the musical influence may have been is impossible to say, but the simple style of many medicine bundle songs may conceivably have been affected by the Great Basin style as it matches its smaller melodic range as well as the presence of forms departing from the "incomplete repetition" plan. The same may be true of the relationship to Salish peoples, although the Flathead, closest associates of the Blackfoot, share the Plains musical style and not that of the Coast Salish.

In certain respects the music history of the Blackfoot may have been affected by their particular position within the Plains culture area and its configuration. The culture area concept as developed by Kroeber and other American anthropologists presumes the existence of a temporal and spatial center or "culture climax," in which the major characteristics of the area appear in their most pronounced form (Kroeber 1947:222–23). In the Plains, this climax is in the geographical center, the culture of the Arapaho, Cheyenne, and Dakota. Given the basic assumptions of the culture area concept, various elements of the Blackfoot style as well as uses of music may thus have come from the south. The Sun Dance is most prominent, but the age-grade societies may also be involved.

On the other hand, the closest associates of the Blackfoot in the nineteenth century were the Cree, to the northeast. The position and role of the Blackfoot on the edge of the Plains culture area may also have had an effect on their music history. Their general musical style is not very different from that of peoples in the Central Plains such as the Arapaho. Nevertheless, there are some things that place the Blackfoot at least somewhat outside the part of the area that has the most typical configuration of Plains musical elements. One is the presence of a large body of songs with small range and with structures other than the "incomplete repetition" form, the medicine bundle songs. Further, the fact that the Blackfoot did not participate in the Ghost Dance movement and also did not take up Peyote makes for a different sort of music history in the late nineteenth century from that of the Arapaho, who had and still have large Peyote and Ghost Dance repertories.

5. AND THE TWENTIETH CENTURY

From a number of kinds of sources, we can thus derive a very rough conjecture of the outline of the earlier history of Blackfoot music. The history of music in the twentieth century is of course more specifically known, and aspects of it can be at least tentatively documented on the basis of recordings. Let me mention some major events, drawing on the comparison of early and recent collections already made in chapter 1. There was the introduction of new or reinterpreted dances and ceremonies, beginning with the Grass Dance from the Assiniboin in the mid-1890s (Ewers 1958:310), followed by the Forty-Nine Dance, the Owl or Rabbit Dance, introduction of North American Indian Days in the 1940s, participation in the pan-Indian powwow culture in the 1950s, beginning of a culture based on records and the general availability to the Blackfoot of music from many Indian cultures in the 1960s. There is the loss of ceremonial material and its replacement first by Blackfoot and then by intertribally current social dances and the accompanying intertribally known body of songs. There is standardization of forms, change in the direction of higher voices, more attention to performance practice and especially drumming, and a gradual increase in women's participation in music generally, and in performance contexts previously reserved for men.

Unfortunately, little is known also about the history of musical instruments in Blackfoot culture. Because of their role in the medicine and age-grade ceremonies, rattles of many types can be presumed to have existed before 1880, but their number declined greatly in the twentieth century. The two types of drum, the large dance drum played by groups and the hand drum beaten by a soloist, both of which still exist but are made with more modernized industrial techniques including metal, were in earlier times complemented by the beating of a piece of rawhide suspended from four stakes. Whistles were used but are now rarely found. Flutes are said by some consultants to have been used but the museum exhibits today include none, except for one that was made of a gun barrel and was possibly of Cree origin (Wissler 1910:86).

Much about the recent history of the Blackfoot can be explained by viewing it as reaction to the culture—including the musical culture—of the whites with whom they had increasing contact after the 1890s. The literature that has developed about the ways in which non-Western societies have reacted to the coming of Western music and musical life into their cultures has identified a considerable number of discrete processes that are serviceable as descriptive categories (Nettl 1978b; Kartomi 1981; Shiloah and Cohen 1983). A list of these reactions (defined in Nettl 1985b:24–28) with abbreviated references to sample cultures or repertories in which they occur is given in Appendix C. Some of these reactions can be identified in Blackfoot culture of the twentieth century. Here is a brief summary.

There has been neither rejection of Western music nor virtual abandonment of the traditional music. In contrast to other Plains tribes, whose adoption of the Ghost Dance and its style symbolized a return to earlier times and ways, there is also no special Blackfoot music that explicitly had the function of nativistic revival. And in general, the Indian repertory of the modern Blackfoot does not in its sound include elements transferred from white music. In the conceptualization of music and musical behavior, elements central to Western musical culture do have a part—for example, the notion that humans compose songs, and the emphasis on group performance.

The process of consolidation plays something of a role; groups of songs with what was originally a group of discrete uses (social dances, age-grade societies, Sun Dance) all today share the same style. One notes the development of a style in which those elements of music that contrast most with their Western analogues are exaggerated, especially in the use of the voice and the relationship of vocal to percussive rhythm. The humorous juxtaposition of Western and Indian music is occasionally practiced, as in the recordings by the Indian Chipmunks, the already mentioned singing group that applies the kinds of distortions used by a white group called the Chipmunks, active in the 1960s, to songs in Indian style. Among the processes noted by Kartomi (1981:236–37), pluralistic coexistence of Western and Indian music is certainly a characteristic of Blackfoot culture. So also is compartmentalization of Indian and white musics, as they are rarely heard together, each being used in certain social contexts (see also Merriam 1964:315 for Flathead examples). In some respects, artificial preservation can be identified: the development of the informally consti-tuted group of older men who are said to know much of the tradition; the election of a ceremonial chief who becomes an authority on matters of older tribal lore; the use of social dances and gambling games, once informal events, as performances for audiences; North American Indian Days, historical pageants, and parades as cultural performances.

It has been suggested (Nettl 1978b:134) that these processes can be grouped into two opposing forces: Westernization, in which central features of Western musical culture are adopted and the entire musical system becomes a subdivision of the Western cultural system, and modernization, in which aspects of Western culture not central to it are adapted in order to permit the traditional system to survive in some form. Of the two, the Blackfoot way selected modernization more frequently than Westerniza-tion. The traditional musical sound remains, and various techniques— exaggeration, artificial preservation, consolidation, coexistence with West-ern music, adopting Western performance practices and conceptions of the sources and functions of music—have been used to retain it as a distinctive part of the culture.

The history of styles and genres is only a part of the history of a music; what happens to individual songs and pieces complements the fate of the larger categories. Histories of Western music have not made much of this component of their field, but were they to do so, they would possibly include studies such as the history of a melody such as the Dies Irae as it is used by composers of sacred and secular music (see, e.g., Tappert 1890); the development of a folk tune into a tune family through the composition of variants and versions; and changes in performance practice of an eighteenth-century work as seen in editions, descriptions, and re-cordings.

Little information is available about the history of individual songs in Blackfoot music. Specific songs said to have existed decades ago seem still to be sung; and this suggests that some songs at least have a certain longevity (McClintock 1910 [1968]:515; Nettl 1968b:182–83). The song about White Dog the Sioux chief recorded in 1909 can still be heard; Witmer in 1968 recorded a song identical in designation and tune to one recorded in 1909; and I was able to record at least three songs again over thirty years after I had first heard them in 1951. By contrast, I found that the Medicine Pipe songs sung by three different singers in 1966 had very little in common (Nettl 1968b:19). And so it is likely also that despite the characteristic Blackfoot conception of the song as unchanging entity, songs do change, and they may enter the repertory and leave it with considerable rapidity. At least they have done so in the last several decades.

This account of Blackfoot music history must remind the reader once again of the reconstructed sculpting of the fabled dinosaur. One can often do little beyond extrapolating from odds and ends of data, using them as the basis of speculation, merely suggesting things that might have happened. At least, and at best, we have some sense of processes, types of events, and trends that characterize the recent and, to a much smaller degree, the earlier music history of the Blackfoot.

6. THE CONCEPT OF MUSIC HISTORY

The purpose of the two preceding sections was to provide an outline of history as best it can be guessed, but mainly as background for a look at the Blackfoot people's own conception of the past as event and pattern.

At least to a limited degree, the Blackfoot do concern themselves with the fact that different repertories of music have different origins. Their division of music into "white" and "Indian" indicates this, and they talk about music of older and more recent origin. The words *old, new, modern, traditional* occur in discussion of songs, though usually, to be sure, in conversations about relatively recent music. But this rhetoric of talking about music may be old and also may have something to do with the Blackfoot tendency to recognize and acknowledge cultural borrowings from other peoples. All of this is further related to the tendency of the Blackfoot to be concerned with origins—if not origins of broad concepts such as culture and music, then at least specific artifacts and components of culture, rituals, and songs. We have seen that they recite the origin myths of medicine bundles, associate songs with those who learned them in visions, recite stories that tell the origins of songs of a secular nature. They are not interested so much in the mode of origination as in the fact and locus of origin, dwelling less on events that occured in visions and more on who had them. The origin myths of rituals do not describe processes so much as they enumerate the events in which the things that constitute Blackfoot culture came to be.

The Blackfoot view of culture as an agglomeration of things, artifacts, songs, rituals, more than a group of processes or of people, seems also to affect their perspective of music history. Let me again turn to other cultures for background. To the educated stratum of Western middle class society, history is a grand march in a chosen and inevitable direction, divided into eras, among them distant ones that are grand and glorious, followed by a brief present. In my experience in Iran, the recent past (since ca. 1900) is lengthy, while major events of the distant past—the Achimenaean Empire, the time of early Islam, the Safavid era—seem, in a telescoped view, close together. Speaking more specifically of music, its history is seen, by Western historians and laymen alike in particular, as a history of styles and periods, each of them with one or a half dozen of the great composers presiding. In Iran and in India, the main points of reference seem to be persons, composers, performers, and theoreticians of the past, and it is how music was done by them, not so much its identity (in the sense of pieces or stable styles), that made the history.

Of course the concept of a music history, in the specific sense, is foreign to the Blackfoot. A man to whom I courageously put the issue said, simply and no doubt appropriately, that it is all part of the history of the Blackfoot people. The Blackfoot view of their own general history is objective in the sense that it divides the story into two main eras, precontact and present, which are its anchors; and the history itself, as it seems to be conceived, is largely the story of the time between the two eras. But if one can persuade them to talk about the history specifically of music, one gets the feeling that it is conceived as a group of isolated events not related to each other or caused and determined one by another, except for the time, era, or moment of origination.

How do the Blackfoot people interpret what happened? What little one can learn by way of fact, as described in our previous sections, comes from the statements of informants, past and recent, and so "objective" and "subjective" are inevitably, at least to an extent, congruent. But we can also derive some benefit from an attempt to separate them. Conversations—very few were productive on this topic—as well as the myths and tales suggest that the Blackfoot conception of history is one that distinguishes origins from a later, stable existence, which is followed by an exceptional, disturbed time resulting from the coming of the whites. I tried to ask older men about the history of their music and found that the first impulse was to talk about "how something got to be the way it is now." The origin myths put things into a world that is essentially like that of modern times.

The Blackfoot see the modern state of affairs as a direct result of the origins. The world is a group of products: songs, rituals, musical repertories, but also hills and streams; all of these are somehow put into existence and then stay, remaining in existence while others may be added to them, not usually affected by what is added except that in some cases they may be eliminated, forgotten, and totally replaced. I asked one man about the visions his father had described to him. Did he change the songs he knew when he learned new ones? Was the ritual he had learned altered when new parts were dreamed? Indeed, had he ever heard of someone saying that a medicine man had been told by his guardian spirit to forget what he had learned and to learn new material? To all of these, the reply was negative. And indeed, one is tempted to speculate that the rejection of Ghost Dance and Peyote, religions that presumed to make qualitative changes in the Blackfoot belief system, occurred in part because of the tendency for the Blackfoot to conceive of change, using Merriam's (1977:813) terminology, as quantitative rather than qualitative. This Blackfoot view of history, if such it is, is tempered by others derived from aspects of Blackfoot ideology, from observation of nature, from ideas taken out of Western culture. Nevertheless the view of the world as a group of concrete units is a powerful theme of Blackfoot culture and plays a role in their view of their past.

A second important area of thought involves the recognition that music is something known to other peoples, with whom exchange is possible. Influences from the outside are important events in Blackfoot music history. Ethnomusicologists have long recognized the existence of a pan-Indian musical repertory and its principal basis in Plains Indian styles (Powers 1968; Thomas 1965). It has been thought that the white American view of Indian music as something inevitably exotic was in part responsible for the adoption of the Plains Indian style, the most removed from Western, as the one to dominate such a repertory. But if there was present a tendency on the part of Plains Indians to accept and recognize musical and other cultural imports from other tribes, this characteristic trait may itself have been "borrowed" by other Indian peoples because they needed it in the nineteenth century in order to permit them to enter into the Plains musical and dance styles. In certain respects, the Blackfoot seem to see their music history as one in which changes took place because new styles and repertories, and in particular types of dances, were adopted from other tribes. While the Blackfoot evidently rejected Ghost Dance and Peyote, in other Northern Plains tribes, the introduction of these repertories followed traditional patterns. The coming of Western music also played out the role of foreign cultural and musical imports. It was adopted as a unit by the Blackfoot, unchanged, not mixed with what was already present, and kept with its cultural context, in a pattern similar to that used to treat Peyote and the Ghost Dance among non-Blackfoot Plains tribes.

It also seems reasonable to suggest that in the Blackfoot conception, different segments of a musical repertory should have different musical

styles. When I played a recent recording for them, my Blackfoot consultants had little difficulty recognizing the functions of songs by their
style, something observed also by Witmer (1982:71–72). They have some
terminology to distinguish characteristics, such as the dotted rhythm of
percussion called "Owl Dance Drum." The recognition of stylistic differences and the identification of outside imports together give us at least
the rudiments of a concept of periodization in Blackfoot musical thought.

In this conception of history as the addition of repertories with distinctive styles, the Blackfoot view corresponds substantially to Western
academics' views of their music history. The units that carry the stylistic
superstructure (which can to an extent be changed without disturbing the
identity of the units themselves) are the songs, corresponding to the pieces,
songs, symphonies, sonatas, and operas of Western music. But the Western
counterparts change during their lifetimes, and the Western conception of
music history gives some, if not much, attention to this phenomenon. The
idea that different performers have their own versions of pieces, that
Beethoven concertos were played differently in the nineteenth century,
that the identity of a repertory may remain but its performane practice
may change, all of this plays a part in the Western conception of music
history. There is, as usual, very little evidence for a Blackfoot counterpart
of this set of ideas, but a few observations may give some insight. The
discussions of songs which I heard did not include much mention of the
ways in which one song is sung by different persons. The notion that a
song may have been sung differently by the person who had given or
taught it to my consultant does not usually emerge. The kind of discussion
of multiple and personal versions that one may hear in the rhetoric of
some European folk singers is not common in Blackfoot parlance. All of
this must again be related to the conception of a song as something given
in finished form and not intended to be changed. The Western conception
of music history importantly includes famous people. So does the Blackfoot
conception of their social and political history, but when asked to answer
questions about their own music history, they didn't deal very much with
prominent individuals who could be considered master musicians, or single
them out. To be sure, they mentioned originators and transmitters of songs.
As we know, in the 1960s they divided people who were concerned with
songs into categories partly (and incidentally) in accordance with their
interest in different song repertories (older, Westernized, Western), although, to be sure, this grouping correlates with other ways of classifying
persons in society, by descent, economic status, and cultural identification.

In certain ways, also, Western academic musicians think of the history
of their music in terms of landmarks—think of the "Missa Papae Marcelli,"
Beethoven's late string quartets, "Tristan," and "The Rite of Spring." In

Blackfoot musical thought, there is surely no concept really close to the "masterwork" of Western culture, but in one way, it is not totally foreign. If the Blackfoot seem rarely to have paid special attention to songs because of their sound and structure, a few songs were and are nevertheless regarded as "favorites of the tribe." McClintock (1910 [1968]:308–11) designates one by implication, and a few others were so labeled by my informant-singers. Properly a subject for chapter 5, they are mentioned here in order to assess any special role they may have in history as now conceived. I was forced to conclude that they do not, but it is interesting that some of them seem to be of rather recent origin, and none was said to be especially old or ancient. The kinds of songs that might have been given to the Blackfoot people by Napi in the earliest period are not the ones in this "favorite" category nor are the songs of medicine bundles. Rather, they are largely social dance and Sun Dance songs, all of an essentially public nature. This wide popularity, as stated or implied, seems related to their use by many persons, not to their presumed supernatural power.

7. THE CONCEPT OF CHANGE

In modern urban American society's conception of music, ubiquity and continuity of change is an important ingredient. Music must always be changing, and the absence of innovation is unacceptable for the health of the musical system. Conventions of composers and educators, informal "rap sessions" of jazz and rock musicians, books about the state of music all concentrate on what is going on that's new—new principally in style, in technology and instruments, in the way of producing sound. Change in the social context of music is not as important, and the rate at which pieces are being composed, that is, innovation in musical content, is also less prominent. But all together, in Western music there is a lot of change, and it is considered essential.

In a somewhat contrasting situation, Madras of the early 1980s, there was a great deal of change taking place in Carnatic music. New instruments were being introduced, and new practices in the social context of music. New ragas were sometimes added, changes in the frequency of performance of certain ragas and talas could be discerned, and the repertory was being expanded by the addition of new songs and the rediscovery of forgotten ones. The fact that much of the music was improvised brought constant changes in microcosm. And yet, in general, musicians were disinclined to admit that change was taking place or that it was desirable.

In looking at the concept of change in Blackfoot culture, it must first be admitted that it is hardly possible even to speculate about ideas of musical change that might have been around in the nineteenth century or before. Conceivably, attitude may have paralleled what we know of behavior, which suggests resistance to change. The myths imply that songs are not to be changed, and the avoidance of Peyote and Ghost Dance religions and musical styles suggests that stability was a value. The notion that history involves origin, after which things remain in place, suggests disapproval of change. The ethnographies published around 1900 do not dwell on the way Blackfoot culture may have changed in earlier times, except to mourn the loss of tradition.

Witmer (1982:117) makes a special point of comparing the remarks of McClintock to the effect that young people were totally uninterested in older tribal traditions before 1910 to his own findings of 1968. By the time he visited the Blood people in Alberta, the old men, who might have been the youths in McClintock's time, were at least moderately informed on ceremonial life and interested in maintaining it. The Montana people in the 1980s seemed to be of a similar mind, old men often being regarded as receptacles of ancient ceremonial material, and many younger people interested at least to some extent.

Over the years, I broached the issues of musical change—in contrast to history—with at least a dozen Blackfoot people. When asked about their attitude toward twentieth century change, they characteristically spoke only of certain issues. They asserted that change had taken place, but then referred mainly to changes in the social context of music, the relative quantity of Indian music as compared to white music on the reservation, the adaptation of certain Western performance practices such as the singing by groups and intertribal star figures, and the Western-derived technologies such as amplification. They spoke of the decline of older ceremonial repertories and the part of the population that still maintains Indian music. They concentrated on aspects of survival and revival. Many gave me the impression that they took a neutral or passive view. Change at the present was neither a good nor an evil. But these people did not speak about the fate of individual songs, or of stylistic changes in form and rhythm, for example. One man in his fifties took a more positive approach. Possibly reflecting an earlier attitude toward culture and change, he pointed out that things had indeed changed a great deal, and said, "We keep getting new songs, and we got to hold on to the old songs, too."

In all of this, one sensed that the concept of musical change was a new one to the Blackfoot, that it was something they felt their ancestors had not thought about, and that it became an issue because other kinds of culture change had also become significant issues in their lives. Probing a bit further, I got the impression that the idea of change was something regarded essentially as quantitative—the addition and subtraction of units, songs, ceremonies, even styles—but that it was not conceived as an ongoing process. It may be argued that earlier Blackfoot society likely took a negative attitude toward musical change. Then, in the twentieth century, the conception that music might change was introduced along with the concept that culture was changing, and indeed, that the Blackfoot had to change their culture if it was to survive at all.

This attempt to match what little is known of actual history with the Blackfoot people's attitudes about their own past and about musical change may have sometimes moved us even past the end of the tail and entirely off the proverbial dinosaur. Nevertheless, the common themes in mythology, nineteenth-century accounts, and recent interviews do tell us something about cultural stability and integrity, demonstrating that in certain respects there is a Blackfoot culture that has persisted through all the change. Much of the Blackfoot way of thinking about musical history and change is governed by the conceptual framework that governs their perception of their culture and the world.

CHAPTER FOUR

Music in Human and Supernatural Societies

1. USES AND FUNCTIONS

In its earlier history, ethnomusicology was prone to distinguish among societies in terms of the degree of "functionality" of their music. The absence of any "art for art's sake" was accepted as a hallmark in the conventional wisdom about tribal societies, as was the idea that true art music was devoid of any but purely artistic function. Some historical musicologists still maintain the distinction, carrying it even further into a dichotomy between Western and non-Western. In a widely quoted statement, Kerman (1985:174) asserts, "Western music is just too different from other musics, and its cultural contexts too different from other cultural contexts." But it is clear that performances of art music in Western culture have "functions" beyond great art for the ages, as some masterpieces were intended to be (and are still) parts of church services, entertainment for parties, background music for dramas, or parts of patriotic rituals. At the same time, cultural contexts of Western art music performance range from the (sociopolitically motivated) ritual of formal concerts to devotional services, from accompaniment of housework and driving to television commercials, from parodied forms in popular dance tunes to musical logos in the world of commerce. The distinctions between art and nonart music and between tribal and high culture and their musics have become blurred, and ethnomusicologists have recently come to view with considerable suspicion the notion that tribal cultures maintain a purely "functional aesthetic" in their view of music.

If we have given up as mistaken the notion that the most important thing about tribal musics in general is their fulfillment of social functions, the Blackfoot people themselves made it clear to me, over and over, that the most important thing about music to them is its relationship to the rest of life, to human culture, to specific activities, and to the supernatural. An emphatic statement of one of my chief consultants put it well: "The right Blackfoot way of doing something is to sing the right song with it." And again, "A good song is one that well fulfills the function of a song," a statement sounding almost as if made by someone who had read Wissler and Ewers. To the Blackfoot, music exists for the purpose of doing something, accomplishing something.

It is a tenet of the anthropology of music that music can best be seen in relationship to other domains of culture. But the domains with which interaction is strongest may vary by society. Steven Feld (1982) looks at the music of the Kaluli of Papua New Guinea in the context of other parts of the spectrum of sound—birdsong, weeping, and speech. Principal points of contact for music, in the conception of the Kaluli, are other kinds of sound. Such an approach must be profitable for any study, yet it seems to shed better light on the workings of Kaluli culture than others. In contrast, for the musical culture of India, aspects of the conception of time and the way it is handled are more promising. One could treat the matter of time, from the rhythmic components of music itself all the way to the importance of the musical calendar, essentially as a continuum. In the Muslim Middle East, it is most helpful to look at music in its relationship to various parts of society that provide opposition to the principal cultural themes—secular entertainment, mysticism, the concept of cultural minority, the requirement of differentiating between theory and practice, intellectual interpretation. There may be universals that apply to all societies—association with the supernatural, marking cultural and social boundaries. But also, there may be relationship among domains of culture that are specific to a society. For the Blackfoot, one can best see the function of music as coming through its relationship to economic life, social structure, political structure, warfare, and religion.

When my consultant said "function," did he mean function in the technical sense, or *use*? The history of these terms in ethnomusicological usage and conceptualization has been discussed elsewhere (Nettl 1983:147–49; Merriam 1964:209–18), so let me simply summarize it by saying that the two were once united, referring simply to activities accompanying music. Later they were separated, use being the overt and obvious, and function, broader and more analytically derived.

It is a complex issue. To ask consultants outright what the function of music in general is or was in Blackfoot culture provided no useful replies. Merriam, in dealing with the Flathead, approached the issue in part by asking why people made music and felt obliged to admit that this question "has not been considered in detail by the Flathead" (1967:28). The variety of answers that led him to this conclusion is probably characteristic also of the Blackfoot. The two recorded occasions on which I asked the question led to answers that distinguished between Indian and white music, like this one: "Well, it's not just to tell stories like your people's songs." Thus, it is statements made in other contexts as well as a look at behavior that are more useful for seeing what, in Blackfoot conceptualization, are the uses and functions of music.

It is not totally inappropriate to say that the Blackfoot distinguish the concepts of use and function somewhat as did ethnomusicologists of the 1970s. Some Blackfoot people are willing to speak differently about the use of one song, and the uses of songs as a whole. On the one hand, in talking about individual songs, the Blackfoot today—and in earlier times, if we can use the classic ethnographies as indicative—speak simply of activities that music accompanies. There is little discussion of songs by themselves; the rhetoric ordinarily associates them with ceremonies, events, actions, or persons. On the other hand, Blackfoot people do talk about the whole body of music, about their songs as a unified concept. While they do not engage in a kind of anthropological discussion of the function of music, I would argue that they definitely consider music as having, on the whole, *a* function or a group of functions distinct from those of other domains of culture, though certainly closely allied with dance.

The very fact that one hears music discussed in these two ways—the song and music as a whole—suggests that in Blackfoot conceptualization, there is a kind of distinction between uses and functions, some notion that the individual piece has a use but that music as a whole plays a larger role. When Merriam (1964:210–211) indicates that *uses* may involve activity to be observed, while *function* is a concept used in analysis and interpretation by the outside observer, he provides a convenient dichotomy for distinguishing the insider's and outsider's views, but it can also be modified to fit an intracultural model. The Blackfoot conceive of songs as having uses; they also, analytically, interpret their songs as a whole to have a generalizable function, or a group of related ones.

Thus, to the outsider observing Blackfoot culture, music symbolizes the contents of life, validates acts, and possesses supernatural power. The symbolic function may be central. Things that are important in life, culture, and nature are symbolized or at least reflected in music, not directly in the sound or style, as may be the case in European "program music," but more abstractly, as in the structure of repertory. The important concepts in Blackfoot culture, the important categories, divisions, and numbers have their musical counterparts.

Music is most closely associated with religion; it is also closely associated with the instrumentalities of society. The important distinctions—between nature and culture, between men and women, among stages in life, among types and degrees of supernatural power, among degrees of formality in behavior—all have their musical aspects. The Blackfoot taxonomy of culture is reflected in the taxonomy of music. So in an important way, the function of music in Blackfoot culture is to symbolize life, and specifically, Blackfoot life.

But this configuration of Blackfoot thought that involves the *function* of music as a separate category is difficult to approach except through analysis, interpretation, and some speculation. In contrast, the Blackfoot very definitely talk about the *uses* of music, stressing association with an activity, and emphatically suggesting that each activity has its proper song.

In earlier times, the idea of "Blackfootness" may have been symbolized by the association of song and action; and in modern times, the correlation between specifically "Indian" activities and "Indian" musical accompaniment is very great. But what actually does the song *do* for the activity, or better stated, what does the actor accomplish by performing or hearing a song? One might look for relationship between act and music in the handling of time—for example, fast action going with fast music, and such. But a close rhythmic relationship is certainly not obvious. Dancers follow roughly the rhythm of a song, although, given the requirement that musicians keep melodic and drum rhythm separate, it is not always clear which musical rhythm is being followed. But in other ways, one cannot really see close relationships between the way time is handled in act and song. The quick tempo of gambling songs is not reflected in rapid body movements. And never was I told, "The rhythm of the song is a guide for our dancing," or anything to that effect.

Why then must one sing "the right song" with an activity? In earlier times, one can imagine that Blackfoot people might have said (e.g., Wissler 1912a:263) that it is simply so because the supernatural figures, giving their power through instructions in visions and myths, directed thus. P. S. in 1966 discoursed at length on the subject; I paraphrase: In the old days, we did nothing without songs. We didn't feel we had done things properly without the songs. Sometimes we forgot the words of those songs, but we still sang. And even when we forgot the right songs, we sang any song that came to us. White people, and some Indians, they do almost anything without songs, and they use their songs only once in a while, for something special. It's different with the Blackfoot. They used to *have* to have their songs.

What is noteworthy in this attitude is the insistence on the importance of music, alongside the relative lack of care as to the specific auditory relationship between song and action, the great emphasis on music per se more than on the right songs. To be sure, the theory of Blackfoot religion requires the right songs to be sung in the ceremonies, but I have pointed out the difference between theory and practice. The lack of agreement on what songs go with what ceremony or belonged to which medicine man was already pointed out by Wissler's informant (1912a:262–66), and in my time on the reservation, there was far less restriction. Yet the idea that music *must* accompany activities, and that this is a Blackfoot cultural feature, is still around.

To interpret the significance of the foregoing further, it may be that the Blackfoot believe that songs validate action (see also Merriam 1964:224). Somewhat in the sense that dress and costume validate participation at various kinds of social events in Western culture, singing the *right* song, but in some cases any song, is what gives an action validity in Blackfoot culture. This thought is a generalization of the idea that in a medicine bundle ceremony, singing the right song with an object is required.

There may have been a time when singing the right song meant singing a song with the right words. The large number of song texts in Wissler's works (1912a:215–19) compared with later ethnographies, and specifically the sixty-six song texts for the opening of the Natóas bundle, part of the Sun Dance ritual, are indicative. Eventually, fewer texts may have been used, there was less specificity in song selection, and eventually there may have remained only the *idea* of singing, singing any Indian music, as a way of validating Blackfoot activity. One cannot claim that songs provide rhythm, that their words narrate what is happening, that the character of melody reminds one of ideas in various actions. Rather, in recent times, it is above all the *act* of singing, pure and simple, that validates actions, not the specific musical content of the song. Possibly the generalized function of music may in part account for the rather homogeneous style of Blackfoot music.

Since this section already has more than its share of speculation, let me also suggest that the relationship of song to culture may be microcosmically reflected in the structure of the relationship of singing to percussive accompaniment. In the accompaniment, there is little variety, and different kinds of rattles and drums are not distinguished by their music, particularly their rhythm. In modern Blackfoot culture, some variation in the drum rhythms, among song types and within the performance of one song, has become characteristic, but older recordings do not have any of this. On the other hand, it is rarely acceptable to sing without drumming. Even in songs elicited by a modern recordist, if no drum is available, some kind of substitute percussive background sound will be produced.

Wissler's musical consultant (1912a:264) points out, "The Blackfoot are given to beating time when they sing. They beat a drum, use a rattle, bells, beat with a stick, or with the foot. They can scarcely sing without beating time." But as the beating may bear no specific rhythmic relationship to the rhythm of the melody or has a relationship to the melody that may be very hard to apprehend, perhaps even explicitly avoiding a specific relationship, "beating time" may actually not be the most descriptive term. The point is that in order for singing to be valid, percussive accompaniment is required. Its simple presence, less than its specific character, is essential.

Another interpretation of Blackfoot musical functions and uses derives from the evidence that, in earlier times, songs not only validated actions but had direct supernatural power, *natóas*, the word or root indicating sacredness in the active sense. My own consultants had evidently become vague about this subject, but Wissler's informants indicated that in the curing of individuals by doctors ("medicine men"), it was the songs themselves that had the supernatural power. The ubiquity of songs in the vision quest readily indicates the important supernatural associations of songs. You can't have a proper vision without songs, they accompany everything else, validate the vision; but in certain situations, it is the songs themselves that have the power. Thus stated Wissler (1912a:270): "On one thing, however, our informants insist, a doctor regards his chief power as associated with one or two songs, songs given him direct by supernatural agencies and which he cannot transfer. It also follows that no other person can use these songs." Wissler then points out that specific songs are associated with various ills—headaches, lung bleeding, bullet wound. A similar situation involves songs owned by individuals to be sung only at times of great crisis, impending death, grave illness, for these are indeed specific songs.

The idea of the special song with its own purpose is probably less developed today than it was a hundred years ago, but it does still exist. In the modern powwow culture, on certain occasions, specific songs are needed to accomplish ceremonial functions such as the grand entry, commemoration of a deceased person, or retrieving a dropped eagle feather. The master of ceremonies emphatically announces that special songs will be sung at these points.

Several ways of dealing with the function of music in society have been proposed in ethnomusicological literature. Merriam (1964:219–21) gives ten functions that music may have and, in his study of the Flathead, pointed out that music today functions "importantly" as a cohesive mechanism for the society, thus leaving the possibility that music may have more than one function. Elsewhere (Nettl 1983:153–61), I suggested two models that might help to understand the difference between use and function and between their perception by the insider and the outsider, and for the Blackfoot, I suggest using these, the "coin" and "pyramid," in combination. If we can look at the Blackfoot people's own ideas of the differences between use and function, and if we can talk about uses of music as observed (by me) and as described by the Blackfoot, we ought also to be able to distinguish somehow between functions as the product of an observer's interpretation and as something that exists in Blackfoot conceptualization. To do this would illustrate the two sides of the ethnomusicologist's coin. In the case of the Blackfoot, who are articulate about the *uses* of "a song" and the uses of songs at large, it makes sense to look at a function for music in relationship to other domains of culture and the function of music in different cultural contexts; that is, we can look for principal and subsidiary functions, arranging them in the shape of a pyramid.

Thus, I suggest that the functions mentioned earlier, symbolizing, validating, and having power, can be subsumed in a single overall function of music in Blackfoot culture, that of mediating between the Blackfoot people and other beings. Various uses of music can be drawn together with this concept. The human-specific or Blackfoot-specific nature of music has been mentioned above. The importance of music in the relationship to the supernatural is obvious. The idea that Blackfoot culture is reflected in the musical system, its various components and important visions reflected in repertorial divisions; the observations made by the Blackfoot about the importance and significant functions of music; the idea that supernatural spirits speak, especially when something important is to be said, in song; all this shows the importance of music in the conception of tribe, and its role as a tribal marker.

In modern times, the use of music as a way of presenting Blackfoot culture to the outside world, Indian and white, replaces the role of music as a way of identifying the Blackfoot people in their relationship to the supernatural. Further, the fact that music is a very generalized activity, that what matters is its presence and not its detailed content, leads us to see it as a form of generalized communication contrasting with speech. That it is in a certain sense outside the culture, a domain of it but also an art that somehow treats of the culture, suggests that it is something separate from but parallel to language. Its content is culture, but its structure is in a sense outside it, something that humans use to communicate their culture, a vehicle more than substance. The energies of music making are directed outside the tribe. In the Blackfoot culture of the 1980s, the social function of music is in part a continuation of earlier Indian customs, in part an adaptation of Western white culture, and in part parallel to the functions of music in other ethnic communities in the United States and Canada. The activities and contexts of music in the 1980s included (1) the North American Indian Days celebration; (2) occasional briefer powwows; (3)

parades; (4) music in public schools; (5) gambling games; (6) listening to recordings at home; (7) academic interests such as use of music in museums, educational pageants, and classes; and (8) reconstruction of older ceremonies. A comparison of these to the contexts of music in a small white American community would show military and patriotic music (which is also used in parades and public schools, in pageants, and in reconstructing older ceremonies such as Civil War battles) to be the closest analogue. Uses of music devised for mainstream American culture are found in modern Blackfoot culture. But at the same time, the function of drawing ethnic boundary lines in a manner similar to that used by European ethnic minorities in American cities is also significant. Cultural performances such as festivals, with the purpose of drawing the group together but also for presentation to the outside, are an American ethnic hallmark (see Porter 1978:8–10), and the most valuable aspects of the traditional culture are accompanied by traditional music. It is not difficult, therefore, to see how the traditional functions of music in Blackfoot culture, mediating between the Blackfoot and some kind of outside world, have been made to syncretize with the mainstream American and also the ethnic minority functions of music.

My experience in hearing people talk about music may shed light. The rhetoric of musical discussion struck me as reflective of the conception of music as something whose task it is to communicate outside the society of humans, or more specifically, outside the society of Blackfoot humans. Within Blackfoot society, people spoke of singing, but not of singing *for* someone; and the listening audience was not mentioned. I asked, "Are you looking forward to singing for all those people?" "They don't pay attention, but it doesn't matter; making some money anyway."

Conversation about the singing groups at modern powwows produced talk of hearing, but not of listening or receiving communication. I had the feeling that the listeners regarded themselves as passive participants. But quite to the contrary, the descriptions of songs and singing that appear in the mythology, while dependent on translation and interpretation by authors and editors, seem to speak more specifically about singing for or to someone. The supernatural figures who sing songs in the presence of humans are said to sing to or for them, definitely communicating to them. Descriptions of singing at medicine bundle rites show singing directed to the supernatural or to the objects in the bundle. Again, a middle-aged consultant commented, in a vein probably familiar to the reader, "Too many radios, too many tapes, the young people don't really care."

In modern life, the counterpart of the supernatural as the principal non-Blackfoot social entity is non-Blackfoot humanity, that is, Indians of other tribes, and whites. It is easy for a cultural outsider to interpret much present-day Blackfoot musical activity as having the function of communicating Blackfoot ethnicity to the outside at powwows and celebrations. In many ways, style and use have been adapted to the needs of this function: the intertribal style, the singing of songs without words, and the adoption of modern mass-media techniques and amplification. The fact that there are few strictly intratribal musical events suggests the conclusion that Blackfoot music exists in good measure for dealing with the outside world; this function is at the top of the pyramid, less general ones, and eventually simple uses, flow from it.

If this is the ethnomusicologist's conclusion, would it also be that of the Blackfoot? We turn to the other side of the coin and, for a bit of circumstantial evidence, to an important statement by one of my principal consultants. Discussion of individual songs leads to talk about a use and fulfilling it properly, but the rhetoric about the concept of song is different: "The songs are some of the most important things we Blackfoot people have." The idea of receiving songs from other tribes but then changing them also speaks to the conception of music as tribal property, and as something that marks the tribe. The association of songs with a revival of Blackfoot ethnicity and of a feeling of tribal self-esteem in the 1950s follows the same line. The combination of music as tribal marker and the lack of music as an intratribal communicator leads me to suggest that the Blackfoot themselves conceive of music as having a function of tribal externalization.

2.   SOCIAL GROUPS AND SONG GROUPS

In important domains of culture—social structure, politics, warfare, religion—music marks the boundaries among sectors of Blackfoot society. In this respect, the Blackfoot are like many societies. In modern Western culture, for example, the relationship of musical and social taxonomies is reflected in the costumes of musicians in performances—tuxedo in the symphony orchestra, long hair and T-shirts in rock groups, Asian dress in concerts of Asian music, sport jackets and sweaters for performances of experimental music, period costumes for Renaissance music. The contemporary Blackfoot don't go quite so far—though the fact that powwow dancers wear traditionally derived costumes while the singers wear farmer's caps is surely significant—but their music does reflect the social system.

We have had occasion above to mention the reflection, in music, of Blackfoot culture and its important divisions, and the tendency of the musical system to underscore things that are essential to the culture. In modern times, this applies particularly to those ideas and activities essential to the specifically *Indian* parts of the culture. Here a function of music is to communicate among the population groups that compose society and to clarify symbolically the relationships of various parts of society to each other. The most important division in society in modern times is between Indians and white people, and within the Indian community, between those Indians who have become (in McFee's [1972] sense) "Indian-oriented" in their values, and those who are "Western-oriented." The major musical distinction is between Indian and white music, and a second one, though much less explicitly stated, between older traditional and modern intertribal musics.

In older traditional culture, a principal social division was between men and women, and this distinction was (and still is) maintained musically through the greater amount of singing done by men and the special though less prominent roles in music assigned to women. While this difference in music is reflective of the contrastive roles of men and women in society, the difference can also be interpreted as a function of the different roles of the sexes in dealing with the outside world. Women ordinarily did not directly confront the supernatural (in visions, for example, or in the Sun Dance), nor in traditional society did they have much to do with members of other tribes or whites (Lewis 1941:221–24). Similarly, they participated only marginally in music, and those of them who sang might be designated as "immodest" (Wissler 1912a:264). The association of men, as the outward-facing segment of society, with music supports the contention that in Blackfoot thought, music had the function of dealing with the outside. It is interesting to read, in Oscar Lewis's account of the "manly-hearted women," who behave more like men than do other women (Lewis 1941:222) and share some of the concerns and prerogatives of men, that they also took part in singing and used a men's singing style.

The association of music with the male, outward-facing, sides of Blackfoot culture is supported by the division of the male population into various components. Aside from division by age-grade society and age, people also divided themselves into groups by adherence to particular supernatural figures such as the guardian spirits. The Beaver Medicine men, the Medicine Pipe men, the Buffalo Rock men all had their own songs, and while each man may have had his own visions and acquired the songs individually, some might also have purchased or inherited medicine bundles or painted tipis and their songs. In any event, they evidently shared a repertory. And yet, personal individuality and an idiosyncratic relationship to human groups and spirits played a major role in life. I got the impression that there was a tendency by men to group themselves informally according to degree of supernatural power, that is, the power of the medicine bundle or guardian spirit one might have or the number of visions and songs one might have learned. The degree of supernatural involvement, and the degree of power and prestige flowing from this, would be directly expressed in identity and quantity of songs.

Children as a category of the population were in some ways treated as a separate group, but in other ways simply as a younger version of adult society. The musical culture of children reflects this, as there appears to be no separate children's repertory. There are songs called lullabies, sung by women *to* children, and there is some mention of children's game songs (Wissler 1912b:58). At the same time, I was told by two older men that as children they had been excluded from ceremonies, but that they made a practice of listening surreptitiously specifically in order to learn ceremonial songs.

If the Blackfoot world of music reflects the social divisions of the tribe in their variety, it appears only recently to have itself produced such divisions in society. The earlier ethnographies make no mention of professional musicians or of particular excellence in performance. Surely there must have been people who were praised for knowing more songs than others, and possibly some were regarded as excellent singers while others were thought abominable. But there is no evidence of a special class of singers or song makers. Knowledge of songs, composition (in visions), frequency of performance, excellence in singing and drumming, all presumably correlated with and resulted from the role of music in other activities, particularly ritual. This is the situation as it has been described for tribal societies at large in older ethnomusicological literature. It is often presented in classrooms as a kind of universal of simpler cultures, and as it is really not an appropriate generalization, we should not emphasize it here. Even so, it seems actually to apply to the Blackfoot. Specialization of labor was not a part of the Blackfoot economy, and thus musician specialists were not developed. Specializations of various sorts in religious life were very much the rule, and musicianship tended to accompany it.

This has changed. Let me recapitulate: In my time on the reservation, certain men were referred to as "singers" or "drummers," the two referring to the same group, and being interchangeable terms. In 1966, about fifty men were so designated in popular parlance; but it was not a title formally bestowed or agreed upon. Singers were members of singing groups who performed at powwows and rehearsed—sometimes publicly—in winter. They were not necessarily the people who sang at gambling games. They were loosely affiliated in groups associated with locations—the towns of Starr School, Browning, Heart Butte, for example. I also found a number of individuals who were said specifically *not* to be singers, but to know a "lot of old songs and traditions of the tribe." They had a major interest in older tribal ceremonials, while the singers were mostly concerned with the intertribal repertory of social dance songs. A few individuals belonged to both groups.

By 1984, the situation had become more formalized. A number of the old-timers were members of the "honorary council" of older men whose job it was to preserve tribal traditions and to advise the Business Council. One member of the honorary council had been elected "ceremonial chief" and served as authority on cultural traditions. In this context, the singers were judged substantially by the repertory, voice, performance practice; the old-timers, by their knowledge of older traditions. In 1984, the singers were more formally divided into singing groups, or "drums," many of whom had made commercial disks and cassettes. Their average age had decreased, and at the core of several of them were the members of an extended family. A singing group was usually also associated with a town or village.

The major events in the lives of individuals and of groups of people in Blackfoot society are variously reflected in musical life, to a degree that it is worth noting as a particular reflection of culture in music. First, the matter of aging. In the older tribal tradition, as a man aged, his musical repertory increased in at least two ways. He would join successive age-grade societies and learn the rituals of each, thus expanding the repertory he knew, although he might not, it is true, add to habitual performance, instead replacing the repertory of one society with that of another every few years. Also, as a seeker and receiver of visions, he would learn additional songs, and his gradually expanding medicine bundle and store of supernatural power would be reflected in the increasing repertory. Thus, on the one hand, men were expected to continue learning more songs, just as they continued learning more of their own culture and of its super-natural superstructure, but on the other hand, they were also expected to have different musical interests at different ages. All of this reflects respect for old age and the conviction that the elderly may most appropriately be the intellectual leaders of society.

There are aspects of modern Blackfoot life that suggest continuity of this structure. The interest in traditional Indian music in most men (and some of the women in singing groups) comes in their late teens or twenties; before this, they seem to be entirely devoted to Western music. Of course many Blackfoot people never take much interest in Indian music, but those who do tend to do so increasingly as they age. After beginning with an interest in the modern, intertribal powwow culture, some Blackfoot men become interested in older Blackfoot traditions, ceremonial songs, and the reconstruction of older ceremonies (Nettl 1968a:206). A modern man's repertory may change and expand gradually, as it did in earlier times. I have no evidence, however, that old men now continue to learn songs. In earlier times, one was expected even in old age to learn more, and what was learned late in life might be most valued. Two consultants told me that the most important personal songs, those that were not to be sung until great need arose, were learned by older men, or in middle age, but in any case they were not among the songs one learned in one's early visions.

All of this contrasts with today's Western urban culture. Musical taste and association may change (from children's and teenage tastes to those of young adults) several times early in life. At the point at which formal education is completed, however, there is a tendency to establish a more or less permanent musical (and social or professional) allegiance. Many of the musical works most valuable to one's life—a body of hymns or a group of pieces from the Western classical repertory or operettas— are learned fairly early, not in old age. In the case of professionals in classical music, knowledge of the musical system and of a certain basic repertory is expected to be completed when formal education—in the early twenties—results in a degree or diploma. While in Western academic musical culture, both content and style of music are expected to change for society at large, the idea of gradual and continued change in the musical experience of the individual seems to be less important.

By contrast, in traditional Blackfoot culture, the individual experienced frequent musical change through life, with significant changes coming in old age, but Blackfoot culture, at least as society conceives of it, was not subject to this same kind of constant gradual change.

3.   THE POWER OF MUSIC

The most important thing about the musical culture of the Flathead Indians, so Alan Merriam (1967:3) asserted, is the supernatural origin of music and its role in the relationship of humans to the supernatural. The same thing applies to the Blackfoot as well, and the statement could be expanded to the effect that the multifarious uses of music in Blackfoot society have their ultimate roots, if not always their functions, in the supernatural associations of music. Music has supernatural power, including the power of mediating between human and supernatural, and it typically validates, or makes properly supernatural, the acts of ritual and religion. The ways humans use music to associate with each other can be interpreted as an analogue to music as a form of communication between humans and supernatural figures.

We have touched on several ways in which this interpretation can be supported: (1) Music is said to have supernatural sources. Songs come from supernatural spirits, and they are the validation of supernatural experience. (2) In the hierarchy of songs, the most valuable have the closest supernatural association. (3) Ceremonies among humans are presented as repetitions or reconstructions of events in which supernatural figures gave power to humans, including songs. (4) Much of the theory about music, such as the supposed ability to learn songs in one hearing and the importance of musical sound as separate from human culture, shows music to be a domain distinct from the rest of human culture. (5) In today's society, the difference between Blackfoot music and white music is stressed far more than the difference between other aspects of Blackfoot and white culture. (6) Some emphatic statements made to me suggest that the musical system is conceived as a particularly perfect and systematically organized reflection of Blackfoot life and culture.

It is hardly necessary to make a case. The religious orientation of music is a cultural universal. Among the origin theories of music that of S. Nadel, presenting music as an invention for the purpose of communicating with the supernatural, is one of the more credible (Nadel 1930:538–44). But while the association is widespread, it differs greatly by culture. Before then turning further to the problem of characterizing the particular supernatural association of music in Blackfoot culture, let me again sample the world context.

Islam presents its principal liturgical text, the *Qur'an*, through a style of performance that is objectively like the singing of Middle Eastern secular music; yet its religiosity is established in part by its theoretical separation from secular music. Baroque composers in Germany, composing choral music for the church, used forms and techniques also found in secular music, but often in better and grander fashion, as a way of inspiring their listeners to praise God. The orchestras of Tibetan Buddhism play loudly in order to gain the attention of deities. There are cultures in which the supernatural is addressed directly in song, and others in which prayer is spoken, while reflections about the deity are sung.

In Blackfoot culture, music is not used so much as a way for humans to approach the supernatural world, but the reverse; it is the language used by the spirits to speak to humans. But, note again, only to humans, not to each other. While there are a great many uses of music, consultants and ethnographies all emphasize the vision and its use of songs as a principal way for spirits to speak to humans in order to give instructions, signify things of great importance, and teach essentials for survival. Songs are the principal way of validating the vision. While Blackfoot people are not accustomed to speak of these matters in the technical terms of ethnomusicologists, they do have ways of insisting that music has the function of receiving communication from the supernatural. The functions of reflecting the cultural system and mediating with the outside can be seen to flow from it, chronologically as well as conceptually.

But if there is a special group of central functions of music, and if music is in a sense outside the culture—reflecting it and acting as a medium for handling culture—it can also be related to a number of cultural themes and thus play a special functional role in different cultural domains. For example, the role of music as a commodity, a medium for exchange, something treated like physical object, the matter of personal ownership—all of these relate music, even religious music, to the economic organization of the Blackfoot. The relationship is clarified in the myth detailing the origin of the powerful beaver medicine bundles. The story begins with an affair of the wife of a great human hunter with a beaver. The child of the union is nurtured by the human stepfather, and beaver decides to reward him by giving supernatural power, visits his house, and one by one exchanges songs for the skins of the local wildlife. The hunter, now in possession of the powerful songs, replaces the skins given to beaver by hunting (Ewers 1958:168–69).

The beaver myth, central to the Blackfoot conceptions of the world and culture as they came to be, shows that songs can be given like objects and, indeed, exchanged for physical objects. The songs are first owned by the beaver, and then by the hunter, and although nothing is said about the beaver's giving up ownership, this is perhaps implied by the exchange of songs for skins. The relationship of the most powerful songs to a collection of skins belonging to all of the local wildlife gives a strong sense of the association of music with the environment, and with the basis of the culture. The myth illustrates the reflection of culture in the musical system. The exchange of songs for the most important symbols of culture—the prepared animal skins—is significant, and the pairing of songs and skins, of animal and human (beaver and hunter), of real world (human and skins) with supernatural underworld (beaver and songs) shows music as a major force with special power, as a way of mediating between humans and others, and as a reflection of the cultural system. This myth and others help greatly in gaining an understanding of the role of music in Blackfoot culture.

It is interesting, therefore, to contemplate further the association of various kinds of supernatural or mythological figures with music. The world of myth and supernatural experience of the Blackfoot is populated by a number of kinds of figures. Most central, I remind the reader, is Old Man, Napi, the culture hero who invented the Blackfoot and much of their surrounding physical environment and culture. He appears in many myths, but in these, as they are presented in Wissler and Duvall (1909:19–39) and in Bullchild's collection (1985:127–228), there are few if any songs. Napi himself is not presented as singer. Nor indeed are heroes of the second rank, Blood-Clot Boy or Scar-Face, heroes who made epic journeys in quests to sun, moon, and stars for important concepts and rituals in Blackfoot culture. Rather, in the myths the singers are most frequently figures who make contact with those human beings who can in some sense be regarded as members of the Blackfoot tribe. To be sure, Napi, Scar-Face and Blood-Clot Boy are felt by the Blackfoot to be very close to them in spirit, but their activities and the era in which they worked are distant from the present. Napi, after all, made mountains; Scar-Face visited the sun and morning star. They are superhuman.

But humans themselves also have roles in myths. This is surely the case of the woman who heard a rock singing and called her husband to point out the strange phenomenon, thus acquiring a set of objects with power. The man who gives all of his animal and bird skins to the beaver in return for the supernatural power and songs of the beaver medicine ritual is presented as an excellent, but human, hunter, and a particularly humane person because he does not punish his wife after her affair. As noted, the singing is almost always done by supernatural figures, particularly animals, but the recipients are ordinary persons. Occasionally in myths, and often in the associated rituals, humans in turn sing to the supernatural figures. Napi, Morning Star, Old Woman (Napi's prototypical wife), and other major figures in the mythology are frequently mentioned or addressed in the ritual songs, as, for example, the sixty-six song texts of the *Natóas* (Sun Dance) bundle ceremony (Wissler 1912a:215–19). Songs are a way in which supernatural figures communicate with humans, but the more remote the figure or myth from humanity, the less singing is involved. One might suggest that in the myths, music is a kind of measure of being human.

I tried to engage one of my elderly male consultants in a conversation regarding the hypothetical existence of songs in the lives of supernatural figures. The questions were of a sort about which he had obviously not thought, and he was a bit startled by the ideas I suggested. I paraphrase slightly.

I asked: "If you imagine the way people used to think about Napi, do you think they felt that he sang songs, that he knew a lot of songs?"

"Well, I don't know. I guess maybe not. Those oldtimers, they knew a lot of stories about Napi, but they didn't think anything about those stories, they just told the stories when they were supposed to."

"But do you think Napi knew songs?"

He laughed: "No, he didn't have anybody to sing them to."

"Weren't there some spirits that could sing songs to Napi?"

"That's a real dumb question. Only people have dreams with songs in them. Not even most people."

I tried it on another man. He replied: "Don't make jokes about those old songs. People used to say those songs very holy. Still are."

It is hard to figure out what kind of a musical persona Napi may have had in the minds of the old-timers. But I continued, "What do you mean by saying the songs are holy?"

"Only supposed to be sung at the right times, I guess. They have power. People get power from the songs."

I asked about the way songs have power.

"If a man sings the right song, he can do anything. Doctor people, get rich, run like wind."

"But how do you know you are singing the right song?"

"Learn from old chiefs. They knew. If I want to do that pipe medicine, open that pipe [bundle], I got to sing the right songs."

"Now, I know the medicine pipe is very powerful. When you open it, when people used to open it, and sang the songs, and danced, and said the prayers, was it the pipe that was powerful, or the songs, or the prayers?"

"All the same. But if you sing that song, without you open the pipe, sometimes something bad might happen. Must be those songs were powerful, used to say they have medicine."

"But if you say the song is powerful, how about if I sing that kind of song, would that song help me?"

"Yeah, it might; no, I don't know. Better if I sing it. I don't have a pipe, but my uncle, he used to. You want me to make you a pipe? Maybe you could learn Indian medicine." He grinned.

The matter of the actual power of songs was one that I also broached to others. A younger man had a more rationalist view: "Songs, they've got no power, it's only what people think."

I replied: "Sure, but what did the Blackfoot people think in the old days? Do you know anything about that?

"I guess they figured if they did those rituals and did them right, like with all the songs, dancing, smoking, looking at those things and the pipe, they had medicine [power]. If you don't do all the things right together, it wouldn't work. Had to have those songs together with everything else."

"Did they sometimes just sing songs without doing anything with them, to get power?"

"No."

And a fourth man, on the same subject, said, "We used to have a lot of songs, but the real, true songs, they all came to us in dreams." This accords, of course, with the way Wissler's consultant (1912a:263) put it.

But my consultant continued: "These songs, they used to be powerful, had what you call medicine, people use them like religion."

"Did the songs have power? Or was it the things you did with the songs?"

"Oh, it was mainly the songs. Somebody had a dream, heard an animal sing, those songs had power."

I asked whether it was the complex of ceremonial actions or the song itself that had power.

"A song could have power. Not like white music. Indian songs had power; but you had to sing them right, and at the right time." But he added, "He didn't dance. Song had no medicine . . . those old men knew the ceremonies, what you had to do when you sang a song." As to the question of the innate power of songs, then, people differed, some assigning songs a role of inherent power, but some feeling that this power was closely associated with the actions that they accompanied and that perhaps the power was manifested only when the song was sung in the proper cultural and ritual context.

These attitudes, present in the late twentieth century and interpreting earlier beliefs, contrast with something else that is often also expressed by residents of Browning in the 1980s: that the old beliefs of the forefathers were quaint, have a historical interest in today's Blackfoot culture, but should not be taken seriously in themselves. Thinking about these things in the abstract was evidently not easy for my own consultants. A characteristic attitude was probably expressed by one woman: "You sure have a lot of funny questions about those songs."

4.   MEDICINE SONGS AND WORDS

It has been established that supernatural power resided in songs, in the act of singing, and in the specifically musical aspects of song. But the words of Blackfoot songs are also important bearers of supernatural power and of messages from the supernatural and are thus significant to an understanding of music as mediator between human and supernatural societies. We turn here briefly to a consideration of religious song texts, supplementing the discussion of the general nature of words in song in chapter 2.

What are the ceremonial songs about? The largest body of text appears in English translation in the early collections of myths and in the descriptions of Medicine Pipe ceremonies, and it may be difficult to gauge precisely how and where within the tune they appeared, especially as there is considerable variety in the lengths of these texts. It is of considerable interest to note their subject matter, narrator, and mood and particularly the fact that they include songs sung by supernatural beings to humans and by humans to the supernatural.

Several kinds of religious text can be distinguished. Some of the songs in medicine bundles address the objects that are being taken out of the bundle. In Wissler's description of the beaver ceremony, the director of the ritual held up a bag that contained two pieces of rawhide and sang,

> It is summer. Let others see you. (Wissler 1912a:179)

In some of the songs, the narrator actually describes the ritual. Thus, in the beaver ceremony:

> It is powerful, this grass, take some of it. I use it for a sacred purpose. (1912a:186)

There are more instances, however, in which actions in a ritual are described, but in terms of instructions from a supernatural figure. Again, in the beaver ritual:

> I am the morning star. Let us have a sweathouse. It is powerful. (1912a: 178)
> The above, he gave me tobacco seed, I have dropped them.
> It is powerful. This here, the earth, he gave me tobacco leaves. It is powerful. (1912a: 189)

The supernatural figures themselves speak in the song texts, indicating actions or stating desires from the myths. Another song from the beaver ritual:

> Old Man, he says, black and white horses, I want them.
> Old Woman, she says, black coyote and white coyote, I want them. Give them to me. (1912a: 188)

Most important in song texts are statements to the effect that what is being done is "powerful," that the act has supernatural power. Over and over, in the words of the rituals, one hears the refrain, "it is powerful." It is this, along with what informants tell and what we can learn from observation, that supports the concept of supernatural power as something that is conferred by song. Thus, in the Sun Dance bundle ceremony, we hear, in three separate songs:

> My necklace, I have taken it. It is powerful.
> Elk are running about; it is powerful.
> The earth is my medicine. It is powerful. (1912a: 218)

Certain songs that appear in myths and are sung by the narrator at appropriate times are the words of characters in the stories. Often they are used in a dramatic way to announce the appearance of a character or to assert a central truth. In the Wissler and Duvall account of the origin myth of the Buffalo Rock Medicine bundle (1909:85–87), a woman hears some singing that is eventually crystallized into a song with the words:

> Yonder woman, you must take me; Yonder woman, you must hear me. It is powerful.

It turns out to be the singing of a rock which reveals itself as having supernatural power by its next song:

> A buffalo rock, I am looking for the place where he is sitting.
> Now I have found him. He is powerful. A buffalo rock, now I have taken him up. He is powerful.

The rock is singing, but in fact the song's narrator appears to be the woman who has taken up the rock. Later, the sacredness of kidney fat in the ceremony is annunciated in three songs sung by the woman in the myth:

> This man says, kidney fat, I want to eat it.

Later:

> Woman says, kidney fat, I want to eat it.

And again,

> I want them to fall [reference is to a buffalo-run where they were to be hunted]. Kidney fat, I want to eat it.

This final song, also sung by the woman in the myth to her husband, reaffirms the sacredness of the Buffalo Rock, and associates it with successful buffalo hunts. The rock first appears by singing, its sacredness is revealed in song, the sacredness of the kidney fat, and the association of the ceremony with buffalo hunting are all explained in the song, more explicitly than is done in the narration itself. The interrelationship of characters, acts, and sacred objects is made clear only in the song texts. In ritual and myth, the songs and their words put the stamp of sacredness on ceremonial objects and on acts of humans and characters in the narration.

5.   MUSIC AND THE HEROIC

In earlier Blackfoot times, much music was associated with behavior and events that can impressionistically be united in the concept of the heroic. The association has not totally disappeared in contemporary Blackfoot culture. The combination of several types of situations under this rubric is at best suggestive, but I hope I can convince the reader. For purposes of definition, we associate the concept of hero with ideas of courage, exposure to risk, isolation, and example. A hero may risk life and reputation, work alone, and instruct by stellar example. It is a concept important in Blackfoot ideology. Counting coup, exposing oneself to risk in war parties, and going on long quests loom large in ethnography and folklore.

Individualism in general underscores the importance of heroism. The Blackfoot want to admire older men for their individual accomplishments. Mythology stresses the heroic deeds of those who made Blackfoot culture what it came to be, and contemporary rhetoric about the recent history of the Blackfoot often revolves about the outstanding and difficult accomplishments of individuals.

Singing partakes of this heroic stance in several ways. Acts of heroism are remembered and, in older times, were represented in song, as men returning from war parties sang about their exploits at the Scalp Dance (Wissler 1912a:266). There is also the quality of heroism as itself transmitted in song. Mythological characters, at moments of great significance or stress, communicate by singing or are given, in high drama, the opportunity to hear songs sung by supernatural figures. The vision quest, itself a heroic act of self-denial as the seeker faces stress and the uncertainties of the natural and supernatural world, is validated by songs.

The insistence of music as something special that is at once intrinsically part of, but also not quite part of, the rest of culture reflects the concept of the hero as a part of, but also somehow outside, ordinary society. The Blackfoot men who are most respected—heroes in warfare and medicine men with many visions and much power—were also distinguished by having many songs. Becoming active in a singing group has recently been a means of raising one's status (McFee 1972:117). A down-and-out person with no supernatural power would not, I was told, have known a lot of songs. The musician who is an outcast of society, essential but barely tolerated, an archetypal character in society and folklore of Europe, Asia, and Africa, is not a Blackfoot phenomenon.

To a Western listener, the style of singing may well suggest the heroic. Whether it also does this in Blackfoot thought is certainly not clear, but there is at least a bit of evidence to support the suggestion. Take the way in which modern Blackfoot people compare Western and Indian music, holding them separate. Western music is the object of discussion very much like other domains of life, as older people speak in approving, disapproving, or casual tones about rock and country music, and younger people make no distinction between Indian and white rock groups. People make jokes about singers and songs of white music. But with few exceptions, however, I found the tone in which Indian music was discussed to be different; it was a serious matter, and there was no question of approving or disapproving it. In conversation, as in behavior, it was treated as something special. Association with heroic deeds, isolation from other domains and musics, use in teaching the values of the culture, all this leads us to conclude that, in the Blackfoot view of things, music and particularly Blackfoot music is part of the heroic side of life.

The concept of heroism is readily associated with politics and warfare, and music is important in both of these domains in cultures around the world. For example, in the culture of the Venda of South Africa (Blacking 1965), music plays a major role in delineating and symbolizing echelons of political power and responsibility, and in some tribal societies, singing, music, and other artificial sounds played a significant part in warfare (Densmore 1918:332–74; Berliner 1978:27; Merriam 1967:79–113). In Blackfoot culture, songs played a prominent role in warfare but a much smaller part in political life. In Blackfoot tradition, there are two distinct forms of warfare: the tribal or subtribal, whose purpose was subjugation of an enemy tribe, preservation of land, or access to natural resources, and the individual or small group war party whose main (though not always exclusive) purpose was to exhibit courage by exposing oneself to danger, to acquire supernatural power, for acquisition of social status, and importantly to learn courage and exposure to risk.

While they may have used the same repertory, each of the two forms of warfare seems to have had a number of separate uses of music (see Ewers 1958:137, 139, 143; Wissler 1912a:267, 270). There was ceremonial music whose purpose was to ensure supernatural help for the warriors but equally to provide punctuation for the beginning of a major event. For example, a war party began its journey after ceremonially riding around the camp singing songs. A second use of music involves songs that were sung by individuals at moments of great danger or impending death, songs that could not be transferred through gift or sale but were the ones that were to be used only by the proper individual owner. Upon returning, warriors would sing songs in which they recounted their deeds, and women sang songs of mourning, a type now known only from occasional verbal references (Ewers 1958:108). The important themes in war of any sort—departure to something unknown, danger, heroism, celebration of deeds, mourning of losses—all these had their special representation in music.

True warfare, other than service in the U.S. armed forces during the various wars of the twentieth century, has of course long been removed from the life of the Blackfoot. It goes without saying that their Western lifestyle, their Christian orientation, the association of tribes in a pan-Indian culture, as well as the aura of U.S. patriotism often present in reservation life all militate against tribal conflict. Yet some of the uses of music in traditional warfare have their descendant forms. The ceremonial departure of the warriors to war is reflected at powwows, particularly North American Indian Days, in the grand entries of dancers to the singing of special songs, in the presentation of military formations on the part of an honor guard of members of the American Legion, and in the formation of the tribal leadership at such occasions; all of these are always accompanied by specifically Indian songs.

The war songs to be sung only at times of great danger or crisis may no longer be widely extant. Two consultants, however, told me that they had received songs from relatives, songs that they were to sing only when they were very ill or on their deathbeds, and that they were saving these songs for such times. They were unwilling to sing or discuss with me the details of these songs. A third group of war songs, those sung upon return of a war party and referred to as "scalp dance songs" in the literature, have also largely disappeared, though a few may still be present.

Tom Many-Guns in 1951 sang for me several songs said to have been sung by young men at the departure of a war party. Characteristic of these is a song with the words:

> Woman, don't worry about me; I'm coming back home, coming back
> home to pick berries.

The concept of picking berries is a symbol of the good life, of a calm, successful existence. Tom Many-Guns also spoke of songs that had been sung by women while their men were busy at war, and sang two of them. They appear to have lived largely in the memory of older persons in the period since 1950, and they may be a remnant without modern counterpart. But some of the songs that are now labeled as love songs, sometimes with humorous texts, sung at powwows to accompany social dances, may conceivably be interpreted as modern forms of those songs of the war complex that mainly concerned the relationship of men and women.

A particular sort of mourning song may be heard in public at North American Indian Days. They commemorate individuals who had passed away in the previous year and are sung at special times designated by the master of ceremonies. At such a point, one of these songs, slow and stately, is sung by one of the attendant singing groups while the bereaved extended family walks slowly but rhythmically around the dance ground, holding a picture of the deceased up for all to see. All together, while the North American Indian Days ceremony can be viewed as a descendant of the Sun Dance, it can also be interpreted as a descendant of ceremonies surrounding the warfare of earlier times. The war complex is one domain of culture whose songs span much of the spectrum of the tribal repertory. Significantly, a domain of culture no longer really functional may nevertheless live on in its ceremonial and symbolic aspects.

If music is an integral aspect of warfare, it is a far less significant component of its peaceful counterpart, political life. In earlier times, political matters seem to have been handled in an informal fashion, contrary to the formality and ritual surrounding warfare (Ewers 1958:96–98). For example, there was little in the way of ranking of individuals or families in political terms. To the extent that individual chiefs exercised political power, it was not by heredity or election but rather by some kind of public consensus, and there appear to have been no ceremonies or rituals that involved the elevation of someone to a position of chief. There were no true social or political classes. Certain families, bands, or men's societies had greater influence than others, but this was a matter of informal and probably temporary recognition. When, in the nineteenth century, certain individuals became unprecedentedly wealthy through hunting, trading, or acquisition of horses, the wealth was supposed to be shared, and someone who gave away what he owned to poorer people thereby acquired status and influence (Ewers 1948:96; McFee 1972:100–101). Such donations could take place at a special ceremony, and the "give-away dances" at modern powwows are probably relics of the practice. But in general, it seems that the Blackfoot did not develop musical rituals to accompany political events.

The absence of a body of music that accompanies the concept of tribal or other political leadership contradicts the model I have suggested that each activity has its appropriate songs. The informal attitude taken toward political matters may lead us to an explanation. In certain ways, the Sun Dance was a tribal act for tribal benefit, with certain political overtones. But on the other hand, chiefs were simply respected older men.

The domain of politics and leadership had quite a bit to do with economic matters. Wealth provided influence, and political leadership had to do with who owned what—individual, family, band, and the tribe in relation to other tribes and to the whites. But again, there is no evidence of a body of songs involving buying, selling, or trading, although songs themselves could be bought or traded.

If music was more important in warfare than in political and economic life, this may have to do with the greater formality of warfare, its more essentially individual activity, its heroic aspects, and its role in relating the Blackfoot to non-Blackfoot beings, human and supernatural. It does not play an important role in the intracultural domains of economics and politics, for it is in a certain sense outside the culture, kept separate, and reserved for occasions when weighty tribal matters or the relationship to the supernatural must be symbolized. It is an essential component of the heroic side of Blackfoot life and thought.

6. OWNERSHIP AND CONTROL

Control of music in creation and performance was and to a degree still is largely vested in individuals. In earlier Blackfoot history, there was evidently an elaborate system of ownership, theoretically recognized but evidently not fully observed in practice. It was first described by Wissler (1912a:265), who presents three classes of ownership which have already been mentioned in other contexts in this study. Considering the kinds of ethnographic information ordinarily provided by ethnomusicologists at the time, one marvels at Wissler's and Duvall's sophistication and powers of observation, their ability to search out interesting and easily neglected facts about a musical culture. Or perhaps this system of ownership of songs was something that the principal Blackfoot consultant emphasized far more than would have been the case in 1980. In any event, the fact that Wissler's rather brief description of Blackfoot musical culture makes quite a bit of this aspect of musical life must be noted; ownership is stressed beyond everything except the association of music and songs with activities and rituals. Given the limited data, one might be inclined to consider ownership to be one of the things to which Blackfoot people themselves gave considerable attention. Wissler's Blackfoot collaborator Duvall (Wissler 1912a:265–71) was able to list eight to ten song types (by use or accompanying activity) that belong to each class of ownership.

Let me recapitulate the three types of ownership: (1) songs that belong to the tribe at large and thus to be performed by anyone more or less at any time; (2) songs that are owned by individuals but may be transferred, i.e., shared with others, given, sold; and (3) songs owned by individuals but not transferable. Among the tribally owned songs, Duvall includes largely those that are performed by groups, that is, general songs of the Sun Dance, dances for social dances. Among the individual but transferable songs are songs of most of the medicine ceremonies. The nontransferable songs include those to be sung at times of great crisis. It is significant that each class is not congruent with a broader type of use or context, i.e., medicine bundles, Sun Dance, age-grade society. For some of the contexts of music there is more than one class of ownership, depending on specific use, origins, and value. There is correlation between transferability, value, and supernatural power: the nontransferable songs have the greatest power and are most valued.

I tried to discuss song ownership and the resulting implications in some detail with three of my older consultants, and now paraphrase some conversations. Yes, P.S. said, he thought people in his youth (1910s) were a good bit concerned with these matters. Owning songs was almost as good as owning horses, one could buy and sell them like horses. However, there wasn't a lot of selling, people used to give songs away as gifts. Why, I wanted to know? Maybe because the Blackfoot people were poor and didn't have other kinds of gifts. But, I asked, what did it mean to own a song? If you own a headdress, you can hold it, store it, wear it, throw it away, do anything you want, isn't that so? Well, you can't do just anything with a headdress either, people would get angry if you threw it away. Well, how about a gun? I see what you mean, he said, a song was more like a headdress, it belonged to a person but also in a way it belonged to the tribe. But a man knew that a song belonged to him, and he could sell it, give it to somebody, often give a song to a good friend, a son, nephew. Could you give it to a woman? Oh, sometimes, but that was more like a joke.

I asked related questions in a conversation with C., a middle-aged man who told me the story of his life. In the old days, could you sing songs that belonged to other men? Did everybody know that a particular song belonged to a person? What does it really mean when you say that *this* song is yours? I received interesting insights. He referred to songs as belonging to himself and did so more or less in equal terms for songs which he said he had "made" or "dreamed" and others that had been given to him by someone—his mother, a cousin, a friend. I asked him about his singing of songs that didn't belong to him. Many of them, he said, belonged to everyone, to the tribe. And some belonged to others, but they had given him permission to sing them. But it is possible that C. made more of this system than might other members of Blackfoot society in the 1960s. After all, a third man to whom I brought up this matter and who was generally cognizant and respectful of older traditions, referred to the idea that people owned songs as (a synonym of) hogwash, saying that as far as he knew, nobody paid attention to it, and everybody sang any song they wished, now and in earlier times. Interestingly, however, C. seemed to be describing, in his own time, a system similar to the one that had been described by Wissler.

What would happen today if a person sang a song that did not belong to him? Well, nothing really, according to C., but one wasn't supposed to do that. As he put it, it was no more than a breach of etiquette. Indeed, the description of ownership and transference in Wissler's time did not include punishments for singing songs one didn't own. Possibly this was viewed a bit like borrowing an object. Only in the Horse Medicine (Ewers 1955:274–75), a rather recent and short-lived medicine cult that combined medicine bundle procedures with elements of men's age-grade society rituals, was strict secrecy observed and the improper singing of songs said to result in supernatural punishments such as injury to the singer's horse.

The idea of individual ownership as it applies to religious objects in general may shed light on the question of song ownership. The belief that medicine bundles belong to individual owners, that they are principal components of cultural capital, that it is desirable to acquire but also to transfer bundles to others—all of this can be adapted to the concept of songs. Early ethnographers present the songs as the validation of the medicine bundles and therefore as important property, things of value. In tracing the continuity of this conception, paraphrase of a conversation with D. B. was enlightening.

"What does it mean to you to own songs, that you have your own songs?" The reply, somewhat edited: "It makes me feel very proud to be a Blackfoot. I have songs that belong to my tribe, but they are songs that I can give to somebody, or I can sing them, and everybody knows they belong to me, and if somebody else sings them, they know these are my songs."

G. K., who was present, commented that white songs probably don't belong to anybody. When I said that whites sometimes do keep track of who made a song, he said, "Yes, but that's not the same thing." And later: "It is very important for a Blackfoot to have songs, have their own songs. My uncle told me, you're not really a Blackfoot if you don't have your songs." This is probably a rather extreme statement of a view once widely held.

Ewers (1958:94–97) depicts Blackfoot society in the nineteenth century as essentially capitalist. Most goods were owned by individuals. It was important to accumulate goods, including those that were largely symbolic in value, such as horses and, as stated, objects with supernatural power, which you bought and sold. A wealthy person gave away things in order to be generous and to illustrate his prestige. Songs were treated as part and parcel of this economic system, and Wissler also speaks of the medicine bundle complex very much in terms of a capitalistic economy. Bundles, rituals, and associations with the supernatural are created in dreams, and it is then religious duty to make medicine bundles and to transfer these to others, somewhat like an investment (1912a:272). Evidently rituals and bundles were constantly being transferred, and thus, songs were constantly being taught. This may account for the common knowledge of the otherwise individually owned and individually known medicine songs. Contrary to Wissler, Ewers relates the transfer of bundles less to economic than to religious and enculturative functions. Just as "a man received his power . . . from a spirit helper, so he could transfer this power to some other human" (1958:163).

In the 1960s, people still gave songs, but I didn't hear of people selling. Singing for a fee and being a master of ceremonies who was paid for leading rituals (Hanks and Hanks 1950:78) may have replaced the selling of songs as a way of seeking remuneration for music. The reaction to the cultural impoverishment that characterized the late nineteenth century may have been to make more of the goods tribal property, material culture as well as entities such as ceremonies and songs. In my experience, singers in the 1960s considered the singing of songs for money to ethnomusicological collectors as something like a sale. When Blackfoot consultants imparted their musical culture to me, they did it mainly in terms of songs. I started the contact by recording songs; they were the centerpieces of discussion. When we talked about reimbursement, it was a price for each song, not for an amount of time, that was agreed upon. A couple of people jestingly suggested selling me their songs in the older sense of the concept, and one told me that I should now learn to sing them, that they would be helpful to me.

7. THE HUMOROUS SIDE

An interesting aspect of some of the figures in Blackfoot and other Plains mythology is their occasionally humorous character. Napi or Old Man, for example, is not only the culture hero who invents customs and rituals and creates mountains and rivers but also a trickster, buffoon, and the butt of pranks. The Blackfoot do not draw as sharp a line between the concepts of supernatural power and humor as do Europeans. The association helps to account for the existence of a repertory of humorous songs, or of songs that can be both taken seriously and considered jokes. As music, like mythology, has a generally sacred and otherworldly nature, the inclusion of funny passages in the sacred myths is paralleled by occasionally funny songs.

The humorous songs are melodically not distinct. An illustration is the considerable number of modern songs called "love songs" that have texts that appear funny to both Blackfoot and whites, texts usually in English. Some of the texts are associated with the intertribal Forty-Nine Dance and are widely distributed through the Plains, Southwest, and Oklahoma. They include the following widely known examples:

> If you wait for me after the dance is over, I will take you home in my purchased wagon.
> I don't care if you're married sixteen times, I will get you.
> My sweetheart, she got mad at me because I said hello to my old-timer.

Around 1900, too, some songs had their humorous side. Wissler (1912a:264) and McClintock (1910 [1968]:391) mention the fact that songs are or may be sung as jokes. The Mice Songs of children are funny, and the songs sung by mice in myths make other characters laugh. The well-known song about the killing of White Dog, the Sioux chief, although associated with the memory of a serious event, is regarded by some Blackfoot as funny.

Considering the fact that music is a weighty matter in Blackfoot culture, one may be surprised at the ease with which the Blackfoot switch attitudes about a song. I broached the issue with one informant; the reader will be painfully aware that in this interview I had difficulty eliciting the information.

"That song about being married sixteen times, is it a funny song?"
"Oh sure."
"When do you sing it?"
"Oh, any time we want to."
"Would you sing it when you are singing for North American Indian Days?"
"Yes, we usually do."
"How about last summer, when you people put on that Sun Dance?"
"Probably did, can't be sure."
"In the old days, do you think a medicine man would have sung a funny song like that when he opened his bundle?"
"It would be all right if he wanted to."
"Why would you sing a funny song when you're doing something serious like that?"
"Why not?"

"Does it have something to do with those funny stories about Napi?"
"Yeah, that's right."

For another example, hand game songs, which usually have no words but a distinct musical style, have a humorous side that seems to derive from the functions of this music. While gambling appears to have been regarded as serious business in earlier times, one function of the singing—so it is generally thought in the literature on American Indian music (Herzog 1935)—was prevention of laughter by the hiding team in order to help the players "keep a straight face." This function may still persist, but the singing exists for its own sake as well, that is, people play the hand game in part for gambling, but also in part in order to be able to sing the songs. An aura of humor surrounds the gambling songs. After completing a part of the game, when the hidden bones or bullets have been found and the song completed, people sometimes break into laughter. I assume this involves the release of tension upon completion of the gambling, but I also noted two or three occasions when singers, after singing a gambling song in special recording sessions, laughed a bit. Once I asked the man why he laughed. "That's a very special song, helps me to win," I was told. The supernatural element may have been present, and the relationship between supernatural power and humor was again established.

The Blackfoot world of the supernatural is importantly a reflection—idealized, to be sure—of human society, and as such it encompasses the many-sidedness of Blackfoot social behavior, fearful reverence as well as confrontation, the heavy and the light, sadness and humor.

On the previous pages I have argued that in Blackfoot culture, music functions principally as a mediator between the tribe and the outside, uniting the tribe by reflecting its culture and its most important social and religious divisions and by validating its actions; that it functions as a form of communication between humans and the supernatural, between the Blackfoot and other tribes or whites; and that it is a medium of communication that flows from the supernatural to the Blackfoot and from them on to other peoples. It may seem strange to the reader to find an interpretation of a Native American musical culture which deals with sacred and secular music virtually in the same breath. I certainly would maintain that the religious component of Blackfoot music is fundamental, but I wish also to argue that music is essentially a social phenomenon, and as such that it binds humans to the society of supernatural beings in much the way that it also ties together the society of the Blackfoot, and various societies of humans.

One question that follows from these considerations concerns the

Blackfoot conception of music as an independent force. Do the songs actually *do* things, or is it the humans, singing songs, that hold supernatural power? It seems to me that in the Blackfoot conception, songs themselves have power to accomplish. They have, as it were, a life of their own.

Two pieces of evidence support this conclusion. One is the rhetoric of the Blackfoot as they talk about songs, for they indeed say that songs "do" things. "This song used to help my mother get well," I was told. Or, "This song has power." And similarly, from one of the elderly tribal authorities: "Those old-timers, they used to have a lot of dreams, dreamed songs, and then they had those songs, and they used those songs. It was the songs that did everything." Unfortunately, I found it difficult to engage in further discussion of the last point; no wonder, it is all very abstract.

A second piece of supporting evidence concerns the large number of song texts that contain action. Few songs are merely contemplative, or descriptive, or state adoration or respect. Most of them describe some forceful action, often directing a singer or listener—or a figure in a myth—to do something. The idea of songs as a medium for giving directions to humans to act is an important aspect of myth and ritual. And in myths, it is often the songs that drive the action forward. This primary association with action, contrasting (for example) with large bodies of lyric song in some European folk music repertories, suggests that in Blackfoot conception, songs themselves have the power to act. Rather than being merely devices with which humans act, they are themselves actors, with a certain degree of independence, in the culture.

CHAPTER FIVE

Musicianship

1. TERMINOLOGY

Our attention so far has been directed principally to questions that are actually tangential to music as a system of sound. We have asked what the Blackfoot think music is and does, how it is related to the rest of culture and particularly to the society of humans and supernatural figures, how it comes about, and how it changes. We now turn to what most readers would probably call the *music itself* and ask what ideas the Blackfoot have about this sector of the musical spectrum.

Like everyone, the Blackfoot talk about music. What they say, the kinds of things they choose to talk about, and the context of the rhetoric inform us about the way they think about music. But all such thought is not necessarily expressed in speech, and thus consideration of music as sound and performance can supplement spoken rhetoric. In turn, we may be concerned about the way matters specifically concerning musical sound are addressed in speech, and so, we come to the question of technical terminology.

To provide a context for considering the Blackfoot musical vocabulary, let me again begin with the familiar world of European classical music, beginning with some observations about European and American encyclopedias of music, as these are the authorities on terminology. They go beyond simply telling the facts, also serving as indicators of styles of thought—including ways of dividing and designating the musical universe. For example, the prominence of certain kinds of entries shows us the importance of the special Western interest in composers and in persons associated with music. But what is the nature of the technical terminology of Western music and for what is it used?

First, it is very much involved with types of pieces, genres, and styles. To Western classical musicians, it is evidently important to separate kinds of music by audible style. An extension of this is the large number of designations of performance styles. Two large areas of Western terminology involve types of pieces, such as operas, oratorios, symphonies, sonatas, trios, quartets, and much more; and tempo or expressive indications, such as allegro, adagio, con brio, and the rest. Interestingly, there is not much terminology involving emotional effects and the matter of affect in general.

Second, terminology tends to be music-specific. The terms that are used—while ultimately derived from other domains of culture—are often used exclusively or principally in music. Thus, "symphony" and "sonata" are not terms borrowed from construction or architecture. But even more, there is—or more accurately, until recently there was—a tendency to use the Italian language for terminology. The reason often given involved the importance of Italy in the development of Western music, but that may not be a sufficient explanation, for after 1750, the great majority of the composers who are most admired are ethnically German. More important may have been a desire to have a separate language for music or at least for art music, to have a terminology that was *not* shared with other domains of culture. So in a way, in English-speaking cultures, musical terminology is music-specific. I could suggest several conceivable reasons: the prestige of nonfunctional art (or as it is often labeled, art for art's sake) or the desire of musicians to have a separate jargon, as expression of their occupational specialization, or even a certain ambivalence of Western culture toward music.

The study of vocabulary as index to musical culture has not been widely explored in ethnomusicology. Among the few relevant publications, a major contribution has been the glossary of Hausa terms by Ames and King (1971), in which a large number of terms, the great majority not specific to music, is presented and discussed in its musical context. For native American societies, Powers (1980) provides a more theoretical but less comprehensive study for Sioux culture. From these studies, it is evident that analytical study of musical vocabulary would tell us a lot about musical thought.

In the case of the Blackfoot, the technical terminology is not music-specific; it consists of terms from everyday life and from the ceremonies, consonant with the Blackfoot concept of music as something that reflects culture, and dissonant with the conception of music as somehow outside culture, looking across at it. Terms dealing with music involve several areas of musical knowledge. Most terms denote (1) instruments; (2) dances and song types; or (3) kinds of performance practice, involving drumming and singing. We make no attempt to provide a comprehensive list here. A complete lexicon would reflect the plethora of uses, and new terms could be devised easily by combining extant words in this highly agglutinative language. But the sample below gives some idea of the kinds of terms that are used:

Selection of Blackfoot Musical Terms.

Singing style:

nínixksini—song
itominíxki—leader of song, introduction of song, also good singer
itomó—leader, first
éspinakki—second singer, second part of song, raises (term used to indicate repetition of first musical line of a song)
ixkane' íxkyan—all sing, main part of song

Song Functions:

káxtsin—game, gambling
kaxtsínsksin—gambling song
akipáskan—Round Dance, or a type of dance known as Women's Dance
piksepásaan—Grass Dance song
natoosítsksin or *natoiinaisini*—sacred song, supernatural power of "medicine"
natóas—sacred
nínsksini—song

Instruments:

istókimaacis—drum
ikinestókkimaya—drumming on rim
sipistwe' istókkiman—Owl Dance drum (alternation of long and short beats, used in Owl Dance as well as certain other songs)
nyinemskapáskan—Chief Maker Dance (designation for a drum roll performed before a song)
auaná—rattle
natóanaa—medicine rattle

These terms were given to me by my consultants and transcribed by me, but they may be found (with some variant orthography) in Uhlenbeck and van Gulick (1930) as well. They give insight into conceptions and attitudes. For example, the notion that the repetition of the first phrase of a song by a second singer, following the song leader, is symbolized by the concept of "raising" is suggestive. I tried to explore the reason for this but received only one reply, and it seemed contrived to me, involving the characteristic melodic descent of the ensuing section. "You have to be raised high before you can go down like that," I was told. There may be a conceptual relationship of repetition to upward motion; in the powwow culture, repetitions of a song are sometimes referred to (in English) as "push-ups," and a song with four "stanzas" is said to have four push-ups. The concepts of high and low pitch were also translated in Blackfoot rhetoric into strength and weakness (well, lesser strength, not outright weakness). A man singing high was singing "strong."

Considering the primacy of vocal music, it is interesting to compare the large amount of terminology about drumming with the relatively smaller amount that deals with singing. The fact that musical differences are minor and not what distinguished instruments from each other is recognized in the terminology, which names instruments not by their shape, sound, and playing technique but by the activity which they accompany.

Terminological differences between earlier and recent times may help to illuminate changes in attitude. Some musical terminology came about as part of the intertribal powwow culture. As described by Hatton (1974:131–33), a variety of musical styles and repertories has developed in the Plains area, the differences among them largely in performance practice. And this is something about which the Blackfoot do speak, largely in English, and there are many terms involving drumming. At the same time, the earlier ethnographies seem to indicate very little in the way of terminology. Singing was then considered mainly a solo or individual activity, and while we know from McClintock and Wissler that it was also carried out by groups, the technical aspects of ensemble performance seem to have been little discussed.

The discrepancy between term and fact is a matter of interest. There seems to have been a tendency to change terminology frequently. Take the songs accompanying a particular social dance type. Its style of dance and music have remained, but the name has changed from "Wolf Song," which seems to have gone out of existence decades ago, to "Grass Dance," which continues but has declined in the last thirty years, further to the same kind of social dance often called "War Dance," for which the term "Intertribal" has recently also been substituted. For a possible reason, we may look to the importance of a hard and fast theoretical system that does not necessarily conform to life, but whose firmness is symbolically important. One thing may have a number of names, just as one set of songs may actually be found in a number of officially discrete ceremonies. The conception that one thing may have a number of designations is consonant with the idea that the form of a song can be conceived of in three ways, as has been described several times above.

The relationship between individual identity and unique form seems in general to be different in Blackfoot thinking than in Western tradition. Two songs may sound alike but have different origins and thus in a sense different identities, and two or three terms may be applied to the same genre without conflict. So, if one is told once that a song is a Grass Dance and, on another occasion, a War Dance, and the conflict is sloughed off, this may refer to a traditional way of correlating terminology and fact rather than simply to culture loss, ignorance, or carelessness.

The greater use of technical musical terminology now than in earlier times, as described in the ethnographies around 1900, may also relate to changing functions. If songs once came ready-made from the supernatural and were above criticism, they may have required little technical discussion. The later use of music principally for social dances and as entertainment for listeners, as well as the competitive aspects of the powwow culture, may all have contributed to increasing discussion of singing and drumming. There may have been a marginal effect of the Blackfoot conception of Western music as something complicated, to be learned, with a lot of technical paraphernalia such as notation. While the Blackfoot distinction between Indian and white music concentrates the much greater emphasis on techniques in white music, there may well have arisen a Blackfoot belief that Indian music could best survive if it became competitive in a technical sense with white music.

Providing interesting comparisons of white and Indian music in Blood Indian thought, Witmer indicates (1982:99) that 46 percent of the Indian homes he visited in 1968 had audio equipment of some sort. In the 1980s, twenty years later, one would have found an even larger percentage of such homes. It is interesting to see that a rather sharp distinction was made by the Blood between Indian and white music, that Indians themselves distinguished categories such as older ("ceremonial") songs, Grass and Chicken Dance, country and western, and rock music (Witmer 1982:22); and at the same time, that the modern genres of both Indian and white music tend to undergo similar kinds of treatment, evaluation, and certain performance techniques. Thus, the modern Indian material is in the hands of a small group of quasi professionals who make and perform songs, compete for fame and money, make records, and are known for producing "hits," much like Indian performers of white music in the popular sphere. McFee (1972:117) points out that being active in a Blackfoot (i.e., Indian music) singing group is a means of raising one's status. While the repertory of ceremonial Indian songs is theoretically thought to be open to addition through composition in visions, Witmer points out that little has been added to this repertory for many years, and that it is a closed corpus, somewhat like the repertory of Western "ceremonial," i.e., church, music.

2. MUSICAL FORM AND FUNCTION

We have had several occasions to mention the close relationship of the concepts of learning and composition, the resulting importance of song learning as a single, one-time, undivided experience, and the resulting belief that a song can be learned in one hearing. The forms of the songs support this conceptualization. There is a tendency for Blackfoot songs and for Plains Indian songs generally to be highly concentrated, to consist of a small number of components, and to present its basic stuff quickly, near the beginning, after which there is little additional material. This high degree of stylistic consistency makes it possible for a singer, once he or she has learned the beginning, to predict rather easily what else will happen in a song.

As far as I know, Blackfoot people don't talk about the forms of the songs in detail or at least in these terms. The three seemingly conflicting Blackfoot descriptions of the same song which I mentioned in chapter 1, section 4 illustrate the limits of analytical discussion in my experience (but for other Plains peoples, see also Hatton 1974; Powers 1980). One consultant said the song was sung through, and then repeated, in part. Another said it consisted of four parts, two short and two long, while a third said it had a beginning, middle, and end.

These three interpretations of what has in the literature been called the "incomplete repetition" form provide emphasis on three aspects of the form and thus tell us important but also conflicting things about the perception of songs. The third interpretation may tell us that the head motif, the descending line, and the final, low section which is often an octave transposition of the first are perceived as radically different sections. At least the emphatic statement to the effect that there are discrete beginnings, middles, and endings suggests this. At the same time, the "incomplete repetition" interpretation may distinguish these songs from others also known to the Blackfoot, as the form is certainly highly separate from that of hymns or popular songs. More important, the placement of verbal text, when there is one, at the beginning of the second main section provides a logical point of division, and it is significant that the Blackfoot sometimes emphasize it. The statement that a song is divided into four parts tells us, as does much in mythology and ritual, about the importance of the number four in Blackfoot ceremonial life, but it also shows that in looking at song structure, the Blackfoot do not consider equality of length (and perhaps symmetry) an issue.

In order for the units of music, the songs, to maintain themselves in oral tradition, a certain degree of unity must be maintained as a mnemonic device. Oral tradition may carry materials of great complexity in controlled fashion, but the limits to human memory do create a difference in essence between orally transmitted and notated repertories (see Treitler 1974:344–46). Among repertories orally transmitted, the Plains style would still have to stand out for its strong set of unifying devices and for the ability of its composers to create variety within a set of constraints that require most of the thematic material of a song to be presented right at the beginning. For example, in the "incomplete repetition" form, the beginning, a kind of head motif, is actually the principal theme of the song, sung by the leader, repeated by a second singer. Its beginning is also often the starting point of the next descending section and often repeated as cadence in a somewhat transformed version, an octave lower. The scales rarely have more than five tones (plus octaves), and the identity of tones separated by an octave is suggested by the use of the same motif octaves apart. Emphasis is often placed on the tones of a triad, and tonic, fourth, fifth, and octave degrees are intoned with a greater degree of consistency than other intervals.

In the case of gambling songs, the form is simple and equally unified. Two phrases may alternate, or several short phrases are united by an isorhythmic structure. In the medicine bundle repertory, too, melodies are brief, have small ranges, and tend to appear in groups that seem to be variants of the same tune. Here, as well, the head motif seems to be the most important aspect of the tune. In all of these respects, while there are thousands of songs, each with distinct melody, a great majority seem to have characteristics that make them easy to learn and to remember, once the beginning has been memorized. There seems to be consistency between the details of form and the conception of a song as an indivisible unit capable of being learned quickly.

But do or did people really learn songs quickly? There is no reason to think so today, and indeed, some of my consultants made fun of the discrepancy between that theory and the well-known practice of bringing cassette recorders to powwows and then playing the tapes repeatedly for the purpose of learning. But some older persons, speaking more seriously, told me that they believed people once had greater capacities for learning quickly, and in general for retaining material such as songs. This is one way in which they see the present as different from the past.

A complex of ideas, quick learning, the notion that a song is indivisible, and the relationship of all this to the vision quest is contrasted to modern life, in which people make up new songs, even from extant ones, or by singing the first half of one and the second half of another, all resulting in a greater lack of thematic concentration in the forms and thus the need to learn songs more slowly. But of course the supposed demise of the fast-learning ability may also be interpreted as related to the Blackfoot perception of major cultural changes, away from a time of purity in Indian life and culture which was unsullied by Western inventions such as literacy, and its disturbance of the oral tradition. At least this is my interpretation of a variety of reactions to such questions. At the same time, the actual increase in the use of the standardized "incomplete-repetition" form as a way of reducing the ingredients of the musical culture must be mentioned as a survival strategy.

The nature of practice sessions is relevant. Rehearsing is said to have been more important in earlier times than in the 1960s, but both earlier and recently, rehearsal sessions consisted of brief runs-through of familiar songs. Western customs such as stopping in the middle of a song to repeat one phrase seemed to be foreign, and songs were always sung completely, sometimes after a single soft run-through by the song leader. Learning new songs seems to have been handled in the same way. But there is some recent evidence of an increase in rehearsal time and emphasis on rehearsing, and in the adoption of more analytic discussion in rehearsal.

The custom of singing simply for the pleasure of making music seems to be a recent introduction, but it has become widespread. Events related to rehearsals are private house party "singsings," one of which is described in detail by Witmer (1982:34–36). An event of this sort that I attended in Starr School conformed to Witmer's description, but it is difficult to be sure about the degree to which it was representative, as it seemed to have been staged partly for my benefit. The singing was done in the fashion of powwow performances, but there were major differences, such as the participation of women and children in the singing. In the 1960s and 1980s, the concept of performance, and the belief that there are different degrees of formality in performance—rehearsal, house party or "singsing," powwow, and possibly beyond that, ceremony—seemed to play a role. Degree of formality correlated with presence of certain elements in performance practice and with the inclusion or exclusion of particular groups of individuals. I was able to find out hardly anything about this kind of music making in earlier times.

The difference between earlier and present is evident in most aspects of Blackfoot life, but I have been concerned here to show that in some respects, there are not only these differences but also continuities in culture, musical thought, and life. The ideas about the technical aspects of song are one area in which the Blackfoot make a major distinction between earlier and recent, the general continuity of musical style notwithstanding.

The change from supernatural to human sources of music is symbolic of the contrast between a past dominated by relationships to the supernatural and a present in which relationship to human groups is essential.

3.   ENSEMBLES AND DRUMMING

Older Blackfoot consultants told me that they thought solo singing predominated over group singing in earlier times. In any event, while early ethnographies mention group singing, its musical structure is not described. And early recordings are largely of singing by individuals. For some understanding of the concept of group musicianship, we must therefore turn to the ensembles or singing groups of recent decades. Here, the Blackfoot share characteristics and practices with the Plains culture at large and with the modern intertribal institution of the powwow, but we can also relate the Blackfoot practices to the characteristics of Blackfoot culture.

In this respect, the importance of the extended family as the nucleus of singing groups or "drums," which I noted earlier, is also mentioned in literature and appears in designations of groups that have made recordings. This as well as the tendency for a singing group to be associated with a particular village or community seems to be a continuation of the importance of families and bands as units in earlier social life. But equally significant is the avoidance of making such associations the exclusive criteria of membership in a group, as social life in earlier times seems indeed to have been regulated by family and band but without great formality or strict adherence to rules.

Authority within the singing groups today reflects what may have been important in earlier social life. The titular leaders of groups are older men who are respected for their accomplishments as singers but also for their general experience in life and their knowledge of tribal traditions. Leadership today sometimes involves little beyond administrative duties of a sort, getting singers to assemble, passing out the drumsticks to them. Some singing groups are named in honor of the senior member, but actual leadership in organization and in the singing devolves upon others. In rehearsal and performance, various members of a group take turns in leading songs, that is, determining what song will be sung and singing the first line, after which others join in, notwithstanding the theory that charismatic leadership is the mark of a good singer.

Witmer (1982:33) interestingly points out that in one group, or drum, which he investigated, three singers, closely related, provided the central musical components—they were composer, lead singer, and second leader;

other singers who joined the group simply duplicated what was already being done. But in other drums, all members participated in leading songs, alternating in a not very systematic manner. In the structure and behavior of these ensembles, one can see replication of the social and political structure of earlier times, suggesting that for the Blackfoot, musical activity provides a way of recalling and preserving older concepts, even in the modern components of the "Indian" part of the Blackfoot musical culture.

The early ethnographic literature and older consultants tell of the prevailingly solo character of singing and performance at large in medicine bundle ceremonies. Yet today, on the rare occasions when medicine bundles are opened, this takes place in ceremonies at which several people sing, dance, and otherwise participate in a performance for which there is also a substantial audience. The Horse Medicine, one of the few rites that appears to have been established in the nineteenth century, described by Ewers (1955:263–70) in detail, was a ceremony in which a number of singers and dancers performed for a large audience of members of the cult.

Contrasting substantially with the older medicine rituals, the Horse Medicine seems to have combined the characteristics of the bundle and tipi ceremonies with those of age-grade societies. While its structure was rather like that of the Beaver and Medicine Pipe ceremonies, its secret character and the restriction to cult members associates it with the age-grade society rituals, but its tendency to have a number of participants can also be related to more recent developments in the practices of older medicine bundle ceremonies, in which the number of participants seems lately also to have increased. Literature and consultants suggest that this resulted from the imperfect knowledge of the ceremony by any one person, due to which a structure would have been developed in which several could contribute. The increased number of participants may also have been supported by the tendency to have group performances of the ceremonial music of Christian worship, and by the general importance of the ensemble in Western musical culture. The significance of the ceremonies in conveying a sense of tribal identity, and the simultaneously declining importance of ceremonies as a way for the individual to communicate with the supernatural were no doubt further factors in the increased significance of ensemble singing. And also contributing may have been the increased use of music as entertainment.

Even so, accounts by three of my consultants as well as early ethnographies specify and imply that solo performance was the norm in most ceremonies, and the singers in early recordings were at least willing to perform alone for the cylinder machines. The attitude, also, survived at least in vestige while actual practice changed. The importance of song leading, the role of soloists in the ensemble, and the absence of a requirement for vocal blending in the group may be among its remnants.

The role and importance of drumming in Blackfoot music of earlier times cannot really be established. Wissler's consultant tells of the omnipresence of drumming and of the singers' proclivity always to be beating on something while singing (Wissler 1912a:264). Yet the technique is nowhere discussed. The role of drumming in modern Indian music is attested to everywhere, and there is much evidence of the care with which it is carried out. In the present Blackfoot musical culture, drumming and the beating of planks is the only kind of percussive accompaniment to singing; the use of rattles seems to have gone out of existence.

The use of drumming as a way of enhancing the interest of performance in the powwow repertory is interesting. In a typical rendition consisting of several repetitions that constitute the performance of a song, the singers often begin by softly and steadily beating the rim of the bass drum around which they sit. As the tempo is increased, the singers drum on the skin, and more loudly. Eventually, a group of "hard beats," loud strokes by an individual, sometimes the leader, may interrupt the ordinary flow of rhythm. In the final rendition, near the end of the stanza, the drummers may cease for the duration of a phrase or two, continuing once more, crescendo, at the very end. In earlier times, we are told, drumming sometimes ceased totally before the end, while female singers or young boys were permitted to finish the last phrase by themselves. All of this applies to Blackfoot music as well as that of the Plains in general. The drumming is characteristically carried out in excellent unison, somewhat off the vocal beat, and the relationship to the vocal rhythm is complex and difficult to analyze. The rhythmic structure of drumbeat and vocal pulse is often related roughly by the proportion of 2:3. It is possible, however, that a much more complex relationship, perhaps thus intended, is really at the root of the seeming disparity of the vocal and percussion rhythm (Pantaleoni 1987).

The rhythmic structure of plank beating by players in the stick game differs somewhat from drumming. There is less accurate blending of the percussive beat by the several players, but there is also a greater tendency than in powwow songs for percussion and vocal beats to coincide. In contrast to singing at social dances, in which each singer beats the drum and no one drums without singing, there may be several gamblers who only beat the plank but leave the singing to two or three players. Percussion in gambling songs is regarded as a less musical activity than is drumming in other kinds of singing.

"Do you have to be a drummer to sing in the stick game?"

"No."

"Just anybody can sing and beat time?"

"A person has to know some of the songs."

The importance of drumming in the performance practice of the modern social dances sung at intertribal powwows is also emphasized by Hatton (1974:129–33). In placing the Blackfoot together with the Crow, Flathead, Cheyenne, Arapaho, and Shoshone into one of four regions, he describes this area as the most tradition-oriented, adding that it is the source for many new songs received by singing groups from other tribes, a statement supporting the concept of the ever-expanding musical universe in Blackfoot culture (p. 132). This area is distinguished from others mainly in its practices of drumming, the use of special rhythms or beats to punctuate stages of the performance, and the importance of drumming off the beat.

Recent changes in drumming may be related to the Westernization of the concept of instruments or, more properly, the contrast between the traditional Blackfoot and the Western conceptions of instruments. We know already that a separate instrumental music is essential to the Western urban concept of music, while music in Blackfoot tradition is quintessentially vocal. But also, in Western culture vocal and instrumental music are in a way regarded as coeval, each a "kind" of music, the two capable of being combined, or replacing each other (as in the optional instrumental performance of songs). In Blackfoot culture, by contrast, instrumental and vocal parts of the music are (1) unequal; (2) interdependent; and (3) quite different in character in the consideration of units of musical creation, repertory, and the handling of time. In one sense, the two parts of the musical system are closer, and in another farther apart, than in Western music. For Blackfoot drumming, there are no songs or pieces, only styles and genres. One could argue that in a way, the symbolic structure of the relationship of music to culture—somewhat outside it, a reflection of it, and yet essential to it—is repeated in the relation of drumming to vocal music. Drumming is essential, as it specifically shows the *music* to be Indian, in the way that the whole musical complex shows the *culture* to be Indian; yet it is predictable and in certain ways not part of the vocal structure. The requirement of beating in a way contrastive to the vocal beat underscores the ambiguity of the relationship.

This interpretation of behavior would probably not be stated in such terms by a Blackfoot consultant, if at all. It has not been brought out to me in conversation, even though the structural relationships are suggestive. But while the traditional relationship of drum and song is still present in performance, instrumentation in the twentieth century has had a fate different from the vocal style. The singing sounds much as it did eighty years ago, and in some ways it now sounds more "extremely Indian," something also suggested by Hatton in his distribution of singing styles. The traditional set of instruments—container, deerhoof, turtle shell and other rattles, different types of drums, possibly a few other idiophones—have been replaced largely by the ordinary bass drum and a few modern hand drums. The bass drum is by far the most used type, essential for maintaining a singing group. Standardization in form of song and instrument is homologous. But instruments have also changed because the Western instruments known to the Blackfoot exist for their sound, not for their ritual or symbolic value, and for strictly musical purposes, the Blackfoot no longer need the great variety of drums and rattles essential to the earlier varieties of ritual and social uses.

4. IDEAS OF PERFORMANCE

In the art music culture of the West, music (i.e., the "sound" sector of Merriam's model) may exist at various levels—as performance, to be sure, but also as a work of art extant only on the page or as the conception of a composer. It exists in ideal performance and in the real world, in theory and also in practice. In considering that music has a kind of ambiguous role in society—integration with and validation of society and its workings, yes, but also a position somehow outside society and a way of dealing with what is outside—we come to the question of musical performance as a concept separate from that of song itself.

In fieldwork, this issue was hard to broach; I lacked concrete questions. One approach is to ask whether it is important for songs to be performed only in their appropriate context by use, or whether they can be sung at any time. Wissler's accounts indicate that songs differ in this respect. The personally owned and nontransferable songs, available for help in times of crisis, were not to be sung at any but the appointed time. Wissler's consultant was quite clear on this matter, but evidently only a few songs are involved. Other songs, at least by implication, could be sung any time, although the constraints of ownership might play a determining role. Who might sing a song was a matter of concern if not outright sanction, but who might hear it was less of an issue. Yet, Ewers (1955:274–75, 278) reminds us that the Horse Medicine songs should not be heard by outsiders to the cult, and one of my consultants told of being punished for listening, in his youth, outside a tent in which a ceremony was taking place.

Restriction on performance seems to correlate with power and value. The situation compares interestingly with that of the Navajo (McAllester 1954:64–65), in whose culture the issue of singing at appropriate times and avoiding danger through misuse is of great importance. Wissler's (1912a:263) consultant said that some songs "are very powerful. It is dangerous to sing them as a joke." Singing is usually a serious matter, performed unsmilingly, although we have shown that in music, as in mythology, there are humorous aspects.

The issue of what is an appropriate performance, or context for performance, is still present today, although it has been mitigated by the tendency in Western musical culture to generalize the question. In Western musical culture, the repertory is divided into classes, each of which is generally and in totality appropriate to certain contexts. There is classical concert music, rock concert music, church music, and music for parades. For the genre of classical concert, which symphony is to be performed is not prescribed, or which hymn in church, or which march for the parade. But one can't simply perform rock music at a classical concert.

It is rather like that in Blackfoot culture today, and to some extent it may have been so for much longer. At Blackfoot musical events in the recent period, the right kind of song must be sung—Grass Dance songs at powwows, gambling songs at games and a selection of ceremonial songs (but sometimes, it seems to me, any ceremonial songs) at rituals. The specifics of rituals have been forgotten to a considerable extent, and the requirement that a certain song accompany a particular action may exist in theory only. Yet it seems that the relationship of specific songs to particular occasions and even moments applied, even in earlier times, only to a minority of songs. There was always a considerable degree of freedom in selecting songs to be sung. The identity of particular songs and certain uses was evidently flexible, as certain groups of songs were associated with more than one ritual.

I suspect, then, that actual practice was often at variance with my consultant's quoted statement that the right way of doing something included singing the right song. Interpretation suggests that it may have been important to the Blackfoot to conceive of music as something that reflected a static and stable culture in all detail, but actually, life was different.

5.   THEORY AND PRACTICE

The Blackfoot, so I have tried to show, see their musical system primarily as a large body of songs, each existing without change, always performed essentially in one way, and learned quickly. The map of musical ownership and control shows some correlation of persons with songs. Songs are thought to belong to or with other activities or domains of culture, but yet they have an existence of their own, often being labeled by tune rather than name. As in many cultures, Blackfoot performance practice does not fully support theory. Singers obviously today do not really learn songs in one hearing, and some of them ridicule the claim that it could be done in the past. The suggestion that changing a note or two in a song constitutes a major error that cannot be allowed is contradicted by the substantial amount of variant singing in groups noted by Witmer and present in my recordings. This tolerance may also be related to the willingness of singing groups to perform with little vocal blend, and in the willingness to accept the singing of songs by nonowners.

Conflict between theory and practice is a commonplace in world cultures, but explanations by musicologists often tend to be normative or to proceed from the assumption that in a typical society, theory and practice must be congruent. In history books one may therefore read that theoreticians were badly informed, not representative, not musicians, or that musicians were poorly trained and could not carry out the theory. The culture hasn't behaved properly, we may hear, or the analyst hasn't seen it correctly, and it is up to scholarship to reconcile the two. Actually, there may be good reason in the structure of a cultural system why a particular theory of how music exists and should work is acceptable to a society, while practice goes its own way.

Traditional Blackfoot culture had a particular lifestyle which included a rather informal and permissive attitude toward many of the rules of life. In myth and recollection, rules were stated forcefully, but behavior was relaxed and informal. And thus, I suggest, in music it was and is important for the Blackfoot to have a concise system of theory and designation, not particularly for describing musical practice, but more in order to show that they have a systematically organized cultural system. Music, as a reflection of culture, lends itself well to this function, and musical theory—the rules articulated for musical behavior—may therefore have a function of its own not related to musical practice.

The Blackfoot today distinguish sharply between earlier and more modern repertories and uses, and one might therefore expect different approaches to musical thought to operate in the two repertories. One function of the modern music, however, continues to be the maintenance of the traditional Blackfoot cultural system. Certain ideas about musicianship in Blackfoot culture have been changed by Western concepts of musicianship—performance practice, the role of the ensemble, the emphasis on instruments. But the modern repertory is also associated with some evidently very traditional ideas of musicianship—what it takes to be a good singer, how one refers to songs, the role of words, the idea of dreaming songs, the indivisibility of song units, and the role of music as a way of reflecting the cultural system. The significant difference between theory and practice may importantly result from the different cultural functions of the two.

An excellent illustration is provided by the relationship of singing to other activities, in the light of the already oft-cited statement that the right way to do something is to sing the right song with it. When performing, Blackfoot musicians engage in kinds of behavior different from that of Western musicians. The concentration on singing and the song of the singers in modern "drums" has been noted. Performance in Western culture ordinarily includes some communication with an audience; in Blackfoot singing it is often notably absent. In Western professional performance, musicians do not ordinarily engage in other activities; yet it is quite conceivable to sing while marching or while acting in a dramatic role. Among laymen, singing while doing almost anything else is of course acceptable behavior.

For the Blackfoot, older ethnographies (McClintock 1910 [1968]:281; Ewers 1958:128–29) tell us that men sometimes sang while they rode or walked, and that the ceremony preceding a war party included circling the camp on the part of the men on horseback, during which they sang songs. They sometimes sang while performing ceremonial tasks. Yet the observer of Blackfoot behavior today is struck by the overwhelming tendency for the singing to be carried out by people who are *not* doing something else. Considering the Blackfoot dictum given above, it seems noteworthy that ordinarily the essential accompanied activity is carried out by someone who is not singing. Thus, I have heard of no songs that were sung while packing a travois or riding on the buffalo hunt. Dancers do not sing at social dances. We don't find Blackfoot songs performed by people engaged in various kinds of labor, a situation widely found, for example, in some Eastern European folk cultures. There is then a significant discrepancy between the Blackfoot theory of music as something that goes with each activity, and the performance of songs by people who are—at least at the moment of performance—acting the role of specialized musicians. While not absolute, the distinction is sufficiently established to warrant attempts at interpretation.

The style of Blackfoot (and northern Plains) singing is such that one could only with difficulty sing and do something else at the same time. Whether one credits this assertion, it is interesting to speculate about the reason for the selection of such a style and its continued maintenance. Let me suggest that specialization, general reflection of culture, the modern function of music, and the particular style of singing, can all be combined in the interpretation of music as an emblem of the difficult and the heroic in Blackfoot life. It is an association already touched upon, but let me recall bits of evidence: the separation of music from the rest of life through aspects of performance practice, a sharp distinction between singing and speaking, the absence of words in many songs, and the use of song texts to impart major points in myth in a condensed and concentrated form all relate music to the heroic aspect of life. There is the close association of music to warfare and the fact that most singing was done by men, and the musical role, even today, of community leaders and principal carriers of tradition. The acquisition of songs as associated with difficult feats— learned in visions brought about through self-denial and torture, required to be learned quickly, sung with the expenditure of great energy, sung in a difficult vocal style—all of this puts songs in the category of the heroic and the difficult. In my experience, I was impressed by singing and drumming as grand gestures, acts in which Blackfoot culture speaks clearly in a heightened manner.

6. QUESTIONS OF EVALUATION

This section is devoted to ways in which the Blackfoot people evaluate music, and relates these to aspects of musical thought at large. Section 7 goes on to an attempt at relating music to the guiding values of Blackfoot culture. Data are not plentiful. In the earlier ethnographic literature, mention of the evaluation of music is difficult to find, and in the modern musical culture, Western musical values play a considerable role.

Let me begin with the consultant who told me that "a good song is one that well fulfills the function of a song." It is a statement suggesting in the abstract that the particular degree to which a song is suitable for dancing, or provides supernatural power, is what determines its quality. In less abstract discussion I did not find people singling out individual songs for such reasons. Rather, it struck me that the statement about "a good song" was a generalization in which I was being told about the principles of the musical system. But do individual Blackfoot songs indeed have quality and value that distinguish them from others?

It seems that they do, but in ways quite different from the Western model. Blackfoot songs have explicitly different meaning for different individuals; they are closely tied to the idea of individualism, one of the important themes in Blackfoot culture. A song to be sung at times of crisis was of great value to the individual who had dreamed it, and beyond this, songs were principally valuable to their originators or owners. When C. B. said to me, "This song is my song, because my uncle gave it to me when I was a boy," he was not suggesting that it had value at large, and was not saying, "This is a very beautiful song," but let the matter of value rest with the statement of personal association. So, while a song was a commodity to be given or sold, it had special value for a particular individual.

I have mentioned the designation of a few songs as "favorites of the tribe," given by some singers of my acquaintance, and suggested that certain of them were special in the view of the Blackfoot people as a whole. Elsewhere (Nettl 1967:298), it was indicated that the style of these songs, as a group, departs slightly, and in various directions, from the Blackfoot stylistic norms, but it is difficult to be at all sure that this is what accounts for their perceived quality. It is more appropriate to consider that musical quality is rarely an issue in individual songs, as they used to be closely associated with activities and their musical character was not thought to be determined by humans anyway. Instead, the value and quality of the musical system (as compared to other domains of culture and to other musical systems) is an issue in Blackfoot aesthetics.

It may seem strange to the reader—though perhaps in keeping with the custom of opinion polling in modern America—to imagine that one might ask what a society thinks of its own music or question whether it even likes its own music. Clearly, there are intercultural differences; all peoples seem not to love their music equally well. My experience in Iran indicated considerable ambivalence on the part of modern Iranians. Music itself was something to be handled at best with care; it was not one of the great or important things in life. But further, even for the majority of people involved directly in the classical system, Iranians did not seem to think music to be one of the great accomplishments of their culture; in their view it could not be compared to Persian poetry, painting, or carpet designs. Western music, they thought, was much more developed. Iranians seemed to believe that they would be better off taking up Western music, but they would not discard their own poetry. By contrast, some of my colleagues in Madras thought the world would be better off if its peoples took up Carnatic music.

The Blackfoot did not share such missionary zeal, and they were realistic about certain values of "white" music, but they felt that their own musical system was a great accomplishment, something very important to them, a matter of great value. This speaks to their evaluation of their own musical system, but it seems to me also related to the Blackfoot conception of music at large. Believing music to be a great universal value might be expected to lead the Blackfoot to exhibit enthusiasm for all kinds of music to which they were exposed, but this was clearly not the case. And so, in describing Blackfoot culture, it is useful to distinguish the value placed on Blackfoot music from the value of music of all types, and to separate this from the evaluation of individual songs and of performances. Songs, as we know, are given by guardian spirits or in general by outside forces, for certain purposes. If one evaluates them at all, it is in terms of their ability to carry out these purposes, the few "favorite" songs notwithstanding. But one may evaluate the way in which humans carry out the instructions of the supernatural, that is, performance.

What, then, is a good performance of a song? This is not usually the way people would talk about it, and I did not hear statements such as, "Wow, they really did that song well." But I did, after a song by a singing group, hear such things as, "They are good singers." It is hard to know how much importance to attach to such field experience, but possibly a structural approach would give insight. Thus, the evaluation of songs is generalized to the whole musical system, and by analogy, evaluation of performance of a song is generalized to the universe of performance by the performer or performers in question. If you have good songs, you have a good music; if you sing songs well, you are a good singer.

To explain, it seems highly unlikely that the Blackfoot people in earlier times would not have reacted to songs with some feelings of like or dislike. But there is little evidence that such feelings were part of the cultural system rather than simply an individual matter. Evaluation of singing may have been similar. Wissler's consultant, although articulate on various matters involving songs, does not really talk about what makes a good song, and his discussion of good singers or good singing involves such general matters as how many songs a person knew.

There is a significant departure from his approach when he discusses women's singing, as he points out that they "are skillful in singing babies to sleep" (1912a:264) and that they "have fine voices and improve the singing" (p. 265) at certain points. It is interesting to find that he gives relatively strong emphasis to the question of women's singing, although one does not know whether the statements resulted from elicitation or came about spontaneously. It is curious to read his statements justifying women's abstinence from singing and at the same time pointing out the degree to which they do participate and in what ways they are good singers. Conceivably, women's role in society was an important issue around 1900, a time of rapid cultural change, and in this context music, that is, singing by women, was seen as a reflection of culture.

But with occasional exceptions, in earlier times, singing was probably so closely associated with ritual and other activity that one may not have judged its performance separately from performance of other ceremonial acts. In the modern culture, substantial knowledge of songs is still a major attribute of a singer, as are personal charisma and a high and strong voice. The guiding principles of a Blackfoot aesthetic place emphasis on the general much more than the specific. One is concerned with the quality of *music* and of *a* singer and not so much with that of individual songs or performances. Even in their statements to me, the Blackfoot emphasized how music fits into culture and what it contributes to the cultural system. This was central to the question of musical value.

7. CULTURAL VALUES AND MUSICAL VALUES

In a study of the music of Iran (Nettl 1978a:20–21), I suggested that the system of Persian classical music reflected and even explicitly symbolized certain values of social behavior, values that were found throughout the culture among various social groups, and that in a sense could be considered as representing some of the central and enduring values of Iranian society. They were these: hierarchy, in several senses of the concept; individualism; surprise and the unexpected; and the framing of events in formal and informal situations. Other values of society might be represented by other musics—culture change and the introduction of Western values and technology, for example, by Western and Westernized music and the interrelationship of traditional and Western components; or regionalism, by folk music. My argument was that music represents and indeed also presents the values of society in clear and unobstructed form.

It may be useful, in this connection, to look also at the way in which music is used to teach the values of a culture. Taking American culture as an example, an admittedly controversial paper (Nettl 1985a:73–75) suggested that the kinds of music taught in public schools, at least in the 1950s and 1960s—the emphasis on marching bands, orchestras, choruses, and large massed works—might well have taught children that what was really important in life was submission to leadership by a dictatorial figure, conformity, hierarchy, avoidance of individual creativity. This is one interpretation; another view might, however, argue that "conformity" ought to be translated as "cooperation," and further, that the mentioned values are clearly intended to be essential only to this particular kind of music making, of strictly technical significance, and nothing else. Or again, one might conclude that in the musical system, the members of a society can be permitted or expected to contradict the guiding principles of their cultural system.

Here, I wish to discuss Blackfoot musical culture along similar lines. In order to do this one should first discover the central cultural values or value systems and then identify various segments of the musical culture in which these may be reflected. In his study of the Montana Blackfeet Reservation, McFee (1972:67) divides the Blackfoot population into two groups, "Indian-oriented" and "white-oriented." My experience supports this grouping, and in the 1960s, the Blackfoot people themselves seemed to follow it, using the terms "full-blood" and "mixed-blood." They recognized the correlation of cultural and biologic groupings that applied in this particular case and used the terms mainly to designate cultural orientation rather than descent. Each of the two groups has its system of values, says McFee (1972:93–101), and while there are overlaps, he was able to extract and name specific values from the bifurcation of population and lifestyle. For the Indian-oriented segment, his list included wisdom, bravery, individualism, and generosity, while the white-oriented group is characterized by self-reliance, acquisitiveness, knowledge, and keeping busy or industriousness.

Considering the affective character of his terms, McFee's set of values sounds in some ways like an idealization of Indian tradition and an indictment of Western capitalistic society. Yet one cannot deny that the white-oriented values play a major role in Blackfoot life today, as it may be seen in part as a subdivision of rural Montana culture. To be a successful small businessman or rancher, one should be self-reliant and avoid the tendency to depend on government help that was thought to characterize the attitude of many full-blooded Blackfoot. Acquisitiveness is a hallmark of success in capitalist society, and keeping busy a sign that you are at least trying to succeed along those lines. Knowledge, in the sense of a large fund of facts and resources that may or may not be related to each other and have specific practical purposes, certainly characterizes aspects of white American education.

In contrast, generosity, individualism, bravery, and wisdom can be easily seen as values in the older Blackfoot tradition. One was expected to accumulate but also to share wealth, and a person's reputation for being rich might be as much enhanced by visible signs of the wealth itself as by the recognized willingness to dispose of it. Wisdom may be defined as the ability to extract the essential from what may be a modest store of factual materials and to use it to deal with the major issues of life; it involves not extent but quality of knowledge. We have seen in many ways the importance of individualism in Blackfoot religion and warfare. Bravery, willingness to face risk, is important in many ways, in warfare, gambling, "counting coup," competition of all sorts, and is related to the mentioned significance of the heroic.

In a very general sense, these values can be related to musical life. It is difficult to compare abstract values to concrete activities, but a few relationships may be suggestive if not thoroughly convincing. Wisdom— in contrast to knowledge—could relate to the ideal of learning songs throughout one's life into old age and to knowing the right songs for occasions. Individualism is expressed in the belief that each person has his or her individual songs, learned in personal visions, and that each song is its owner's even when it sounds like someone else's.

The concept of individualism may also play a role in the idea of songs as unchanging entities. It is harder to make a musical analogy for bravery, but it may be reflected in several aspects of musical thought. These include the ideas of exposing oneself to risk in seeking visions, expecting to learn songs quickly, and singing without formal preparation. Also relevant here are the importance of song in warfare and, as suggested in chapter 4, the relation of music to the heroic. Generosity is found in the custom of giving songs. Musical life, if not the songs themselves, expresses and may even be in part governed by the mentioned values of the Indian-oriented segment of Blackfoot society.

Self-reliance, acquisitiveness, knowledge, keeping busy—these sound like the values of Western culture as stated by someone who does not totally admire them. Some indeed are reflected in modern Indian musical culture. But the congruency is weaker than for the Indian-oriented values. There is now, among the singing groups at powwows, the belief that one should rehearse, learn new songs, keep up one's repertory, with an attitude that rewards industriousness. Learning new songs shows that you are not a lazy person, and when you have nothing else to do, practicing your songs is an option. The ideas of knowing many songs, learning more from sources outside the tribe, making up songs, and getting paid for performing them puts such singing groups in the mainstream of modern American-style acquisitive music making. One never knows enough songs, it is now believed, but to be sure, Blackfoot singers and medicine men a hundred years ago may have already had this opinion. Self-reliance too has always been a factor in ritual and musical culture and is therefore a bit hard to relate specifically to modern group performance.

The sound and style of Blackfoot music lack some of the technical complexities normally expected in Western or Asian Indian or Indonesian art music. In most respects, such a statement is irrelevant to the concerns of ethnomusicology. But it is nevertheless worth saying that the need to juxtapose theory with practice, composition with performance, singing with drumming, older with newer styles, solo with ensemble, men's with women's singing, and the traditional with the Westernized shows that Blackfoot music is a musical system of great complexity and sophistication. Its relationship to other domains of culture is constant, but our examination of musical and social values shows us an apparent but probably very significant inconsistency in the relationship. The two configurations of values, Indian-oriented and white-oriented, and their accompanying illustrations in musical behavior exhibit the totality of musical life to be more reflective of the values of the Indian-oriented portion of Blackfoot society than of those of the white-oriented.

This incongruency seems anomalous, but a credible explanation rests on the tendency of the entire society of Blackfoot—full-blooded and mixed-blooded, Indian-oriented and white-oriented—to use the traditional music (in contrast to white music) as an emblem of tribal and ethnic identity. Simply put, for conservative as well as for modernized Blackfoot Indians, traditional music (Indian, old or recent) is a reminder—more than that, an emblem—of the unique origin and history of their people.

A Blackfoot Theory Text?

This essay has consistently suggested that there is a system of ideas about music in Blackfoot culture that is coherent and relates music to the other domains of culture. In a sense, therefore, all that has been said might be considered the "music theory" of the Blackfoot people and their culture, just as the set of ideas about music held by Western musicians and intellectuals is in one sense of the word conventionally labeled as the Western "theory of music." I should now like to ask, perhaps as a logical concluding question, whether there may not be something in Blackfoot culture that could be considered more specifically *the* Blackfoot theory of music.

In considering the kinds of sources which I could use for this study, I continually tried to imagine how a historian or ethnographer of Western musical culture might proceed in an analogous situation and what kinds of sources might be available to him or her. Many of the problems with which I was faced in working with the Blackfoot would surely also confront someone working in the contemporary era of the history of Western academic music. The difficulty of bringing a variety of sources, older and newer, authoritative and general, written and oral, all to bear on a general panorama would duplicate the problems faced by a student of a tribal society today. But for data on musical thought, and for synthesis and evaluation, traditional historical musicology relies most on works usually designated as theoretical treatises. In European music history, the theoretical treatise is the paradigm of the conspectus of ideas about music, their authority and established tradition. Whether this is the best or the only way of encapsulating musical ideas or concepts is not at issue here, and musicologists do not claim that it is (Kerman 1985:60–61).

There are no Blackfoot theoretical treatises on music, written or orally transmitted. We may thus ask ourselves whether for a theory to exist there must also be a text that embodies and communicates it and, given the Blackfoot situation, if the culture does not present it overtly, whether there is a way of deriving one. Such a need might be filled by myths, yet in the Blackfoot case they contain little that is specifically about music. There is also no set of rules orally transmitted ready for an observer such as myself to explicate. Nevertheless, certain ideas and themes were so strongly expressed in the musical culture that I determined (stimulated by suggestions in Haefer 1981) to find a way of extracting a text that could serve as a basic Blackfoot statement of music theory, and I proceeded as follows.

Consulting my notes of several years, and recorded conversations, I found eighteen statements that seemed to me to have been made to me by consultants with particular emphasis, sometimes as if the purpose were to impart to me matters of broad and general import. Some were made in the context of other conversation, others were almost lifted out above such a context. In several cases it was clear that a consultant wished to point me in an important direction. I have had occasion to quote some of them in the preceding pages. Needless to say, they were not equally significant, and the line between them and other statements made with less emphasis is quite unclear. And of course the perception of emphasis may be my own. But for a start, and as a kind of conclusion to a description of a system of musical thought, I should like to restate them here, arranged in an order reflecting the organization of my chapters. I suggest that they, or something like them, may in a way be regarded as the Blackfoot equivalent of formally recognized texts such as theoretical treatises in Western and Asian musical cultures. The statements deal with many aspects of musical life, but together they indicate a consistent attitude toward music and refer to a number of the themes that have dominated my presentation.

The Concept of Music

1. The songs are some of the most important things we Blackfoot people have.
2. Our songs are different from white people's songs, they are special; for one thing, they sound special, and they don't just have a lot of words.
3. Our songs came back to us (i.e., after 1950) when our Blackfoot feelings came back.
4. This Blackfoot song is one of the favorite songs of the tribe.
5. Our songs have a lot of stories that go with them.

Origins and History

6. The real songs of our tribe, our true songs, they mostly came in dreams.
7. Our songs (i.e., the style of our songs) are so old, they must go back to the days of Napi (the culture hero) (followed by a chuckle).
8. When I made up songs, dreaming had a lot to do with it.
9. Sometimes I hum a song, over and over, and that way I catch a new song.
10. We learned a lot of dances and songs from other tribes—like the Cree, Assiniboine, Gros Ventres—but then we changed them too.
11. Our tribe keeps getting new songs, there are always new songs come into our reservation. But we try to hold on to them old songs too. Sometimes we can't, but we should.

Uses and Functions of Music

12. A good song is one that fulfills well the purpose of the song.
13. The right Blackfoot way to do something is to sing the right Blackfoot song with it.
14. We used to have a lot of different kinds of songs, you can't imagine how many kinds of songs.

Musicianship

15. A good song leader knows a lot of songs and has a good strong voice; he can get other singers to follow him.
16. Most Blackfoot people can sing a song after they heard it sung only one time.
17. People used to have a better memory for songs than they do now. It's because they depend so much on reading and writing.
18. Our songs have a beginning, middle, and end. After beginning, somebody raises the leader, and then all sing.

Am I right in singling out a small number of statements from many conversations to make up a kind of rudimentary systematization of musical thought? It is difficult to know how helpful such an analytical procedure may be. But other conversations and observations led to similar configurations of thought, and therefore I believe that the above-cited statements, even had they not been presented with the kind of emphasis that made me take notice, might in any event have become the pillars of this modest edifice.

What I have been able to present here is still just a small part of the totality of a musical culture viewed synchronically and diachronically.

Brevity of field experience, lack of historical depth, a long period of rapid change, the Blackfoot people's own belief that much of their tradition has been forgotten, all make necessary the admission that at best I have reconstructed a dinosaur from a bone in its tail. These eighteen statements represent the Blackfoot people's way of helping me move from fragment to synthesis. I have presented them as a statement of the Blackfoot theory of music, but they may also function appropriately as a summary of the chapters that precede.

This study has been an essay in the identification and interpretation of some of the ideas about music that are components of Blackfoot culture, trying to see these in the light of musical sound and behavior and to understand them in their relationship to the character of other domains of Blackfoot culture. I have tried to follow them through a period of cultural upheaval for the Blackfoot people, identifying continuities and changes. It has been necessary to do this with the use of a small amount of data that bears directly on the subject and some additional material that provided indirect evidence from general ethnography; from observation of musical behavior; from the structure of music; and from mythology, song texts, and various other sources. It has also been necessary frequently to rely on extrapolation and interpretation and, far more than one might wish, on speculation. To say that I have tried to construct a credible dinosaur from an extant tailbone has all too often seemed a fitting metaphor.

The complexity of the Blackfoot system of ideas about music and its close interaction with the central features of the culture points to the great significance of the songs to the Blackfoot people. Providing a reflection of the culture as a whole, music abstracts and clarifies cultural values. In particular, it functions as a force that mediates between human and supernatural, Blackfoot and non-Blackfoot, the traditional and modernized segments of society and, in its existence at the center of society, and somehow also outside, perhaps even nature and culture. In the last hundred years of Blackfoot history, a period of unprecedented difficulty, conflict, and crisis, music in all of its aspects has continued to be closely woven into the cultural fabric, a significant symbol and a major force.

Chronological List of Recorded Collections of Blackfoot Music (1897–1986)

F = Collection of field recordings housed in an archive
CLP = Commercial LP record
CT = Commercial cassette recording
C78 = Commercial 78-rpm recording

1897	F	George Bird Grinnell. Collection of 40 songs on 20 wax cylinders, recorded at Piegan Agency, Montana. Originals at Indiana University Archives of Traditional Music, Bloomington.
1898	F	Walter McClintock. Collection of about 51 songs on 36 gramophone cylinders, recorded in Montana. Originals at Southwest Museum, Los Angeles.
1903–1904	F	Clark Wissler. Collection of about 200 songs on 121 wax cylinders, made for the American Museum of Natural History, recorded in Montana. Originals at Indiana University Archives of Traditional Music, Bloomington.
1908–1909	F	Joseph K. Dixon. 5 songs on 5 wax cylinders, recorded for the Wanamaker Expedition to the American Indians no. 2, at Crow Agency, Montana. Originals at Indiana University Archives of Traditional Music, Bloomington.

1909	F	Edward S. Curtis. Collection of around 43 songs on 20 wax cylinders. Originals at Indiana University Archives of Traditional Music, Bloomington.
1910–1920(?)	F	Truman Michelson. Collection of about 17 songs, plus some spoken material, on 15 wax cylinders. Originals at American Folklife Center, Library of Congress.
1914	C78	Two commercial records, with a total of 5 songs, recorded at New York City. Victor 17611 and 17635.
1926	F	Jessie Donaldson. Collection of 21 songs, on 11 cylinders, recorded in Montana. Originals at the Museum of Anthropology, University of California, Berkeley.
1926	F	James Willard Schultz. Collection of 20 songs on 10 cylinders, recorded in Montana. Some are not salvageable. Originals at Indiana University Archives of Traditional Music, Bloomington.
1939	F	Jane Richardson Hanks. Collection of about 45 songs on 32 cylinders, recorded at Gleichen, Alberta. Originals in possession of collector; copies at Indiana University Archives of Traditional Music, Bloomington.
1949	F	Donald D. Hartle. Collection of 28 songs on wire recordings, made on a field trip sponsored by the University of New Mexico. Originals in possession of collector; copies at Indiana University Archives of Traditional Music, Bloomington.
1950	F	Ralph McFadden. Collection of 36 songs on wire, recorded at Browning, Montana. Original in possession of collector; copy at Ethnomusicology Archive, University of California, Los Angeles.
1952	F	Howard K. Kaufman. Collection of 17 songs on tape, recorded at Browning, Montana. Originals at Indiana University Archives of Traditional Music, Bloomington.
1952	F	Bruno Nettl. Collection of 107 songs on tape, recorded at Bloomington, Indiana. Originals at Indiana University Archives of Traditional Music, Bloomington.
1966	F	Bruno Nettl. Collection of about 160 songs on tape, recorded at Browning, Heart Butte, and Starr School, Montana. Originals at University of Illinois Archives of Ethnomusicology, Urbana.

1966	CLP	*Indian Music of the Canadian Plains.* Recorded by Ken Peacock. Ethnic Folkways Library, FE 4464. Includes 9 Blackfoot and Blood songs.
ca. 1967	CLP	*Blackfeet Tribal Grass Dance.* American Soundchief, BLKFT–104. Sung by Edward Morning Owl and Wilbur Morning Owl. Recorded in Canada. 12 songs.
ca. 1967	CLP	*Blackfeet Grass Dance Songs.* Soundchief, B–100 (R–2271). 11 Grass Dance songs, sung by Allen White Grass, Pat Kennedy, and Stanley Whitemen.
ca. 1967	CLP	*Crow Tribal Circle Dances: Blackfoot Owl Dance Songs (Circle Dance).* Soundchief, BLKFT–204. Includes 5 Blackfoot songs.
1967	F	Bruno Nettl. Collection of 3 hours of tape, including 10 songs, largely interviews. Originals in possession of collector.
1968	F	Robert Witmer. Collection of about 366 songs, plus some 50 "white" songs sung by Blackfoot musicians, on tape. Recorded on Blood Reserve, Alberta. Originals at University of Illinois Archives of Ethnomusicology, Urbana.
1972	CLP	*Blackfoot A-1 Club Singers,* vols. 1–2. Indian House, 4001–4002. Recorded by Tony Isaacs at Gleichen, Alberta. 20 songs.
1972	CLP	*Crow Celebration: 10 Great Drums at Crow Fair.* Canyon Records, C–6089. Includes selection by Cardston Blood Singers led by Edward Little Bear. 10 songs.
1972	CLP	*From the Land of the Blackfeet.* Canyon Records, C–6095. Sung by Pat Kennedy and Blackfeet Singers, at North American Indian Days, Browning, Montana, 1972. 11 songs.
1973	CLP	*Old Agency Singers of the Blood Reserve,* vol. 1. Indian House, 4051. Recorded by Tony Isaacs at Stand Off, Alberta, 1972. 8 songs.
1973	CLP	*Kyi-Yo Pow-wow.* Canyon Records, C–6111. Includes songs by Kanai Blood Singers, Starr School Singers, and Heart Butte Singers. Recorded by Raymond Boley at Missoula, Montana. 9 songs.
1973	CLP	*Old Agency Singers of the Blood Reserve.* Indian House, 4052. Recorded by Tony Isaacs at Stand Off, Alberta, 1972. 8 songs.
1974	CT	*Blackfeet Powwow Songs: Blackfeet Singers of Browning, Montana.* Canyon Records, CR–6119. 12 songs. Also issued on LP.

1975	CLP	*Blackfoot A-1 Singers.* Canyon Records, 6132. Recorded by Raymond Boley at Calgary, Alberta. 11 songs.
1975	CLP	*Northern Plains Society Singers.* Blackfeet, Blood, and other singers. Canyon Records, C–6122. Recorded by Raymond Boley. 12 songs.
1975	CLP	*Songs from the Battleford Powwow.* Canyon Records, C–6142. Sung by Blackfoot and other singers, Pat Kennedy, Alex Scalp Lock, and Francis Greene. 12 songs.
1975	CLP	*Songs from the Blood Reserve.* Canyon Records, 6133. Performed by the Kai-Spai Singers. Recorded by Raymond Boley in Calgary. 11 songs.
1975	CLP	*Twelve Blackfeet Songs.* Indian Records, IR 220. Recorded at Browning, Montana. 12 songs.
1977	CT	*Young Grey Horse Society: Songs of the Blackfeet.* Canyon Records, CR–6164-C. Recorded by Raymond Boley in 1976 at Browning, Montana. 12 songs.
1979	CLP	*An Historical Album of Blackfoot Indian Music.* Edited by Bruno Nettl. Ethnic Folkways Records, RE 34001. Recordings from various collections listed above, 1897–1966.
1980	CT	*Calgary Drummers: Blackfoot.* Canyon Records, 9002-C. 12 songs.
1980	CT	*Old Songs from the Past: Blackfoot Oldtimers.* Canyon Records, 9004-C. Recorded in Alberta. 12 songs.
1981	CT	*A-1 Club Singers (Blackfoot, Alberta),* vol. 2. Canyon Records, CR–9007-C. Recorded by Raymond Boley, 1981. 12 songs.
1981	CT	*Heart Butte Singers.* Canyon Records, CR–6177-C. Recorded by Raymond Boley in Heart Butte, Montana, 1981. 12 songs.
1981	CT	*Kicking Woman Singers.* Canyon Records, CR–6178-C. Recorded by Raymond Boley in Browning, Montana, 1981. 10 songs.
1981	CT	*Scalp Lock Singers (Blackfoot, Alberta).* Canyon Records, CR–9013-C. Recorded by Raymond Boley, 1981. 11 songs made by Alex Scalp Lock.
1981	CT	*Two Medicine Lake Singers (Blackfeet, Montana).* Canyon Records, CR–6176-C. 10 songs.
1981	CT	*Crowfoot Drummers (Blackfoot, Alberta).* Canyon Records, CR–9009-C. Recorded by Raymond Boley at Cluny, Alberta, 1981. 12 songs.

1982	CLP	*The Canadian Blackfoot Indians.* Performed by the Scalp Lock Singers. Lyrichord, LLST 7373. 12 songs.
1982	CT	*Carlson Singers (Blackfeet, Montana).* Canyon Records, CR–6179-C. Recorded by Raymond Boley in Heart Butte, Montana, 1981. 12 songs.
1984	CT	*Kicking Woman Singers: Pow-wow Songs.* Canyon Records, CR–6181-C. Recorded by Raymond Boley at Browning, Montana, 1983. 12 songs.
1984	CT	*Two Medicine Lake Singers (Blackfeet, Montana),* vol. 2. Canyon Records, CR–6182-C. 12 songs.
1984	CT	*Young Grey Horse Society,* vol. 2. Canyon Records, CR–6184-C. 12 songs.
1984	F	Bruno Nettl. Collection of about 40 songs on 4 tape cassettes, made at North American Indian Days, Browning, Montana, July 1984. Originals in possession of collector.
1985	CT	*Kicking Woman Singers: Pow-wow Songs,* [vol. 2]. Canyon Records, CR–6182-C. 12 songs.
1986	CT	*Heart Butte Singers (Blackfeet, Montana),* vol. 2. Canyon Records, CR–6187-C. 12 songs.
1986	CT	*Kicking Woman Singers: Contest & Intertribal Pow-wow Songs,* [vol. 3]. Canyon Records, CR–6183-C. 12 songs.
1986	CT	*Little Corner Singers: Pow-wow Songs. Blackfeet, Montana.* Canyon Records, CR–6189-C. 9 songs.
1986	CT	*Seven Hand Game Songs: Thomas Big Spring & Floyd Heavy Runner (Blackfeet, Montana).* Canyon Records, CR–6188-C.

Appendix A

Blackfoot song types by use, as found in the various recorded collections

	Grinnel 1897	McClintock 1898	Wissler 1903–1904	Dixon 1908–1909	Curtis 1909	Donaldson 1926	Schultz 1926	Hanks 1939	Hartle 1949	Nettl 1952	Kaufman 1952	Nettl 1966	Witmer 1968	9 commercial recordings 1972–1980	9 commercial recordings 1981–1984
Medicine Songs															
Beaver	14	5	16		3	2	9	3	2			3	14		
Medicine pipe		6	58		2			5	4	12		11	9		
Tipi			16					2					1		
Crow water	2												26		
Buffalo rock		2						3					2		
Other medicine or personal		3	10			8		7		16		3	6		
Sun Dance		4	7		8			4	2	4		9	9		
Societies															
Parted hair	8												7		
Deer society	2		4												
Crazy dog	3	2	10		3			5			3	4	10		
Others			23	18				2				17	16		
Social Dances															
Owl and rabbit							8		4	18	2	21	57	25	8
Grass and war			12				9		6	11	3	45	113	41	36
Tea dance	5		6										2		
Round dance											3			4	4
Chicken dance									3				2	6	3
"Intertribal"															13
Sioux dance													12		

	Grinnel 1897	McClintock 1898	Wissler 1903–1904	Dixon 1908–1909	Curtis 1909	Donaldson 1926	Schultz 1926	Hanks 1939	Hartle 1949	Nettl 1952	Kaufman 1952	Nettl 1966	Witmer 1968	9 commercial recordings 1972–1980	9 commercial recordings 1981–1984
Fast and fancy														4	15
Giveaway dance												4	6		
Sneak-up															4
Women's and squaw dance						2	1			8					
Other social dances			4						4				16	2	2
War Complex and Remnants															
Honoring, memorial, flag												2	6	10	10
Wolf songs		5	5								2	5			
War complex and other		4	28	3	1	2		4	2	3	6	3	17		
Songs in Myths (not including those under Medicine Songs)		3		3											
Gambling (stick and feather games)		1	7			1	4		1	4		18	23	2	
Children's Game Songs and Lullabies		1	3							2		4			
Riding Songs			7	1		1									
Love Songs	3	1		1		1	3	1		3		4	9		
Other (mainly social)		2				3	4				2	10	19		
Not identified or otherwise problematic	5									22			3		

Appendix B

Three Blackfoot Songs

1.

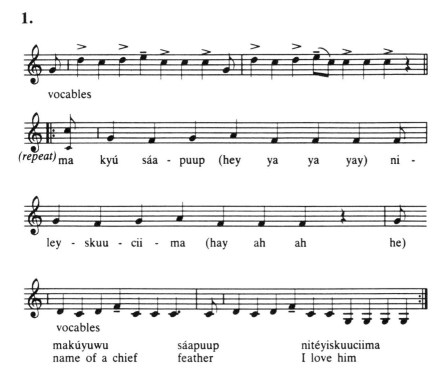

vocables

(repeat) ma kyú sáa - puup (hey ya ya yay) ni -

ley - skuu - cii - ma (hay ah ah he)

vocables

makúyuwu	sáapuup	nitéyiskuuciima
name of a chief	feather	I love him

2.

i - máa - yaa - kii   či - ta - a - páss - to

ï - máa - yaa - kii   či - taa - páss - to (hey - ey - ey - ey - e,

wi - yei   ey ey   hey ey   ey ey   ey ey)

imáayaakiičitaapássto   ɛsstookɛitáamsoop
you're going to die and be alone   in the graveyard

3.

vocable text

repeat three times

a - kee - yé — wii -

noo - táa - mo - ket (to mey ey ey ey)

(me ne) — takk xyaa po yo (ma ha ____ haw __

yaw __ he ye he yo ho yo ho yo yo.)

akeeyé   wiinootáamoket   tákxyaapaapówi
woman   don't worry about me   I'm coming back home

takxkyaaowimfinii
I'm going back home to eat berries

Appendix C

**Responses of non-Western musics to Western influences:
development of concepts in three studies**

Nettl (1978) (general)	Kartomi (1981) (general)	Shiloah & Cohen (1983) (Israel only)
(Related concepts and processes are horizontally and vertically aligned.)		

WESTERNIZATION (becoming part of the Western system by adopting central features of Western music)

Nettl (1978) (general)	Kartomi (1981) (general)	Shiloah & Cohen (1983) (Israel only)
Abandonment (e.g., Australian aborigines' vestigial retention of didjeridu)	Virtual abandonment (Restating of Nettl's "abandonment")	Fine art music Ethnic art music
Reduction or impoverishment (e.g., Plains Indian reduction to one main form or Japanese reduction of repertory)	Transculturation (adoption of clusters of traits from Western musical culture)	Popular music Pseudoethnic music
Diversification (diverse styles of a culture in one concert, film, or record)	Pluralistic coexistence (e.g., of Indian and white music in Blackfoot culture)	Transitional music
Humorous juxtaposition of Western and other music (as in some Indian film songs and some Mexican mariachi music)		

MODERNIZATION (modifying tradition by adapting noncentral features of Western music)

Consolidation (e.g., the creation of coherent styles from several cultures—e.g., the pan-Indian and Peyote styles of North America)	Transfer of discrete traits (e.g., using Western harmony in music otherwise traditional)	Neotraditional music Museumized music
Syncretism (fusion of compatible elements—e.g., African and Afro-Caribbean musics)	Compartmentalization (e.g., in Japan)	Conserved music
Exaggeration (non-Western traits emphasized; e.g., Plains Indian and Arabic singing styles)	Nativistic revival (e.g., North American Indian Ghost Dance and West African Juju)	
Artificial preservation (e.g., musicians who are "national treasures" in Japan and Korea)	Virtual rejection of Western music (e.g., in portions of musical culture of India)	Traditional music
Reintroduction (e.g., Afro-Caribbean influences in Africa)		

Bibliography

(Publications cited or otherwise directly relevant)

al-Faruqi, Lois Ibsen. 1979. "The Status of Music in Muslim Nations: Evidence from the Arab World." *Asian Music* 12(1): 56–85.

Ames, David W., and Anthony V. King. 1971. *Glossary of Hausa Music and Its Cultural Context.* Evanston, Ill.: Northwestern University Press.

Berliner, Paul. 1978. *The Soul of Mbira.* Berkeley and Los Angeles: University of California Press.

Blackfeet Community College. 1985. *Blackfeet Bilingual Teacher Training Program, Annual Report.* [Browning, Montana, 1986].

Blacking, John. 1965. "The Role of Music in the Culture of the Venda of the Northern Transvaal." *Studies in Ethnomusicology* (New York) 2:20–57.

———. 1967. *Venda Children's Songs.* Johannesburg, South Africa: Witwatersrand University Press.

Bullchild, Percy. 1985. *The Sun Came Down.* New York: Harper and Row.

Curtis, Edward S. 1911 [1970]. "The Piegan." In *The North American Indian,* by Edward S. Curtis, 6:3–83. New York: Johnson Reprint Company.

Dahlhaus, Carl. 1977. *Grundlagen der Musikgeschichte.* Cologne: Hans Gerig.

Davis, Leslie B. 1961. *Peyotism and the Blackfeet Indians of Montana: An Historical Assessment.* Studies in Plains Anthropology and History, no. 1. Browning, Mont.: Dept. of the Interior, Office of Indian Affairs.

Dempsey, Hugh Aylmer. 1968. *The Blackfoot Ghost Dance.* Glenbow-Alberta Institute Occasional Papers, no.3. Calgary, Alberta.

———. 1972. *Crowfoot, Chief of the Blackfeet.* Norman: University of Oklahoma Press.

Densmore, Frances. 1910. *Chippewa Music.* Bureau of American Ethnology, Bulletin no. 45. Washington, D.C.

———. 1913. *Chippewa Music II*. Bureau of American Ethnology, Bulletin no. 53. Washington, D.C.

———. 1918. *Teton Sioux Music*. Bureau of American Ethnology, Bulletin no. 61. Washington, D.C.

———. 1932. *Menominee Music*. Bureau of American Ethnology, Bulletin no. 102. Washington, D.C.

———. 1938. *Music of Santo Domingo Pueblo, New Mexico*. Southwest Museum Papers, no. 12. Los Angeles.

Driver, Harold E. 1961. *Indians of North America*. Chicago: University of Chicago Press.

Ewers, John C. 1942. "Were the Blackfoot Rich in Horses?" *American Anthropologist* 45:602–10.

———. 1955. *The Horse in Blackfoot Indian Culture*. Bureau of American Ethnology, Bulletin no. 159. Washington, D.C.

———. 1958. *The Blackfeet, Raiders on the Northwestern Plains*. Norman: University of Oklahoma Press.

———. 1965. "Deadlier Than the Male." *American Heritage* 16(4): 10–13.

Farr. William E. 1984. *The Reservation Blackfeet, 1882–1945: A Photographic History of Cultural Survival*. Seattle: University of Washington Press.

Feld, Steven. 1982. *Sound and Sentiment: Birds, Weeping, Poetics, and Song in Kaluli Expression*. Philadelphia: University of Pennsylvania Press.

Fenton, William N. 1953. *The Iroquois Eagle Dance: An Offshoot of the Calumet Dance*. Bureau of American Ethnology Bulletin no. 156. Washington, D.C.

Fletcher, Alice C. 1904. *The Hako, a Pawnee Ceremony*. Bureau of American Ethnology, 22nd Annual Report. Washington, D.C.

Fogelson, Raymond D., and Richard N. Adams, eds. 1977. *The Anthropology of Power*. New York: Academic Press.

Frisbie, Charlotte J. 1980. "Vocables in Navajo Ceremonial Music." *Ethnomusicology* 24:347–92.

Gillis, Frank J. 1984. "The Incunabula of Instantaneous Ethnomusicological Sound Recordings." In *Problems and Solutions,* edited by Jamie Kassler and Jill Stubbington, 314–21. Sydney, Australia: Hale & Ironmonger.

Grinnell, George Bird. 1892 [1962]. *Blackfoot Lodge Tales: The Story of a Prairie People*. Reprint. Lincoln: University of Nebraska Press.

Gurlitt, Willibald, ed. 1967. *Riemann Musik Lexikon*. Mainz: Schott.

Haefer, J. Richard. 1981. *Musical Thought in Papago Culture*. Ph.D. diss., University of Illinois.

Hanks, Lucien Mason Jr., and Jane Richardson Hanks. 1950. *Tribe under Trust: A Study of the Blackfoot Reserve of Alberta*. Toronto: University of Toronto Press.

Harris, Marvin. 1968. *The Rise of Anthropological Theory*. New York: Crowell.

Harrod, Howard L. 1971. *Mission among the Blackfeet*. Norman: University of Oklahoma Press.

Harwood, Dane L. 1976. "Universals in Music: A Perspective from Cognitive Psychology." *Ethnomusicology* 20:521–33.

Hatton, Orin T. 1974. "Performance Practices of Northern Plains Pow-wow Singing Groups." *Yearbook for Inter-American Musical Research* 10:123–37.
———. 1986. "In the Tradition: Grass Dance Musical Style and Female Pow-wow Singers." *Ethnomusicology* 30:197–222.
Herndon, Marcia. 1980. *Native American Music*. Darby, Pa.: Norwood Editions.
Herzog, George. 1935. "Special Song Types in North American Indian Music." *Zeitschrift für vergleichende Musikwissenschaft* 3(1–2): 23–33.
———. 1938. "Music in the Thinking of the American Indian." *Peabody Bulletin* (May), 1–5.
Hinton, Leanne. 1966–67. Personal communication and unpublished papers on Havasupai musical culture, University of Illinois.
———. 1980. "Vocables in Havasupai Song." In *Southwestern Indian Ritual Drama*, edited by Charlotte J. Frisbie, 275–306. Albuquerque: University of New Mexico Press.
———. 1984. *Havasupai Songs: A Linguistic Perspective*. Tübingen, West Germany: Gunter Narr Verlag.
Hood, Mantle. 1985. "All Musical Cultures Are about Equally Complex." In *More Than Drumming*, edited by Irene V. Jackson, 21–30. Westport, Conn.: Greenwood Press.
Hornbostel, E. M. von, and Curt Sachs. 1914. "Systematik der Musikinstrumente." *Zeitschrift für Ethnologie* 43:556–90.
Howard, James H. 1951. "Notes on the Dakota Grass Dance." *Southwestern Journal of Anthropology* 7:82–85.
———. 1955. "Pan-Indian Culture of Oklahoma." *Scientific Monthly* 81:215–20.
Hungry Wolf, Adolf, and Beverly Hungry Wolf. 1983. *Shadows of the Buffalo: A Family Odyssey among the Indians*. New York: Morrow.
Hungry Wolf, Beverly. 1982. *The Ways of My Grandmothers*. New York: Quill.
Kartomi, Margaret J. 1981. "The Processes and Results of Musical Culture Contact: A Discussion of Terminology and Concepts." *Ethnomusicology* 25:227–50.
Katz, Ruth. 1968. "The Singing of Baqqashot by Aleppo Jews." *Acta Musicologica* 40:65–85.
Keil, Charles. 1979. *Tiv Song*. Chicago: University of Chicago Press.
Kerman, Joseph. 1985. *Contemplating Music: Challenges to Musicology*. Cambridge: Harvard University Press.
Knepler, Georg. 1982. *Geschichte als Weg zum Musikverständnis*, 2d ed. Leipzig: Reklam.
Kolstee, Anton. l982. *Bella Koola Indian Music*. Ottawa: National Museum of Canada.
Kroeber, A. L. 1902. *The Arapaho*. Bulletin of the American Museum of Natural History, vol. 18. New York.
———. 1947. *Cultural and Natural Areas of Native North America*. Berkeley and Los Angeles: University of California Press.
Kroeber, A. L., and Clyde Kluckhohn. 1952. *Culture: A Critical Review of Concepts and Definitions*. Papers of the Peabody Museum of American Archeology and Ethnology, vol. 47. Cambridge, Mass.

Laade, Wolfgang. 1975. *Musik der Götter, Geister und Menschen.* Baden-Baden, West Germany: Valentin Koerner.

LaBarre, Weston. 1959. *The Peyote Cult.* Hamden, Conn.: Shoe String Press.

Lah, Ronald. 1980. *Ethnoaesthetics of Northern Arapaho Indian Music.* Ph.D. diss. Northwestern University.

Lewis, Oscar. 1941. "Manly-Hearted Women among the North Piegan." *American Anthropologist* 43:173–87. Reprinted in *Anthropological Essays,* by Oscar Lewis, 213–30. New York: Random House, 1979.

———. 1942. *The Effects of White Contact Upon Blackfoot Culture.* New York: American Ethnological Society. Reprinted in *Anthropological Essays,* by Oscar Lewis, 137–212. New York: Random House, 1979.

Lowie, Robert H. 1924. *Primitive Religion.* New York: Liveright.

———. 1935. *The Crow Indians.* New York: Rinehart.

McAllester, David P. 1941. "Water as a Disciplinary Agent Among the Crow and Blackfoot." *American Anthropologist* 43:593–604.

———. 1954. *Enemy Way Music. Papers of the Peabody Museum of American Archeology and Ethnology,* vol. 41, no. 3. Cambridge, Mass.

———. 1980. "Shootingway, an Epic Drama of the Navajos." In *Southwestern Indian Ritual Drama,* edited by Charlotte J. Frisbie, 199–237. Albuquerque: University of New Mexico Press.

McClintock, Walter. 1910 [1968]. *The Old North Trail.* Reprint. Lincoln: University of Nebraska Press.

———. 1930. *The Tragedy of the Blackfoot. Southwest Museum Papers,* no. 3. Los Angeles.

McFee, Malcolm. 1968 [1972]. "The 150% Man, A Product of Blackfeet Acculturation." In *Native Americans Today: Sociological Perspectives,* edited by Howard M. Bahr, Bruce A. Chadwick, and Robert C. Day, 303–12. New York: Harper and Row.

———. 1972. *Modern Blackfeet: Montanans on a Reservation.* New York: Holt, Rinehart and Winston.

Merriam, Alan P. 1964. *The Anthropology of Music.* Evanston, Ill.: Northwestern University Press.

———. 1967. *Ethnomusicology of the Flathead Indians.* Chicago: Aldine Press.

———. 1977. "Music Change in a Basongye Village (Zaire)." *Anthropos* 72:806–46.

The Montana-Wyoming Indian. 1965. Billings, Montana: U.S. Department of the Interior, Bureau of Indian Affairs.

Monts, Lester P. 1983. "The Conceptual Nature of Music among the Vai of Liberia." *The Black Perspective in Music* 11:143–56.

Mooney, James. 1896. *The Ghost-Dance Religion and the Sioux Outbreak of 1890.* Bureau of American Ethnology, 14th Annual Report. Washington, D.C.

Nadel, Siegfried. 1930. "The Origins of Music." *Musical Quarterly* 16:531–46.

Nettl, Bruno. 1953. "Observations on Meaningless Peyote Song Texts." *Journal of American Folklore* 66:161–64.

————. 1954a. *North American Indian Musical Styles.* Philadelphia: American Folklore Society.

————. 1954b. "Text-Music Relations in Arapaho Songs." *Southwestern Journal of Anthropology* 10:192–99.

————. 1955. "Musical Culture of the Arapaho." *Musical Quarterly* 41:325–31.

————. 1956. "Unifying Factors in Folk and Primitive Music." *Journal of the American Musicological Society* 9:196–201.

————. 1963. "A Technique of Ethnomusicology Applied to Western Music." *Ethnomusicology* 7:221–24.

————. 1967. "Studies in Blackfoot Indian Musical Culture," Parts 1, 2. *Ethnomusicology* 11:141–60, 292–309.

————. 1968a. "Biography of a Blackfoot Indian Singer." *Musical Quarterly* 54:199–207.

————. 1968b. "Studies in Blackfoot Indian Musical Culture." Parts 3,4. *Ethnomusicology* 12:11–48, 192–207. (Part 4 written by Bruno Nettl with Stephen Blum.)

————. 1978a. "Musical Values and Social Values: Symbols in Iran." *Journal of the Steward Anthropological Society* 10(1): 1–23.

————. 1978b. "Some Aspects of the History of Music in the Twentieth Century: Questions, Problems, Concepts." *Ethnomusicology* 22:123–36.

————. 1979. *An Historical Album of Blackfoot Indian Music*, with notes. Ethnic Folkways Records, FE 34001.

————. 1983. *The Study of Ethnomusicology.* Urbana: University of Illinois Press.

————. 1985a. "Montana and Iran: Learning and Teaching in the Conception of Music in Two Contrasting Cultures." In *Becoming Human Through Music*, edited by David P. McAllester, 69–76. Reston, Va.: MENC.

————. 1985b. *The Western Impact on World Music: Change, Adaptation, Survival.* New York: Schirmer Books.

Neuman, Daniel M. 1980. *The Life of Music in North India.* Detroit: Wayne State University Press.

Nevin, Arthur. 1916. "Two Summers with Blackfeet Indians in Montana." *Musical Quarterly* 2:257–70.

Pantaleoni, Hewitt. 1987. "One of Densmore's Dakota Rhythms Reconsidered." *Ethnomusicology* 31:35–55.

Porter, James. 1978. Introduction to *UCLA Selected Reports in Ethnomusicology* 3(1):1–24.

Powers, William K. 1968. "Contemporary Oglala Music and Dance: Pan-Indianism Versus Pan-Tetonism." *Ethnomusicology* 12:352–71.

————. 1975. *Oglala Religion.* Lincoln: University of Nebraska Press.

————. 1980. "Oglala Song Terminology." *UCLA Selected Reports in Ethnomusicology* 3(2): 23–41.

————. 1982. *Yuvipi: Vision and Experience in Oglala Ritual.* Lincoln: University of Nebraska Press.

Radin, Paul. 1920 [1963]. *Autobiography of a Winnebago Indian.* Reprint. New York: Dover.

Rice, Timothy. 1980. "Aspects of Bulgarian Musical Thought." *Yearbook of the International Folk Music Council* 21:43–66.

Richardson, Jane, and L. M. Hanks, Jr. 1942. "Water Discipline and Water Imagery among the Blackfoot." *American Anthropologist* 44:331–33.

Rouget, Gilbert. 1985. *Music and Trance.* Chicago: University of Chicago Press.

Sachs, Curt. 1930. *Vergleichende Musikwissenschaft: Musik der Fremdkulturen.* Heidelberg, West Germany: Quelle & Meyer.

———. 1962. *The Wellsprings of Music.* The Hague: M. Nijhoff.

Sahlins, Marshall. 1976. *Culture and Practical Reason.* Chicago: University of Chicago Press.

Sakata, Hiromi Lorraine. 1983. *Music in the Mind: The Concepts of Music and Musicians in Afghanistan.* Kent, Ohio: Kent State University Press.

Samek, Hana. 1987. *The Blackfoot Confederacy, 1880–1920: A Comparative Study of Canadian and U. S. Indian Policy.* Albuquerque: University of New Mexico Press.

Schaeffer, Claude E. 1962. *The Bison Drive of the Blackfeet Indians,* Information Leaflet Series. Browning, Mont.: Dept. of the Interior, Bureau of Indian Affairs.

Schneider, Albrecht. 1984. *Analogie und Rekonstruktion.* Bonn, West Germany: Verlag für systematische Musikwissenschaft.

Schneider, David M. 1980. *American Kinship,* 2nd ed. Chicago: University of Chicago Press.

Schultz, James Willard. 1907. *My Life as an Indian.* Boston: n.p.

———. 1962. *Blackfeet and Buffalo.* Reprint. Norman: University of Oklahoma Press.

———. 1974. *Why Gone Those Times? Blackfoot Tales,* edited by Eugene Lee Silliman. Reprint. Norman: University of Oklahoma Press.

Seeger, Charles. 1971. "Reflections Upon a Given Topic: Music in Universal Perspective." *Ethnomusicology* 15:385–98.

Shiloah, Amnon. 1979. *The Theory of Music in Arabic Writings (c. 900–1900).* Munich, West Germany: G. Henle.

Shiloah, Amnon, and Erik Cohen. 1983. "The Dynamics of Change in Jewish Oriental Ethnic Music in Israel." *Ethnomusicology* 27:227–52.

Smith, Richard Chase. 1970. "Delivery from Chaos for a Song." Cornell University. Typescript.

———. 1984. "The Language of Power: Music, Order and Redemption." *Latin American Music Review* 5:129–60.

Spier, Leslie. 1921. *The Sun Dance of the Plains Indians: Its Development and Diffusion.* Anthropological Papers of the American Museum of Natural History, vol. 6, part 7. New York.

Steward, Julian. 1934. *The Blackfoot.* Berkeley: National Park Service.

Stocking, George W., Jr. 1968. *Race, Culture and Evolution.* Chicago: University of Chicago Press.

Stumpf, Carl. 1911. *Die Anfänge der Musik.* Berlin: J. E. Barth.

Tappert, Wilhelm. 1890. *Wandernde Melodien.* 2nd ed. Leipzig: List & Francke.

Thomas, Robert K. 1965. "Pan-Indianism." *Midcontinent American Studies Journal* 6(2): 75–83.

Thompson, Stith. 1946. *The Folktale.* New York: Dryden Press.

Treitler, Leo. 1974. "Homer and Gregory: the Transmission of Epic Poetry and Plainchant." *Musical Quarterly* 60:333–72.

Uhlenbeck, C. C. 1911. *Original Blackfoot Texts.* Amsterdam: Koninglijke Akademie van Wetenschappen, Verhandelingen, Part 12, no. 1.

Uhlenbeck, C. C., and R. B. van Gulick. 1930. *English-Blackfoot Vocabulary.* Amsterdam: Koninglijke Akademie van Wetenschappen. Afdeeling Letterkunde, Verhandelingen n.s. 29 (4).

———. 1934. *A Blackfoot-English Vocabulary, based on Material from the Southern Peigans.* Amsterdam: Koninglijke Akademie van Wetenschappen, Afdeeling Letterkunde, Verhandelingen n.s. 33 (2).

Vennum, Thomas. 1982. *The Ojibwa Dance Drum.* Smithsonian Folklife Studies, no. 2. Washington, D.C.

Wachsmann, Klaus. 1971. "Universal Perspectives in Music." *Ethnomusicology* 15:381–84.

Wallaschek, Richard. 1893. *Primitive Music.* London: Longmans, Green.

Willcomb, Roland H. 1970. "Bird Rattle and the Medicine Prayer." *Montana* 20(2): 42–49.

Wissler, Clark. 1910. *Material Culture of the Blackfoot Indians.* Anthropological Papers of the American Museum of Natural History, vol. 5. New York.

———. 1912a. *Ceremonial Bundles of the Blackfoot Indians.* Anthropological Papers of the American Museum of Natural History, vol. 7, part 2. New York.

———. 1912b. *Social Life of the Blackfoot Indians.* Anthropological Papers of the American Museum of Natural History, vol. 7, part 1. New York.

———. 1913. *Societies and Dance Associations of the Blackfoot Indians.* Anthropological Papers of the American Museum of Natural History, vol. 11, part 4. New York.

———. 1918. *Sun Dance of the Blackfoot Indians.* Anthropological Papers of the American Museum of Natural History, vol. 16, part 3. New York.

———. 1936. *Changes in Population Profiles Among the Northern Plains Indians.* Anthropological Papers of the American Museum of Natural History, vol. 36, part 1. New York.

———. 1940. *Indians of the United States: Four Centuries of Their History and Culture.* New York: Doubleday, Doran.

Wissler, Clark, and D. C. Duvall. 1909. *Mythology of the Blackfoot Indians.* Anthropological Papers of the American Museum of Natural History, vol. 2, part 1. New York.

Witmer, Robert. 1973. "Recent Change in the Musical Culture of the Blood Indians." *Yearbook for Inter-American Musical Research* 9:64–93.

———. 1982. *The Musical Life of the Blood Indians.* National Museum of Man. Mercury Series. Canadian Ethnology Service Paper, no. 86. Ottawa.

The World of Music. 1977. "Universals" [Special issue on universals] 19(1–2): 2–141.

Zemp, Hugo. 1978. " 'Are'are Classification of Musical Types and Instruments." *Ethnomusicology* 22:37–68.

————. 1979. "Aspects of 'Are'are Musical Theory." *Ethnomusicology* 23:6–48.
Zonis, Ella. 1973. *Classical Persian Music: An Introduction*. Cambridge: Harvard University Press.

Index

Afghanistan, music in, 11
American Museum of Natural History, 19
Ames, David W., 11, 148
Amuesha (of Bolivia), 50, 58, 91
Anthropology: fieldwork of, 25, 28; and the study of tribes, 3–4
Anthropology of Music, The (Merriam), 1
Apikuni, *See* Schultz, James Willard
Arapaho Indians: and Blackfoot Indians, 44; and Ghost Dance movement, 63; language of, 13; musical style of, 43, 71, 106, 158; research on, 11, 22
Assiniboin Indians, 44, 106

Beaver, mythological importance of, 14
Beaver Medicine cult: importance of, 37; origin of, 130, 134; songs associated with, 33, 34, 36, 39, 94, 125
Behavior (of music), 1–2, 11
Bella Coola Indians, 59
Bells, use of, 37–38, 121
Benedict, Ruth, 20
Berliner, Paul, 11
Bible, origins of music in, 91
Blackfeet: Raiders on the Northwestern Plains, The (Ewers), 12
Blackfeet Community College, 16, 27, 69
Blackfeet Indian Reservation, 16
Blackfoot Indians: adaptation to white culture, 9, 107–8; age-grade societies among, 14, 33, 35, 40, 75, 85, 105, 106, 107, 125, 127; concept of history among, 12; concept of music among, 3, 10, 48–52, 171; cosmology of, 13–14, 58; culture of, 10, 32, 63, 110–111; employment among, 15; fieldwork among, 3, 23–24; gender differentiation of roles among, 15, 83–84, 125; groups among, 13; history of, 13, 64, 105; and humor, 143–45; informants from, 23, 24, 25–27; men's societies among, 22, 33, 105; modern, 15; musical culture of, 10, 32, 34–35, 50, 166–68, 170–71; mythology of, 18, 34, 74–75, 89, 92–93, 95, 101, 102, 110, 130–33, 136, 143; perception of Western ("white") music, 5, 50, 60, 66, 67, 103, 137, 151; politics among, 15–16, 139–40; population of, 3, 13; reason for studying, 3; relationships with whites, 15; religion of, 14, 64, 93, 94–96; research on, 12–13, 17–23; reservation life of, 15; schooling among, 15; taxonomy of, 52–53; tribal name variations, 16; warfare among, 14, 34–35, 64, 137–39
Blackfoot Indians and music: associations for, 54–58, 73, 77, 117; calendar of, 37; concept of, 3, 10, 48–52, 171; evaluation of, 163–66; heroic, 136–40; history of, 103–6, 109–13, 171–72; as human activity, 59–60, 129, 131; and identity, 122–24; importance of, 17; kinds of, 76–82; learning of, 6, 37, 62, 97, 99, 101, 152, 153–54; meaning of, 5, 70, 73; modern, 106–9; for mourning, 84, 139; origins of, 89, 92–94, 110, 171–72; performance of, 159–60; quantity of, 61–65, 99; recordings of, 17, 18, 19–20, 21, 24, 25, 26, 32–33, 35, 41, 43, 82, 108–9, 156; research on, 17–18; ritual use of, 12, 14, 34, 94–96, 119–22, 129; and singing, 49, 50, 60, 67, 69–73, 82–83, 123, 155–56, 162–63; and social differentiation, 124–

28; sound of, 4–5, 65–68, 158–59, 168; sources of, 5–6, 31, 53, 55, 56–57, 62–63, 97–100, 101–3, 110–11; and specialization of musicians, 126–27, 151; style of, 43–44, 67–68, 112, 162, 168; and supernatural power, 128, 129–33, 146; synchronic view of, 8; taxonomy of, 53–58, 77–78, 79–82, 119, technical view of, 12; terminology for, 148–51; uses and functions of, 117–24, 130, 172; vocables in, 69, 71; and words, 5, 33, 37, 69–73. *See also* Dance, Blackfoot; Language, Blackfoot; Songs, Blackfoot

Blacking, John, 4

Blood Blackfoot Indians: music of, 13, 17, 24, 85, 114, 151; use of musical instruments by, 87

Blood-Clot Boy, myth of, 131

Buffalo Rock, myth of, 66, 135

Buffalo Rock Medicine cult, 125, 135

Buffalo Society, 83

Bulgaria, music in, 11

Bullchild, Percy: medicine bundle rituals described by, 38; mythology recorded by, 13, 21, 95, 131; origin myths recorded by, 92, 93

Business Council. *See* Tribal Council, Blackfoot

Cheyenne Indians, 13, 43, 63, 158

Chicken Dance, 36

Children, songs associated with, 35, 85, 126, 144

Chippewa Indians, 23, 44, 64

Circle Dance, 41

Concept (of music), 1–2, 9, 46–48

Cosmology, Blackfoot, 13–14, 58

Cree Indians, 13, 44, 102, 106, 107

Crow Indians, 13, 22, 44, 83, 158

Culture: continuity of, 8; definition of, 7, 29; heterogeneity of, 28–30; musical universe of, 1; synchronic view of, 8, 89

Curtis, Edward S., 20

Curtis, George, 32

Czechoslovakia, music in, 48

Dakota Indians, 22, 43

Dance, Blackfoot, 48; Chicken Dance, 36; Fast-and-Fancy Dance, 36; Feather Dance, 36; Forty-Nine Dance, 63, 106, 144; Grass Dance, 35, 36, 41, 63, 105, 106, 150, 151; Owl Dance, 36, 41, 105, 106; Rabbit Dance, 36, 63, 106; Scalp Dance, 34, 136; War Dance, 36, 41, 77, 150, 151. *See also* Ghost Dance movement; Social dances; Sun Dance

Densmore, Frances, 22, 23, 64

Dixon, Joseph K., 19–20, 32

Donaldson, Jessie, 32

Drums: musical instruments, 37, 43, 44, 49, 86, 87, 107, 120, 150, 157–58; and singing, 41, 67, 82, 83, 126, 127, 155–56

Duvall, D. C.: abilities of, 140; mythology recorded by, 19, 92, 94, 95, 130, 135

Eskimo songs. *See* Inuit songs

Ethnicity, and music, 122–24

Ethnography, synchronic view of culture in, 8

Ethnomusicology: and comprehension of entire musical systems, 4; conventional fieldwork in, 5, 7, 24–25, 28; normative assumptions of, 161; and the study of tribes, 4

Ethnomusicology of the Flathead Indians (Merriam), 1

Ewers, John: Horse Medicine ceremony described by, 156, 159; medicine bundle rituals described by, 38, 143; research on Blackfoot Indians by, 12, 20, 63, 142; women's mourning chants mentioned by, 84

Farr, William E., 12, 21

Fast-and-Fancy Dance, 36

Feather Dance, 36

Feld, Steven, 11, 117

Forty-Nine Dance, 63, 106, 144

Four, importance of, 12, 14

Flathead Indians: compared to Blackfoot Indians, 1, 13, 23, 43, 44, 105; development of songs among, 96, 97, 158; ethnomusicology of, 1, 59, 118, 128

Flutes, 37, 66, 107

Frisbie, Charlotte J., 69

Gambling: and Hand Game, 42, 145; performances for, 108; songs for, 35, 36, 37, 40, 43, 77, 82, 104, 105, 119, 153

Games, songs associated with, 35, 85, 126

Ghost Dance movement, 107; Blackfoot non-participation in, 43, 63, 106, 111, 114; role of, 44
Gilbert, Henry F., 20
Gillis, Frank J., 20
Glacier National Park, 15, 18, 22
Grass Dance: also called War Dance, 36, 41, 150, 151; introduced among Blackfoot Indians, 63, 106; prominence of, 35; style of songs associated with, 105
Grinnell, George Bird, 18, 32, 92, 93, 95
Gros Ventre Indians, 13, 44

Haefer, J. Richard, 11, 59
Hako, 64
Hand game (stick game), 42, 87, 104, 145, 157
Hanks, Jane Richardson, 21, 32, 83
Hanks, Lucien, 21, 83
Harmonicas, 66
Hartle, Donald, 21, 32
Hatton, Orin T., 44, 84, 150, 158, 159
Hausa tribe, 11, 148
Havasupai Indians, 58, 64, 65, 91, 95
Herzog, George, 10, 42, 65, 104
Hinton, Leanne, 58, 65, 91
Honor Lodge. *See* Sun Dance
Hornbostel, E. M. von, 86
Horse Medicine cult, 34, 38, 156, 159
Humor, Blackfoot, 143–45
Hungry Wolf, Adolf, 21
Hungry Wolf, Beverly, 21

India, music in, 50, 62, 78, 110, 113, 117
Indian Chipmunks, 68, 108
Informants, Blackfoot, 23, 24, 25–27
Instruments. *See* Musical instruments
Inuit songs, 62, 96
Iran, music in, 47–48, 50, 59, 61–62, 66, 78, 80, 110, 166
Iroquois Indians, 64

Jubal, 91

Kaluli (of Papua New Guinea), 11, 117
Kartomi, Margaret J., 108

Kaufman, Howard K., 21, 32
Keil, Charles, 11, 48
Kerman, Joseph, 116
King, Anthony V., 11, 148
Kiowa Indians, 63
Kolstee, Anton, 59
Kroeber, A. L., 8, 22, 105

Laade, Wolfgang, 91
Lah, Ronald, 11
Language, Blackfoot, 27; family of, 13; and musical culture, 48–49; and musical terminology, 148–51; research on, 20; and singing, 69–73; transcription of, 16–17; use of, 16, 68–69
Lewis, Oscar, 20, 69, 70, 84, 125
Lewis, Ruth, 20
Lowie, Robert H., 8, 22

McAllester, David, 4, 59, 79
McClintock, Walter: ceremonies and songs described by, 39, 40, 83, 84, 113, 144; information about singing described by, 150; recordings by, 32; research on Blackfoot Indians by, 18, 56, 58, 114
McFee, Malcolm, 12, 21, 29, 151, 166–67
Many-Guns, Tom, 23, 24, 138
Masnavi (Mowlavi), 66
Mbira music (of the Shona of Zimbabwe), 11
Medicine, songs for, 77, 82, 104, 121, 133–36
Medicine bundle ceremonies: fieldwork at, 27; origin myths of, 97; performance of, 38–39, 94; recording of, 27, 43; songs associated with, 19, 33, 34, 36, 51, 75, 82, 100, 105, 106, 143, 153; timing of, 14
Medicine Lodge. *See* Sun Dance
Medicine Pipe cult: importance of, 37, 94, 133; number seven in, 39; recordings of, 36; songs associated with, 33, 34, 74, 82, 109, 125, 133
Menomini Indians, 23, 64
Merriam, Alan P.: and comprehension of entire musical systems, 4; and functions of music, 121; and Inuit music, 62; model of music by, 1–2, 9, 10–11; study of Flathead Indians by, 1, 23, 43, 59, 97, 118, 128
Mide, 64

Mirasis (of northern India), 11
Monts, Lester P., 11
Morning Star, myth of, 131
Mourning, songs for, 84, 139
Mowlavi, 66
Museum of the Plains Indian, 16, 20, 21
Music: changes in, 5–6, 8, 113–15; definition of, 46–47; function of, 116; Merriam's model of, 1–2, 9, 10–11; relationship to culture, 2–3. *See also* Blackfoot Indians and music; Western music
Musical instruments: types of, 37, 107; use of, 37, 43, 44, 49, 66, 86–87, 107, 120, 150, 157–58. *See also* Bells; Drums; Flutes; Harmonicas; Pianos; Rattles; Violins; Whistles
"Music in the Thinking of the American Indians" (Herzog), 10
My Life as an Indian (Schultz), 18
Mythology, Blackfoot, 18, 34, 74–75, 89, 92–93, 95, 101, 102, 110, 130–33, 136, 143

Nadel, Siegfried, 59, 129
Napi. *See* Old Man
Natóas bundle, 39, 40, 120, 131
Navajo Indians, 59, 79, 159
Neuman, Daniel M., 11
Nevin, Arthur, 17, 20
New Guinea, music in, 11
North American Indian Days: introduced to Blackfoot Indians, 106; and mourning songs, 139; performance at, 37, 40–42, 54, 69; and preservation of Blackfoot ethnicity, 108, 122; recording of, 27; and warfare songs, 138
Northern Arapaho Indians, 44
Northern Blackfoot Indians, 13

Oglala Sioux Indians, 11
Old Man (Napi), myth of, 14, 92, 93, 95–96, 97, 102, 113, 130–33, 143
Old North Trail, The (McClintock), 18
Old Woman, myth of, 131
Owl Dance, 36, 41, 105, 106

Papago Indians, 11
Pawnee Indians, 63, 64
Peyote religion: Blackfoot nonparticipation in, 43, 63, 106, 111, 114; role of, 44; songs associated with, 69, 96
Pianos, 66
Piegan Blackfoot Indians, 13, 85
Pima Indians, 59, 62, 64–65, 95, 96
Politics, Blackfoot, 15–16, 139–40
Powers, William K., 11, 22, 148

Rabbit Dance, 36, 63, 106
Radin, Paul, 23
"Raising the Pole" (Blackfoot song), 40, 57
Rattles, 37, 86, 87, 107, 120, 159
Religion, Blackfoot, 14, 64, 93, 94–96; and ritual use of music, 12, 14, 34, 94–96, 119–22, 129
Rice, Timothy, 11
Riemann Musik Lexicon (Gurlitt), 47

Sachs, Curt, 86
Sakata, Hiromi Lorraine, 11
Salish Indians, 105
Samek, Hana, 12
Scalp Dance, 34, 136
Scar-Face, myth of, 131
Schultz, James Willard ("Apikuni"), 18–19, 32, 56, 95
Second Wanamaker Expedition, 20
Seven: importance of, 12, 14; songs in medicine bundle ceremonies, 39
Shoshone Indians, 44, 105, 158
Siksika. See Language, Blackfoot
Singing, Blackfoot, 49, 50, 60, 67, 69–73, 82–83, 123, 155–56, 162–63
Singsings, 154
Sioux Indians, 63, 148. *See also* Oglala Sioux Indians; Teton Sioux Indians
Social dances, songs associated with, 35, 82, 105, 107, 108, 113. *See also* Dance, Blackfoot
Songs, Blackfoot: as basic units of musical thought, 51, 77; brevity of, 73; "favorites of the tribe," 113, 164; forms of, 100–101, 152–54; heroic, 136–40; history of, 108–9; learning of, 6, 37, 62, 97, 99, 101, 152, 153–54; origins of, 93, 95; ownership and control of, 30, 55, 140–43; political, 139–40; quantity of, 61–65, 99; sources for, 5–6, 31, 97–100, 101–3, 110–11; vs. speech,

69–73; stability of, 52, 63–64, 66, 98, 99, 114–15; "titles" for, 58, 70, 77; types of, 73–75
Sound (of music), 1–2
Steward, Julian, 20
Stick game. *See* Hand game
Sun Dance: as part of general Plains culture, 22; performance of, 39–40; and preservation of Blackfoot ethnicity, 139; research on, 19; songs associated with, 33, 34, 36, 43, 75, 77, 105, 106, 107, 113, 134–35; timing of, 14, 37

Teton Sioux Indians, 22
Thompson, Stith, 94
Tipis, ceremonial painting of, 94, 97
Tiv (of Nigeria), 11
Tribal Council, Blackfoot, 15–16, 127
Tribes: anthropological study of, 3–4; ethnomusicological study of, 4; origins of music among, 91

Uhlenbeck, C. C., 16, 20, 27, 72, 87, 149

Vai (of Liberia), 11
van Gulick, R. B., 16, 27, 87, 149
Venda (of South Africa), 137
Vennum, Thomas, 23
Violins, 66, 87
Vision quests, and origins of songs, 22, 31, 33, 56–57, 62, 96, 97, 99–100, 121, 127

Vocables, use of, 69, 71

Wannamaker Expedition, 56
War Dance, 36, 41, 77, 150, 151
Warfare, Blackfoot, 14, 34–35, 64, 137–39
Western music: Blackfoot perception of, 5, 50, 60, 66, 67, 103, 137, 151; change in, 8–9, 113; kinds of, 76–77, 80–81; origins of, 90–92
Whistles, 87, 107
White Dog, song of, 56, 57, 75, 108, 144
Winnebago Indians, 23
Wissler, Clark: information on use of musical instruments, 87; medicine bundle ceremonies described by, 38, 134, 135, 143; origin myths recorded by, 92, 94, 95, 97, 130, 135; and performance of songs, 150, 157; recordings by, 32, 33; research on Blackfoot Indians by, 8, 19, 36, 37; songs described by, 81, 83, 84, 98, 99, 120, 121, 140, 144, 165
Witmer, Robert: information on origins of songs recorded by, 98–99, 102; information on use of musical instruments recorded by, 87, 155; recordings by, 108; research on Blackfoot Indians by, 17, 21, 114, 154; songs described by, 65, 67, 80, 112
Women, "manly-hearted," 20, 84, 125
Words, importance of in songs, 5, 33, 37, 69–73

Zemp, Hugo, 11